Remembering Genocide

In *Remembering Genocide*, an international group of scholars draws on current research from a range of disciplines to explore how communities throughout the world remember genocide. Whether coming to terms with atrocities committed in Namibia and Rwanda, Australia, Canada, the Punjab, Armenia, Cambodia and during the Holocaust, those seeking to remember genocide are confronted with numerous challenges. Survivors grapple with the possibility, or even the desirability, of recalling painful memories. Societies where genocide has been perpetrated find it difficult to engage with an uncomfortable historical legacy.

Still, to forget genocide, as this volume edited by Nigel Eltringham and Pam Maclean shows, is not an option. To do so reinforces the vulnerability of groups whose very existence remains in jeopardy and denies them the possibility of bringing perpetrators to justice. Contributors discuss how genocide is represented in media, including literature, memorial books, film and audiovisual testimony. Debates surrounding the role museums and monuments play in constructing and transmitting memory are highlighted. Finally, authors engage with controversies arising from attempts to mobilize and manipulate memory in the service of reconciliation, compensation and transitional justice.

Nigel Eltringham is Senior Lecturer in Social Anthropology at the University of Sussex. He is the author of *Accounting for Horror: Post-Genocide Debates in Rwanda* (2004) and editor of *Framing Africa: Portrayals of a Continent in Contemporary Mainstream Cinema* (2013). He is currently working on a monograph on the International Criminal Tribunal for Rwanda.

Pam Maclean is an Honorary Fellow, Alfred Deakin Research Institute, Deakin University, Australia. She has published widely on Holocaust memory, particularly in relation to Holocaust videotestimony, and her publications include *Testifying to the Holocaust* (2008), co-edited with Michele Langfield and Dvir Abramovich.

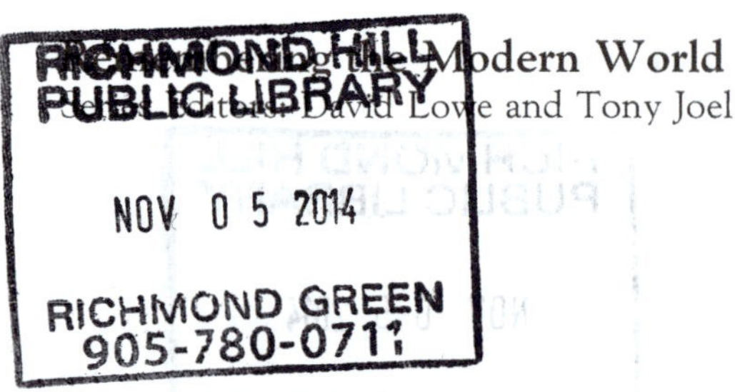

Remembering the Modern World

Series Editors: David Lowe and Tony Joel

The *Remembering the Modern World* series throws new light on the major themes in the field of history and memory in a global context. The series investigates relationships between state-centred practices and other forms of collective and individual memory; looks at the phenomenon of anniversaries and national days in the context of global and national identities; shows how some cities and sites play active roles in generating acts of remembrance and asks why some phenomena and events are remembered more widely and easily than others.

Remembering the Cold War
David Lowe and Tony Joel

Remembering Genocide
Edited by Nigel Eltringham and Pam Maclean

Forthcoming titles in the series:

Remembering the Great War
Bart Ziino

Remembering Genocide

Edited by
Nigel Eltringham and Pam Maclean

LONDON AND NEW YORK

First published 2014
by Routledge
2 Park Square, Milton Park, Abingdon, Oxon OX14 4RN

And published by Routledge
711 Third Avenue, New York, NY 10017

Routledge is an imprint of the Taylor & Francis Group, an informa business

British Library Cataloguing in Publication Data
A catalogue record for this book is available from the British Library

Library of Congress Cataloging in Publication Data
A catalog record for this book has been requested

ISBN: 978-0-415-66011-2 (hbk)
ISBN: 978-0-415-66012-9 (pbk)
ISBN: 978-1-315-79766-3 (ebk)

Typeset in Goudy
by Taylor & Francis Books

Printed and bound by CPI Group (UK) Ltd, Croydon, CR0 4YY

Contents

List of illustrations

Figures

Maps

Contributors

Dr Avril Alba is the Roth Lecturer in Holocaust Studies and Jewish Civilization in the Department of Hebrew, Biblical and Jewish Studies at the University of Sydney. From 2002 to 2011 she was the Education Director at the Sydney Jewish Museum, where she also served as the Project Director/Curator for the refurbishment of the Sydney Jewish Museum's permanent exhibition Culture and Continuity in 2008–2009. She is currently working on a book-length monograph exploring the largely unexamined topic of museums as sacred spaces.

Dr Nigel Eltringham is Senior Lecturer in Social Anthropology at the University of Sussex. He is the author of *Accounting for Horror: Post-Genocide Debates in Rwanda* (2004) and editor of *Framing Africa: Portrayals of a Continent in Contemporary Mainstream Cinema* (2013). He is currently working on a monograph on the International Criminal Tribunal for Rwanda.

Dr Donna-Lee Frieze is the Prins Senior Fellow at the Center for Jewish History in New York City and Visiting Fellow at the Alfred Deakin Research Institute at Deakin University, Australia. She has published widely on genocide and film, and is the editor of Raphael Lemkin's autobiography *Totally Unofficial* (2013).

Dr Nicki Hitchcott is Associate Professor and Reader in African Francophone Studies at the University of Nottingham. She is the author of *Women's Writing in Francophone Africa* (2000) and *Calixthe Beyala: Performances of Migration* (2006), and has edited a number of volumes on African literature in French, most recently *Francophone Afropean Literatures* (with Dominic Thomas), which is forthcoming in 2014. She is currently writing a book on fictional responses to the genocide in Rwanda.

Tricia Logan is a PhD candidate at Royal Holloway, University of London. Her dissertation topic focuses on memory of residential schools and the history of settler colonial genocide in Canada. From 2010 to 2013, she was Curator of Indigenous Content at the Canadian Museum for Human Rights in Winnipeg, Canada. Her publications include 'Memory of

Atrocity in Canada: How Do You Engage Canadian Civil Society in Truth and Reconciliation?' (*London Journal of Canadian Studies* 26, 2010/2011).

Pam Maclean is an Honorary Fellow, Alfred Deakin Research Institute, Deakin University, Australia. She has published widely on Holocaust memory, particularly in relation to Holocaust videotestimony, and her publications include *Testifying to the Holocaust* (2008), co-edited with Michele Langfield and Dvir Abramovich.

Dr Henning Melber is Senior Advisor/Director Emeritus of The Dag Hammarskjöld Foundation in Uppsala, Sweden and Extraordinary Professor in the Department of Political Sciences at the University of Pretoria and the Centre for Africa Studies at the University of the Free State in Bloemfontein in South Africa. He is co-editor of the *Africa Yearbook* and author of *Understanding Namibia* (forthcoming in 2014).

Elena Lesley-Rozen is a graduate student in the Division of Global Affairs at Rutgers University. She is completing a Master's thesis on genocide memorial sites in Rwanda and Cambodia for which she received fieldwork funding from the Council of American Overseas Research Centers. A forthcoming chapter about this research will appear in Antonius Robben and Francisco Ferrandiz (eds), *Down to Earth: Exhumations in the Contemporary World* (forthcoming in 2014 from University of Pennsylvania Press).

Dr Damien Short is Director of the Human Rights Consortium and Senior Lecturer in Human Rights at the Institute of Commonwealth Studies, School of Advanced Study, University of London. His research interests include indigenous peoples' rights, reconciliation initiatives, genocide studies and environmentalism. He has published widely in these areas. A new monograph, *Genocide and Colonization*, is forthcoming in 2014.

Dr Pippa Virdee is Senior Lecturer in South Asian History at De Montfort University, UK. Her research interests include the history of the Punjab, the South Asian diaspora in Britain and women's history in Pakistan. She is the Convenor of the Punjab Research Group. Her publications include *Coming to Coventry: Stories from the South Asian Pioneers* (2006) and the co-edited *Refugees and the End of Empire* (2011).

Series editors' foreword

Organized thematically, this ambitious new series takes a broad view of what constitutes remembering great historical events and phenomena in the late modern period (i.e. since 1789). Volumes in the series draw on such things as: ceremonies associated with anniversaries and national days; episodes of memorialization and commemoration including museum exhibitions; filmic representations and popular culture; public discourse and debate as shaped and reflected by speeches of political and civic leaders; and school curricula. *Remembering the Modern World* makes a fresh contribution to memory studies by placing much emphasis on narrative (with substantive introductory chapters addressing the main theoretical and methodological issues) and by drawing on the strengths of complementary disciplines such as History, Cultural Heritage, Anthropology, Journalism Studies, Sociology, International Relations and Law. To complement the text, wherever appropriate volumes are encouraged to make widespread use of maps, timelines, illustrations and especially photographs taken by contributing authors during field research.

The series offers a comparative glance across the contemporary world in a manner that explores both the reach of globalization and the insistence of localizing forces. As for themes projected for examination throughout the series, these include, *inter alia*, war and peace; genocide; political and social emancipation; imperialism; decolonization; terrorism; sporting triumphs, tragedies, and rivalries; heroes and villains; political revolutions and constitutional crises; and feminism.

Each book in the series will start with an overview of the most significant theoretical and methodological approaches historians and other scholars have deployed in relation to the kind of material being explored within the volume. The aim is to sketch the theoretical and methodological landscape, enabling interested readers to follow key references to what has become a well-theorized field. The substantive chapters/sections thereafter might be theoretically suggestive, but focus primarily on presenting narrative constructed around whatever case studies are being remembered.

Remembering the Modern World throws new light on key themes for students, scholars and general readers of contemporary history. The series aims to provide greater understanding of relationships between state-centred practices and other forms of shared or common memories; examine the phenomenon of anniversaries and national days in the contexts of global and national identities; explore the 'transition zones' between narrative histories and explorations of history's significance in contemporary societies; and ponder why some phenomena and events are remembered more widely and easily than others. In its ambitious geographical and topical reach, the series suggests connections and invites new research questions that inform further historical enquiry.

David Lowe
Tony Joel

Acknowledgements

This volume would not have been possible without the Alfred Deakin Research Institute, Deakin University, Australia, initiating the project through the *Remembering the Modern World* series and its series editors, Professor David Lowe and Dr Tony Joel. David and Tony have provided invaluable advice and encouragement throughout the preparation of the volume. At Routledge, Eve Setch, Paul Brotherston and Geraldine Martin have been model editors. We are especially grateful to Paul for his patience as the volume slowly took shape. Michael Helfield, as copyeditor, also made an invaluable contribution to the quality of the volume. We are, of course, indebted to the contributors for producing rich and insightful work and for their good humour and efficiency when asked for revisions, and to Lisa Couacaud for compiling the index. As with any undertaking, we could not have seen this volume to completion without the support of our partners Anna and Rod.

Remembering genocide

Nigel Eltringham and Pam Maclean

> ... Memory, so far from being merely a passive receptacle or storage system, an image bank of the past, is rather an active, shaping force; that is dynamic – what it contrives symptomatically to forget is as important as what it remembers ... memory is historically conditioned to the emergencies of the moment; that so far from being handed down in the timeless form of 'tradition' it is progressively altered from generation to generation. It bears the impress of experience, in however mediated a way. It is stamped with the ruling passions of its time. Like history, memory is inherently revisionist and never more chameleon than when it appears to stay the same.
>
> (Samuel 1994: x)

Critical to the process of countering genocide has been the desire that details of genocidal events, the victims and the worlds they inhabited are not forgotten. And yet, as the quote above indicates, remembrance is in continual flux. What is remembered is determined by *present* social and political needs (see Friedländer 1992:1; Santner 1992:143). What does 'remembrance' entail if its object is so ephemeral? Alongside the unstable quality of what is remembered, there is a need to appreciate the relationship between individual memory and public testimony. It can be argued that there is a continuum of remembrance; at one end there is the 'event *before* it has become public – the immensely personal phenomenon of individual survivors struggling to reconstruct life', while at the other end there is the 'public ritual' of official commemoration (Wajnryb 1999: 83). This volume is not concerned with the, ultimately inaccessible, inner memory of the survivor, but rather with the inter-subjective, shared remembering where the witness is, in turn, witnessed as inner memories are articulated in an encounter with others. This reflects a critical feature of genocide remembrance: what is remembered may be individual memory of trauma, but that individual memory is appropriated for the 'group' of which the survivor is a member. Survivor memory is, in other words, mobilized by (often self-appointed) spokespersons for a group and used for strategic purposes, so that an individual memory of genocide is deployed as evidence for the experience of the group as a whole. Ultimately, the relationship of individual memory to genocidal memory is synecdochal, such that individual memory comes to stand as an illustration of a broader group memory.

Public or collective memory is, however, heterogeneous. Aleida Assmann (2010b) argues that memory takes a number of 'formats', including the 'social' (passed from generation to generation), the 'political' (constructed for instrumental purposes) and the 'cultural' (as systematically preserved through cultural media). This insight is reflected in many of the contributions to this volume. Each of the formats differs in terms of 'extension in space and time, size of group, and volatility and stability' (Assmann 2010b: 40). While individual memory is inherently fragmented, volatile and subject to change and, ultimately, eradication, social memory is to some extent a more stable form of memory because it is not embedded in an individual. That said, with the disappearance of survivors, it too is subject to change and impermanence. By contrast, political memory is oriented towards imposing memory from the top down through institutions and commemoration with the objective of preservation over time for a clearly defined purpose. It thus tends towards homogenization and stasis. Finally, cultural memory, with its propensity to capture experience within symbols and media, sustains memory – like its political counterpart – beyond a limited period of time and across spatial boundaries, but does so while making room for more heterogeneous interpretation. Assmann (2010b: 44) concludes that, although political and cultural memory are both intentionally designed to preserve memory over the long term, '(b)oth are permanently challenged and contested, and it is to a large part, this very contestation that keeps this memory alive'.

This volume is concerned with the way 'long-term' memory (including that which denies genocide) is constructed and 'permanently challenged and contested'. By way of introduction, the discussion below will concentrate on survivor memory (rather than the memory of perpetrators, bystanders or descendants of survivors). It will reflect on the way private memory is transformed into public memory in a context in which genocide survivors speak to 'multiple audiences – survivors in the local community, perpetrators in the local community, the dead, national government officials, and international human rights advocates' (French 2009: 98).

The impulse to remember

In terms of what is remembered, scholars have called for the collection and preservation of survivor memory that is otherwise excluded from political remembrance (Leydesdorff 2009: 23). There is a call for survivors' experience of death and loss to be gathered, preserved and acknowledged lest survivors be 'condemned to dwell alone and nameless in the ruins of memory' (Das 1996: 69). Further, because scholars believe that survivor memory can act as a spur to moral engagement, they are critical of any attempts to devalue the role of victim testimony. Robert Melson (2011: 284–285), for example, has argued that rehabilitation of victims' memories serves to counter those effects of genocide that go beyond killing and that genocide 'is also about seizing property, destroying their culture, denying their memories, and silencing their voices. It is incumbent upon us as scholars to give voice to the victims and not to cooperate, even if inadvertently, with their persecutors'. Unfortunately, enabling victim groups to 'give voice' to their suffering, is not inherently positive. Telling does not automatically break the cycle of community destruction, because, more often than not, the act of telling continues within the context of the powerlessness of the victim group in relation to the perpetrator group. Indeed, attempts by perpetrator groups to reassert their power over victim groups through denial or lack of genuine remorse constitute a continuing act of genocide (Theriault 2012; see also the works of Melber and Short in this volume). Most notably, the Turkish government's suppression of 'dissidents' seeking acknowledgement of the Armenian Genocide is viewed with consternation by the Armenian community, which feels its identity remains under threat.

The position held by some scholars that survivor experience must be collected and preserved at all costs does not necessarily correspond to what survivors want. While the Holocaust survivor Primo Levi (Levi and Woolf 1979: 15) writes that he was driven by a 'violent impulse' to tell his story, research suggests that other survivors of genocide may not wish to engage in remembrance through testimony and that they choose silence, for pragmatic reasons, for socio-economic survival (Eastmond 2007). Drawing on fieldwork in multi-ethnic communities in Bosnia-Herzegovina in which crimes against humanity and war crimes were committed in the 1990s, Marita Eastmond and Johanna Mannergren Selimovic (2012: 507) suggest that silence is a strategy actively employed in everyday interactions with 'ethnic others' in ways that 'empower by communicating respect and even trust, thus forming and sustaining relations important to viable local life' (see Stefansson 2010). Silence, therefore, must be seen as an act of social communication rather than as an absence, that is, as 'a pragmatic and, given the circumstances, successful strategy for coexistence' (Eastmond and Selimovic 2012: 524). Furthermore, silence is not simply erasure or forgetting. Rather, as everyone in those communities knows what happened, 'open acknowledgement would be counterproductive' to rebuilding a 'normal life' (Eastmond and Selimovic 2012: 512), which is the objective of those living in difficult socio-economic circumstances.

Writing in the context of the aftermath of the 1994 Rwanda genocide in which as many as one million Tutsi were killed, Bert Ingelaere (2007: 22–24) makes almost identical observations, saying that 'silence on the past was the order of the day. Things "from before" were known or suspected but not spoken aloud'. Ingelaere continues:

> Due to necessity life turned to a form of normality and co-habitation. Life in the hills is highly pragmatic. Tensions and conflicts are kept in

> the dark because neighbours and villagers depend upon each other in their daily activities and their fight for survival in mutual impoverishment.
>
> (Ingelaere 2007: 22)

These authors make clear, of course, that in Bosnia-Herzegovina and Rwanda silence is not really a 'choice', but rather a pragmatic strategy determined by socio-economic imperatives. While that may be contrary to the 'revealing is healing' paradigm promoted by, for example, truth commissions and unpalatable to some scholars, such pragmatism on the part of survivors cannot be wished away.

Alternatively, while survivor silence may be necessary to establish a 'normal life', there is also the possibility that silence is imposed by the inability of language to express the experience of genocide (Agamben 1999: 39; Caruth 1996: 5–9; Scarry 1985: 4) or the fear on the part of survivors that they will not be believed (Langer 1991: xiv). As a consequence, 'the urge to tell meets resistance from the certainty that one's audience will not understand' (Langer 1991: xiii). As Ruth Wajnryb (1999: 88) suggests, 'So few are the shared assumptions between speaker and listener that no common ground exists in which a narrative can begin to be constructed'. At the same time, however, 'silence' may not be an inadequate term given the fact that oral silence does not mean that inter-subjective remembering is not present. Rather, remembrance may be present as 'implicit transmission' (Wajnryb 1999: 84). Julia Dickson-Gómez (2002: 420), for example, describes how in El Salvador survivors of state violence[1] displayed *nervios*, a catch-all term for illness caused by trauma (including headaches, stomach problems and insomnia). Dickson-Gómez suggests that trauma is 'transmitted implicitly to children as parents' *nervios* creates an environment of distrust, confusion, and resentment in the family' given that *nervios* results in 'emotional withdrawal or inability to function effectively in his or her expected role' (see Alba in this volume for a discussion of inter-generational memory).

Such research reveals the realities in communities that have suffered mass atrocity, including genocide, and suggests that remembrance is not as straightforward as some scholars may wish. Remembrance may, on the one hand, be eschewed for pragmatic reasons; on the other hand, it may be implicit in somatic illness and mutually agreed silences. The apparent absence of explicit remembrance does not mean that remembrance is absent.

The fact that survivors may avoid testimony for socio-economic imperatives or a lack of adequate language leads to another aspect of remembrance: survivors rarely testify in isolation. The collection of survivor testimonies is often assumed to involve unmediated recall, a 'kind of "pure" utterance and "authentic" transmission of experience' (Douglass 2003: 56). But even in the absence of intentional embellishment, remembrance is not a 'pure' unmediated utterance. Survivors rarely simply tell their stories. Rather, their stories are elicited and produced dialogically as co-productions with an 'auditor', i.e., an interviewer (Jackson 2002: 22; see Eastmond 2007; Langfield and

Maclean 2009; Vansina 2006 [1961]: 29; and Maclean in this volume). The questions the auditor (human rights activist, lawyer, scholar) asks are then excised from the text, and what was a two-way conversation is presented as a monologue (Gelles 1998: 16; see Eltringham this vol.). Making personal memory legible to a wider audience, therefore, always relies on the framing grammar of the solicitor; the stories are the 'result of a relationship, a common project in which both the informant and the researcher are involved together' (Portelli 1981: 103; Vansina 2006 [1961]: 29). The co-production of survivor memory alerts us to the fact that such texts reflect a 'collage of intervening presences – witness, editor, transcriber, translator, reader', so that the text 'reflects the different voices, styles of expression, perceptions of "truth", and political agendas of each and every participant in its chain of production' (Douglass 2003: 68).

One can go further. In one sense, the remembered event only comes into existence when it is called forth by and narrated to another person:

> The emergence of the narrative which is being listened to – and heard – is, therefore, the process and the place wherein the cognizance, the 'knowing' of the event is given birth to. The listener, therefore, is a party to the creation of knowledge de novo. The testimony to the trauma thus includes its hearer.
>
> (Laub 1992: 57)

What this also further indicates is the way in which memory is 'inherently revisionist' (Samuel 1994: x), that stories are '*nowhere* articulated as personal revelations, but authored and authorized dialogically and collaboratively in the course of sharing one's recollections with others' (Jackson 2002: 22).

Utilitarian remembrance – therapy and deterrence

A substantial literature argues that survivors must remember in order to 'heal' themselves (Agger and Jensen 1990; Minow 1998) and deter future crimes. The therapeutic benefits of storytelling have, however, been questioned (Brounéus 2008; Fletcher and Weinstein 2002: 592–595; Summerfield 1999). Furthermore, Rosalind Shaw (2007), writing in the context of Sierra Leone, argues that the assertion that survivors must remember is based on Eurocentric assumptions. By contrast, in Sierra Leone:

> the work of memory is not primarily to store and retrieve information but to create a relationship between oneself and a remembered event or person: the verbal recollection of violent events (especially in public) is undesirable because it makes that violence present and connects it to the person remembering.
>
> (Shaw 2007: 195)

Despite such insights, mobilization of memory is increasingly justified by reference to serving a utilitarian function for the future. Remembering for the future, reflects, according to Louis Bickford and Amy Sodaro (2010: 68), the emergence of a new memorial paradigm that has replaced a focus on national or sub-national memory, with the idea that the purpose of memorialization is an 'accumulation of knowledge' to assist in the future. For example, in his 2008 report to the UN Security Council the President of the International Criminal Tribunal for Rwanda stated that, 'Among the most basic and most important of the Tribunal's achievements has been the accumulation of an indisputable historical record' (United Nations 2008; see Eltringham 2009), a record generated, of course, from the memory of survivors who have testified in the trials. Another example of this use of memory is evident in the global educational context (Assmann 2010a), where governments or transnational organizations mandate specific programmes such as teaching the Holocaust as a form of moral education designed to inoculate children against intolerance and hatred. Erica Lehrer and Cynthia Milton analyse the ethical role played by museums tasked with the display of 'dark knowledge' and are somewhat sceptical of naïve assumptions about the educative role such museums can play in influencing behaviour. They conclude that there is a growing recognition that confronting visitors with macabre exhibits will not, in themselves, prevent future atrocities and that alternative strategies need to be adopted to solicit empathetic responses from visitors (2011: 1; see the works of Alba, Eltringham, Hitchcott and Lesley-Rozen in this volume).

The idea that memory must have a utility combined with Assmann's (2010b) notions of political memory can introduce an element of coercion as regards survivor memory. Legal interventions (human rights investigations, truth commissions; international tribunals) enforce and popularize formulaic (coercive) templates of testimony through which 'memory' is mediated and 'mythologised' (Tal 1996: 6; see Douglass 2003; Beverley 1996; Ross 2003; Wilson 2001: 111–121). Human rights reporting, for example, deploys preordained modes of soliciting, corroborating and packaging stories (Schaffer and Smith 2004: 27, 36–37, 45; Wilson 1997; see Eltringham in this volume). Christopher Colvin (2006: 172) describes a 'global political economy of traumatic storytelling', a form of storytelling that lacks any ambiguity and in which events are 'reduced to the most important, shocking and morally obvious details of harm' framed by the psychotherapeutic language of trauma and the assumption that 'revealing is healing'. One of the effects of the 'global political economy of traumatic storytelling' is that 'what sells and what does not become part of shaping the stories people tell'. In other words, at the very moment a memory is elicited, there is anticipation of the form that will be willingly consumed by global audiences.

As Colvin (2006: 173) notes, there is a 'constant stream of journalists, researchers, politicians, priests and psychologists who fly to the next hot spot … asking permission to record, interpret and circulate victims' stories' globally to a diverse array of audiences' (see Madlingozi 2010). Uli Linke (2009: 155) also notes how the 'global media rapidly appropriate and circulate images of people's suffering: the memories of victimhood are commoditized:

the remembrance of pain is commercialised'. Having once remembered publicly, survivors can be quickly alienated from their remembrance when others 'subject the narrative to different and unpredictable readings [and put it] to different and unpredictable uses' (Schaffer and Smith 2004: 32; see Tal 1996: 7).

This relates to the complaint from survivors that remembrance and the uses to which their testimony is put reduces them to mono-dimensional figures. Werner Weinberg (1985: 150–152), a survivor of Bergen-Belsen, suggests that 'survivor' becomes 'a constricting designation that can easily make its bearer appear – to others and himself – as a museum piece, a fossil, a freak, a ghost'. Survivors, it can be argued, are 'produced through the occupation of the signs of injury' that suppresses their subjectivity and who they were before the catastrophe (Ross 2003: 12). Rwandan survivors have also complained that they are only acknowledged at (politicized) commemorations (Brauman et al. 2000; see Ibreck 2010: 336).

These coercive expectations (what 'outsiders' will wish to 'consume') are evident in the controversy surrounding Rigoberta Menchú's (Menchú and Burgos-Debray 1984) account of violence (including genocide)[2] perpetrated against Mayan indigenous peoples in Guatemala, the veracity of which was challenged by David Stoll (1999; see Sanford 1999). Reflecting on this controversy, Ana Douglass suggests that 'we need to reconsider the role of the Western reader in creating an unreasonable set of expectations of what constitutes "authenticity" of speech' (2003: 81) and the assumption that 'the witness is necessarily innocent, truthful, and above conscious manipulation in the telling of his or her story' (2003: 81). For Douglass (2003: 80–81), 'Menchú's conscious manipulation of the facts ... reveals more about her level of awareness of the expectations of her readership and international politics than about her own character'. In other words, survivors of genocide and mass atrocity are required by those who will consume their stories to frame those narratives in a particular way which may result in what is misunderstood as 'embellishment' and 'inaccuracy'. Douglass argues that Menchú, 'by consciously using the rhetorical construct of the eyewitness, [made] "an unbelievable story" believable to the otherwise detached Western readership'. In doing so, Menchú (who was awarded the Nobel Peace Prize in 1992) prepared the way for the trial of José Efraín Ríos Montt (de facto President of Guatemala 1982–1983) who was convicted of genocide and crimes against humanity, and who was sentenced to eighty years, imprisonment on 10 May 2013.

Truth: forensic and psychological

As the previous section indicated, when remembrance is explicit and public, there is always the delicate question of the 'truth' of such remembrance. Elie Wiesel (quoted in Cargas 1986: 5) suggests that 'any survivor has more to say than all the historians combined about what happened'. The problem with

Wiesel's statement is that it implies these are two comparable epistemologies. In reality, there is a difference between 'factual or forensic truth' and 'personal or narrative truth' (TRC 1:112), which reflects the difference between a historical truth and a survivor's psychological truth (Felman and Laub 1992: 59–60; Leydesdorff 2009: 23; Payne 2008: 197–228). As Nora Strejilevich (2006: 703) – a survivor of the 'Dirty War' (1976–1983) in Argentina – writes, 'testimony after genocide does not abide by the rules established by the scientific/academic/legal apparatus. Rather, it voices the intimate, subjective, deep dimension of horror'. We should not exaggerate the gulf between personal memory and historical truth given that both are intrinsically subjective. As Jan Vansina (1980: 726) notes, 'the study of memory teaches us that all historical sources are suffused by subjectivity right from the start. As the source is created, even anticipated in the act of perceiving, the subjectivity is already there'. Likewise, Strejilevich (2006: 707–708) reminds us that 'historical discourse – which hides the historians' viewpoint while a third person narrator tells the story … is an interpretation' and that 'all "truth" presupposes a degree of fictionalisation'. Subjectivity cannot be avoided.

'Psychological truth' is inevitable, caused by the way in which memory evolves. As Michael Jackson (2002: 15) observes, 'To reconstitute events in a story is no longer to live those events in passivity, but to actively rework them, both in dialogue with others and in one's own imagination'. There is an incremental process of inter-subjective redescription telling the same story each time with additional detail (Wilson 2001: 43), so that memory is transformed 'as it is replayed, recited, reworked and reconstrued' (Jackson 2002: 22). Under such circumstances, the survivors' 'factual understanding of what they actually heard or saw' is always evolving, and this evolution includes the incorporation of secondary 'foreign material' (Levi 1986: 130).

These issues relate to the debates over *testimonio*, which originated in Latin America (Douglass 2003: 61–62), but whose characteristics correspond to the testimony of genocide survivors. John Beverley (1996: 24) defines *testimonio* as 'a novel or novella-length written narrative … told in the first person by a narrator who is also the real protagonist or witness of the events he or she recounts, and whose unit of narration is usually a "life" or a significant life experience'. The distinction between *testimonio* and autobiography is that the narrative of the former is 'always linked to a group or class situation marked by marginalisation, oppression and struggle' (Gelles 1998: 16). Examples include Marie Béatrice Umutesi (2004) for Rwanda and Haing S. Ngor (Ngor and Warner 2003) for Cambodia. Again, it has been argued that it is ill-founded to evaluate such accounts according to 'forensic' truth. Rather, as Strejilevich (2006: 703) argues, the 'essential meaning of testimony is lost when defined as a means to provide information and knowledge based on facts'. Rather, 'A truthful way of giving testimony should allow for disruptive memories, discontinuities, blanks, silences and ambiguities' (Strejilevich 2006: 704).

'Inaccurate' memory also relates to the question of silence discussed earlier. The past does not exist independently of our *present* relationship to it. Rather, as indicated earlier, the present 'replete with its own preoccupations, struggles, and interests appropriates the past' and in so doing 'revises the way the past *appears* to us' (Jackson 2005: 356; see Eltringham 2004). In fact, 'even at the moment of reproducing the past our imagination remains under the influence of the present social milieu' (Halbwachs and Coser 1992: 49), so that from the 'continuous mass of mere happenings' (Hastrup 1992: 8) we 'notice only those things that are important for our immediate purposes. The rest we ignore' (Berger 1963: 71). And because our 'immediate purposes' change, the past is not a fixed, concurrent 'foreign country', but is always a *potentiality*.[3] In other words, the past becomes a resource to reconstruct life (see Eltringham 2011). An example of this can be seen in the embellished stories Lee Ann Fujii (2010: 234) encountered among genocide survivors in Rwanda which give insight into the 'speaker's state of mind, aspirations and desires'. Rather than attempts to deceive, these stories were instructive as attempts to 'invent a new life history' that make it easier to cope with a present reality.

There is a need, therefore, to appreciate this potentiality of the past *in the present*, that the purpose of memory 'is not to preserve the past but to adapt it so as to enrich and manipulate the present' (Lowenthal 1985: 210) through forms of 'fabulation', that is, the creation of stories that serve purpose in response to present needs (Vansina 1980: 266). With this understanding, attention can turn to the *purpose* this fabulated remembering serves. For example, Eugenia Zorbas's (Zorbas 2009: 173–175) respondents in post-genocide Rwanda expressed a desire to 'live like we lived before', a situation in which 'we had mixed marriages, we helped carry each other's sick, we shared beer' (see Buckley-Zistel 2006: 140–142). Asked to describe what a reconciled community would look like, Zorbas's respondents 'recalled' a *fabulated* 'highly partial, idyllic picture of life before the genocide'. Such idealized remembrance is a form of hopeful anticipation. Here fabulated remembering of good relations in the past is a means to envisage and evaluate a common future because 'any narrative of the past is interwoven with a vision of the future' (Leydesdorff 2009: 36).

And yet, deploying such fabulated remembrance is not always possible. Selma Leydesdorff indicates that female survivors of the Srebrenica Genocide of July 1995 in the former Yugoslavia found it too difficult to recall the pre-war past of peaceful co-existence; the memory of the betrayal of friends and neighbours preventing them from 'developing any vision of the future, for such a vision can only be based on feelings about what was perceived as "good" in the past' (2009: 25). These pre-genocide memories held no potential for envisaging the future.

The assertion that survivors do not tell the 'truth' or even a 'truth' (narratives change over time) can be disconcerting and perhaps even offensive. The challenge, however, is to 'develop an attentiveness to each person's grasp of the past' while not abandoning judgement about facts that can challenge testimony (Minow 1998: 129). Such alternatives imply that the real issue is that we do not seek a 'remembering' that is an unproblematic reconstruction of the past, but a 'remembering' that is primarily a commentary on the present (and a vision for the future).

Both silence and psychological truth are contrary to the invocation to remember forensic truth. But, alongside these two responses there is a third response, in which, rather than an unproblematic reconstruction of the past, 'remembering' is primarily a commentary on the present (and a vision for the future). This response is humour. Carol Kidron, for example, has demonstrated the important place that 'serious humour' can play in how episodes of genocide are commemorated. Drawing on fieldwork at the 'House of Being', a 'tiny Holocaust memorial museum-pedagogic center that doubles as a survivor geriatric center' in central Israel, Kidron (2010: 432) demonstrates the way 'humour, as a key cultural mechanism, functions to allow descendants to explore the incongruity between national memorial narratives and the familial lived experience of the Holocaust'. She notes how the commemorative practices of the Israeli state celebrated the heroism of the Warsaw Ghetto Uprising, but disdainfully dismissed non-combatant victims of the Holocaust as 'sheep to the slaughter' (2010: 431). It is this hegemonic discourse that is undermined through humour, a practice encouraged by Tzipi Kichler, the larger-than-life founder and manager of the centre. Through humour, 'Israeli mainstream society and the survivor in-group are satirised for constructing a hierarchy of survivor suffering' (2010: 442). For example, on the eve of the national Holocaust Memorial Day (renamed 'Holocaust Holiday' by centre members), descendants jokingly heckle each other as they give testimony at a vigil at the centre. When the child of a Hungarian survivor of Auschwitz finishes his testimony, a descendant of Polish origin shouts out, '"Wait a minute, you're from Hungary! I'm sorry, you people were also on vacation, what's a year in school, we were there for three" (Polish Jews were sent to camps in 1943, Hungarian Jews in 1944)' (2010: 448). On the one hand, Kidron sees such humour as an act of resistance to state hegemonic remembrance that denigrates the non-combatant Holocaust survivor, while on the other hand it is also an act of remembrance of parents by 'highlighting the heroism of parental "passive" endurance [and] resilience' (2010: 442).

Humour is also employed in other contexts of genocide and mass atrocity. Anna Sheftel (2012: 158) found in post-war Bosnia-Herzegovina that humour was used to reject conventional means of remembering the past. Sheftel (2012: 150) notes that the idealistic transitional justice paradigm promotes a 'liberating and healing' counter-memory that will speak literal truth to power. And yet, this is not appropriate for many Bosnians because claims to 'literal truth' are precisely what ethno-nationalist propagandists claim to be speaking. Humour, therefore, as a form of counter-memory, is employed to challenge ethnically divisive narratives. Humorous stories about the way Bosnians naïvely thought that they would always remain safe during the conflict allows them to laugh at their own *naïveté*. This 'self-aware use of ironic humour serves to make present-day Bosnians, laughing at themselves' regain their dignity (2012: 151). Furthermore, because such humorous stories position the tellers as neither victims nor heroes, they can 'avoid the traps of dominant narratives in the region that try to push them into one or both of those roles' (2012: 151).

Humour, it appears, can play a part in disarming hegemonic forms of remembrance. Writing on the comic and humorous in three books about the Holocaust (Tadeusz Borowski's *This Way for the Gas, Ladies and Gentlemen*; Leslie Epstein's *King of the Jews* and Art Spiegelman's *Maus*), Terrence Des Pres (1988: 220, 227) suggests that these works are, on the one hand, acts of resistance that 'refuse to take the Holocaust on its own crushing terms' and in so doing, they free the reader 'from the hegemony of terror in the spectacle we behold'. On the other hand, Des Pres also argues that humour counteracts the fact that images of the Holocaust (and other genocides) become over-familiar and clichéd. When this happens, 'inappropriate' humour can compel 'new attention to an old story' (1988: 229). Des Pres (1988: 232) suggests that genocide seen only as tragedy is overwhelming and incapacitating, but that humour means that 'pity and terror are held at a distance', enabling a 'tougher more active response'. This response is reflected in Kidron and Sheftel's research, where survivors of genocide and mass atrocity exercise agency by using humour to resist the subject position of hapless victim that is offered.

Memorial sites

In her discussion of humour, Sheftel also draws attention to the role played by memorial sites. Sheftel (2012 157–158) notes that artworks such as the giant can of canned beef in Sarajevo (entitled 'Monument to the International Community, From the Grateful Citizens of Sarajevo'), the monument to Bruce Lee in Mostar and the monument to Rocky in Zitiste all represent a 'sarcastic rejection of the post-war project of commemoration and remembering that has been promoted and institutionalised by the international community'. The memorial site at Srebrenica-Potočari,[4] for example, was created by the executive powers of the Office of the High Representative in 2000 (Mannergren Selimovic 2013). The idea for the Srebrenica-Potočari Memorial Room was initially the idea of Lord Ashdown (the Fourth High Representative in Bosnia-Herzegovina) after a visit to the Holocaust Exhibition at the Imperial War Museum in London (Bardgett 2007). In a similar way, the Beth Shalom Holocaust Centre in Nottingham (run by the Aegis Trust) was created after a visit by its founders to Yad Vashem (Smith 1999), and in turn, having visited the Beth Shalom Holocaust Centre in 2003, the Rwandan Minister for Youth, Sports and Culture and the Mayor of Kigali requested that the Aegis Trust take over responsibility for the creation of the Kigali Memorial Centre and the Murambi Genocide Memorial Centre (see Sodaro

2011). Such links and the way in which forms of genocide memorialization are replicated from one context to another are not new (see Eltringham in this volume). Paul Williams (2004: 248) notes that designing the Tuol Sleng exhibition in Cambodia, Vietnamese General Mai Lam travelled to Poland to study the Auschwitz-Birkenau Memorial and Museum in order to portray the Khmer Rouge as 'fascist' communists (see Young 1993: 49; see Lesley-Rozen in this volume).

This raises a question of whether there is a transnational aesthetic to genocide commemoration. In her study of the Bangladesh Liberation War Museum (BLWM) which commemorates the 1971 war between East and West Pakistan, Nayanika Mookherjee (2011: 74) notes that the museum was built on the template of the Holocaust Museum in Washington DC and how 'descriptions of genocides in different instances draw from each other, cross-referencing those various violent encounters' (2011: 80). Mookherjee suggests that there is a process of 'genocidal cosmopolitanism' which 'describes genocides through the evocation of various local, national and global tropes' (2011: 80). She sees, for example, the display of bones and skulls at the BLWM as recreating a trope associated with Cambodia and Rwanda (2011: 83). As a consequence, 'genocidal events and their exhibition in museums are not only made in relation to each other, but their specificity is decontextualised. This is necessary as they need to be presented as a global moral-historical lesson' (2011: 88).

Johanna Mannergren Selimovic (2013) comes to similar conclusions in her comparative study of the Srebrenica-Potočari Memorial in Bosnia-Herzegovina and the Kigali Memorial Centre in Rwanda. Employing Daniel Levy and Natan Sznaider's (2006) notion of 'de-territorialised cosmopolitan memory', she notes how a globally recognized template of genocide promoted by 'global memory entrepreneurs' obscures contextual complexities. She notes, for example, how an unqualified comparison between the Rwanda genocide and the Srebrenica genocide, Armenian genocide and the Holocaust promoted at the Kigali Memorial Centre serves to obscure a distinct feature of the Rwanda genocide absent from the exhibition, namely, that the Rwandan Patriotic Front, currently in power, is accused of committing crimes against humanity in Rwanda in 1994 and later in the Democratic Republic of the Congo (see Straus and Waldorf 2011). In this case, the 'global memory template' contributes to the silencing of certain victims (see Conway 2011), suggesting that 'the packaging of the conflictual past for global consumption has little to do with the realities on the ground' (Mannergren Selimovic 2013: 348). As with the packaging of 'traumatic storytelling' for global consumption by memory 'entrepreneurs' (see Colvin 2006; Madlingozi 2010), so memorialization follows a format designed, it would appear, for mobile cosmopolitans.

Conclusion

There are many forms of genocide remembrance that have not been considered in this introduction, including cinema (see Eltringham 2013; Hirsch 2004;

Wilson and Crowder-Taraborrelli 2012; Frieze in this volume; Virdee in this volume); photography (see Hughes 2003; Morrison 2004); art (Kyriakides 2005; Young 2000); and theatre (Kalisa 2006; Skloot 1990). These omissions reflect the sheer breadth of sites and forms through which genocide is remembered.

The need to understand how genocide is remembered takes on a more urgent quality if one accepts Dirk Moses's contention that memory (of the perpetrator) is the *primary* motivation for and agent of genocide, rather than a *secondary* effect of the original atrocity. Moses (2011: 294) argues that 'genocides generally are driven by traumatic memories of past events in which, for various reasons, a group is construed as disloyal and held collectively guilty and then collectively punished, deported, or destroyed pre-emptively to prevent the feared repetition of the previous traumatic experience'. Perpetrators' actions, therefore, are a 'fantastic' response to perceived, but totally unfounded, threats from the victim group based on 'remembrance'. As a consequence, 'traumatic perpetrator memory' replaces ideology as the catalyst for genocide. Seen in this light, memory is, as always, as much about the present and the future as about the past.

Notes

1 The Salvadoran Civil War (1979–1992) was a conflict between the military-led government and the *Farabundo Martí National Liberation Front*, a coalition or 'umbrella organization' of five left-wing guerrilla groups.
2 According to the report of the Commission for Historical Clarification, 'agents of the State of Guatemala, within the framework of counterinsurgency operations carried out between 1981 and 1983, committed acts of genocide against groups of Mayan people which lived in the four regions analysed' (Commission for Historical Clarification 1999: para 122). See http://s3.documentcloud.org/documents/357870/guatemala-memory-of-silence-the-commission-for.pdf.
3 As Michael Jackson (2005: 356) suggests, the past is 'never one thing, but *many*; and it is characterised less by necessity than *potentiality*'.
4 In July 1995, more than 8,000 men and boys were killed by Bosnian Serb forces.

Bibliography

Agamben, G. (1999) *Remnants of Auschwitz: The Witness and the Archive*, New York: Zone Books; London: MIT Press.

Agger, I. and S.B. Jensen. (1990) 'Testimony as Ritual and Evidence in Psychotherapy for Political Refugees', *Journal of Traumatic Stress*, 3.1: 115–130.

Assmann, A. (2010a) 'The Holocaust – A Global Memory? Extensions and Limits of a New Memory Community', in A. Assmann and S. Conrad (eds) *Memory in a Global Age: Discourses, Practices and Trajectories*, Basingstoke: Palgrave Macmillan.

——. (2010b) 'Re-framing Memory. Between Individual and Collective Forms of Constructing the Past', in K. Tilmans, F. Van Vree and J. Winter (eds) *Performing the Past: Memory, History and Identity in Modern Europe*, Amsterdam: Amsterdam University Press.

——. (2012) 'To Remember or to Forget: Which Way out of a Shared History of Violence?', in A. Assmann and L. Shortt (eds) *Memory and Political Change*, Basingstoke: Palgrave Macmillan.

Bardgett, S. (2007) 'Remembering Srebrenica', *History Today*, 57.11: 52–53.

Berger, P.L. (1963) *Invitation to Sociology: A Humanistic Perspective*, Garden City: Doubleday & Co.

Beverley, J. (1996) 'The Margin at the Center: On *Testimonio* (Testimonial Narrative)', in G.M. Gugelberger (ed.) *The Real Thing: Testimonial Discourse and Latin America*, Durham: Duke University Press.

Bickford, L. and A. Sodaro. (2010) 'Remembering Yesterday to Protect Tomorrow: The Internationalization of a New Commemorative Paradigm', in Y. Gutman, A.D. Brown and A. Sodaro (eds) *Memory and the Future: Transnational Politics, Ethics and Society*, Basingstoke: Palgrave Macmillan.

Brauman, R., S. Smith and C. Vidal. (2000) 'Rwanda: politique de terreur, privilège d'impunité', *La Revue Esprit* August/September: 147–162. Available at: http://rwandanet.tripod.com/articlerwandaseptembre2000.html (accessed 24 March 2014).

Brounéus, K. (2008) 'Truth-Telling as Talking Cure? Insecurity and Retraumatization in the Rwandan Gacaca Courts', *Security Dialogue*, 39.1: 55–76.

Buckley-Zistel, S. (2006) 'Remembering to Forget: Chosen Amnesia as a Strategy for Local Coexistence in Post-Genocide Rwanda', *Africa: The Journal of the International African Institute*, 76.2: 131–150.

——. (2012) 'Between Pragmatism, Coercion and Fear: Chosen Amnesia after the Rwandan Genocide', in A. Assmann and L. Shortt (eds) *Memory and Political Change*, Basingstoke: Palgrave Macmillan.

Cargas, H.J. (1986) 'An Interview with Elie Wiesel', *Holocaust and Genocide Studies*, 1.1: 5–10.

Caruth, C. (1996) *Unclaimed Experience: Trauma, Narrative, and History*, Baltimore: Johns Hopkins University Press.

Colvin, C.J. (2006) 'Trafficking Trauma: Intellectual Property Rights and the Political Economy of Traumatic Storytelling', *Critical Arts: A Journal of South-North Cultural and Media Studies*, 20.1: 171–182.

Commission for Historical Clarification. (1999) *Report of the Commission for Historical Clarification: Conclusions and Recommendations*. Guatemala City.

Conway, P. (2011) 'Righteous Hutus: Can Stories of Courageous Rescuers Help in Rwanda's Reconciliation Process?', *International Journal of Sociology and Anthropology*, 3.7: 217–223.

Das, V. (1996) 'Language and Body: Transactions in the Construction of Pain', *Daedalus*, 125.1: 67–91.

Des Pres, T. (1988) 'Holocaust Laughter?', in B. Lang (ed.) *Writing and the Holocaust*, New York: Holmes and Meier.

Dickson-Gómez, J. (2002) 'The Sound of Barking Dogs: Violence and Terror among Salvadoran Families in the Postwar', *Medical Anthropology Quarterly*, 16.4: 415–438.

Douglass, A. (2003) 'The Menchú Effect: Strategies, Lies and Approximate Truths in Texts of Witness', in A. Douglass and T.A. Vogler (eds) *Witness and Memory: The Discourse of Trauma*, New York: Routledge.

Eastmond, M. (2007) 'Stories as Lived Experience: Narratives in Forced Migration Research', *Journal of Refugee Studies*, 20.2: 248–264.

Eastmond, M. and Selimovic, J.M. (2012) 'Silence as Possibility in Postwar Everyday Life', *The International Journal of Transitional Justice*, 6.3: 502–524.

Eltringham, N. (2004) *Accounting for Horror: Post-Genocide Debates in Rwanda*, London: Pluto Press.

——. (2009) '"We are not a Truth Commission": Fragmented Narratives and the Historical Record at the International Criminal Tribunal for Rwanda', *Journal of Genocide Research*, 11.1: 55–79.

——. (2011) 'The Past is Elsewhere: The Paradoxes of Proscribing Ethnicity in Post-Genocide Rwanda', in S. Straus and L. Waldorf (eds) *Remaking Rwanda: State Building and Human Rights after Mass Violence*, Madison: University of Wisconsin Press.

——. (2013) 'Showing What Cannot Be Imagined: "Shooting Dogs" and "Hotel Rwanda"', in N. Eltringham (ed.) *Framing Africa: Portrayals of a Continent in Contemporary Mainstream Cinema*, Oxford: Berghahn Books.

Felman, S. and D. Laub. (1992) *Testimony: Crises of Witnessing in Literature, Psychoanalysis, and History*, London: Routledge.

Fletcher, L.E. and H.M. Weinstein. (2002) 'Violence and Social Repair: Rethinking the Contribution of Justice to Reconciliation', *Human Rights Quarterly*, 24: 573–639.

French, B. (2009) 'Technologies of Telling: Discourse, Transparency, and Erasure in Guatemalan Truth Commission Testimony', *Journal of Human Rights*, 8.1: 92–109.

Friedländer, S. (1992) 'Introduction', in S. Friedländer (ed.) *Probing the Limits of Representation: Nazism and the 'Final Solution'*, Cambridge: Harvard University Press.

Fujii, L.A. (2010) 'Shades of Truth and Lies: Interpreting Testimonies of War and Violence', *Journal of Peace Research*, 47.2: 231–241.

Gelles, P.H. (1998) 'Testimonio, Ethnography and Processes of Authorship', *Anthropology News*, 39.3: 16.

Halbwachs, M. and L.A. Coser. (1992) *On Collective Memory*, Chicago: University of Chicago Press.

Hastrup, K. (1992) *Other Histories*, London: Routledge.

Hirsch, J.F. (2004) *Afterimage: Film, Trauma, and the Holocaust*, Philadelphia: Temple University Press.

Hughes, R. (2003) 'The Abject Artefact of Memory: Photographs from Cambodia's Genocide', *Media, Culture and Society*, 25.1: 23–44.

Ibreck, R. (2010) 'The Politics of Mourning: Survivor Contributions to Memorials in Post-Genocide Rwanda', *Memory Studies*, 3.4: 330–343.

Ingelaere, B. (2007) '"Does the Truth Pass across the Fire without Burning?" Transitional Justice and its Discontents in Rwanda's Gacaca Courts', Antwerp: Institute of Development Policy and Management.

Jackson, M. (2002) *The Politics of Storytelling: Violence, Transgression, and Intersubjectivity*, Copenhagen: Museum Tusculanum Press.

——. (2005) 'Storytelling Events, Violence, and the Appearance of the Past', *Anthropological Quarterly*, 78.2: 355–375.

Kalisa, C. (2006) 'Theatre and the Rwandan Genocide', *Peace Review: A Journal of Social Justice*, 18.4: 515–521.

Kidron, C.A. (2010) 'Embracing the Lived Memory of Genocide: Holocaust Survivor and Descendant Renegade Memory Work at the House of Being', *American Ethnologist*, 37.3: 429–451.

Kyriakides, Y. (2005) '"Art after Auschwitz is Barbaric": Cultural Ideology of Silence through the Politics of Representation', *Media, Culture and Society*, 27.3: 441–450.

Langer, L.L. (1991) *Holocaust Testimonies: The Ruins of Memory*, New Haven: Yale University Press.

Langfield, M. and P. Maclean. (2009) 'Multiple Framings: Survivor and Non-Survivor Interviewers in Holocaust Videotestimonies', in N. Adler, S. Leydesdorff,

M. Chamberlain and L. Neyzi (eds) *Memories of Mass Repression: Narrating Life Stories in the Aftermath of Atrocity*, New Brunswick: Transaction Publishers.

Laub, D. (1992) 'Bearing Witness or the Vicissitudes of Listening', in S. Felman and D. Laub (eds) *Testimony: Crises of Witnessing in Literature, Psychoanalysis, and History*, London: Routledge.

Lehrer, E.T. and C.E. Milton. (2011) 'Introduction: Witnesses to Witnessing', in E.T. Lehrer, C.E. Milton and M.E. Patterson (eds) *Curating Difficult Knowledge: Violent Pasts in Public Places*, Basingstoke: Palgrave Macmillan.

Levi, P. (1979) *If This is a Man/The Truce*, Trans. S. Woolf, Harmondsworth: Penguin.

——. (1986) 'The Memory of Offense', in G. Hartman (ed.) *Bitburg in Moral and Political Perspective*, Bloomington: Indiana University Press.

——. (1989) *The Drowned and the Saved*, London: Abacus.

Levy, D. and N. Sznaider. (2006) *The Holocaust and Memory in the Global Age*, Philadelphia: Temple University Press.

Leydesdorff, S. (2009) 'When Communities Fell Apart and Neighbours Became Enemies: Stories of Bewilderment in Srebenica', in N. Adler, S. Leydesdorff, M. Chamberlain and L. Neyzi (eds) *Memories of Mass Repression: Narrating Life Stories in the Aftermath of Atrocity*, New Brunswick: Transaction Publishers.

Linke, U. (2009) 'The Limits of Empathy: Emotional Anesthesia and the Museum of Corpses in Post-Holocaust Germany', in A.L. Hinton and K.L. O'Neill (eds) *Genocide: Truth, Memory, and Representation*, Durham: Duke University Press.

Lowenthal, D. (1985) *The Past is a Foreign Country*, Cambridge: Cambridge University Press.

Madlingozi, T. (2010) 'On Justice Entrepreneurs and the Production of Victims', *Journal of Human Rights Practice*, 2.2: 208–228.

Mannergren Selimovic, J. (2010) 'Perpetrators and Victims: Local Responses to the International Criminal Tribunal for the Former Yugoslavia', *Focaal*, 57: 50–61.

——. (2013) 'Making Peace, Making Memory: Peacebuilding and politics of Remembrance at Memorials of Mass Atrocities', *Peacebuilding*.

Melson, R. (2011) 'Critique of Current Genocide Studies', *Genocide Studies and Prevention*, 6.3: 279–286.

Menchú, R. and E. Burgos-Debray. (1984) *I, Rigoberta Menchú: An Indian Woman in Guatemala*, London: Verso.

Minow, M. (1998) *Between Vengeance and Forgiveness: Facing History after Genocide and Mass Violence*, Boston: Beacon Press.

Mookherjee, N. (2011) '"Never Again": Aesthetics of "Genocidal" Cosmopolitanism and the Bangladesh Liberation War Museum', *Journal of the Royal Anthropological Institute*, 17 (Suppl. 1): S71–S91.

Morrison, W. (2004) '"Reflections with Memories": Everyday Photography Capturing Genocide', *Theoretical Criminology*, 8.3: 341–358.

Moses, A.D. (2011) 'Revisiting a Founding Assumption of Genocide Studies', *Genocide Studies and Prevention*, 6.3: 287–300.

Ngor, H. and R. Warner. (2003) *Survival in the Killing Fields*, London: Robinson.

Payne, L.A. (2008) *Unsettling Accounts: Neither Truth nor Reconciliation in Confessions of State Violence*, Durham: Duke University Press.

Portelli, A. (1981) 'The Peculiarities of Oral History', *History Workshop*, 12.1: 96–107.

Ross, F.C. (2003) *Bearing Witness: Women and the Truth and Reconciliation Commission in South Africa*, London: Pluto Press.

Samuel, R. (1994) *Theatres of Memory. Volume 1: Past and Present in Contemporary Culture*, London and New York: Verso.

Sanford, V. (1999) 'Between Rigoberta Menchú and La Violencia: Deconstructing David Stoll's History of Guatemala', *Latin American Perspectives*, 26.6: 38–46.

Santner, E.L. (1992) 'History Beyond the Pleasure Principle: Some Thoughts on the Representation of Trauma', in S. Friedländer (ed.) *Probing the Limits of Representation: Nazism and the 'Final Solution'*, Cambridge: Harvard University Press.

Scarry, E. (1985) *The Body in Pain: The Making and Unmaking of the World*, Oxford: Oxford University Press.

Schaffer, K. and S. Smith. (2004) *Human Rights and Narrated Lives: The Ethics of Recognition*, Basingstoke: Palgrave Macmillan.

Shaw, R. (2007) 'Memory Frictions: Localizing the Truth and Reconciliation Commission in Sierra Leone', *The International Journal of Transitional Justice*, 1.2: 183–207.

Sheftel, A. (2012) '"Monument to the International Community, from the Grateful Citizens of Sarajevo": Dark Humour as Counter-Memory in Post-Conflict Bosnia-Herzegovina', *Memory Studies*, 5.2: 145–164.

Skloot, R. (1990) 'Theatrical Images of Genocide', *Human Rights Quarterly*, 12.2: 185–201.

Smith, S.D. (1999) *Making Memory: Creating Britain's First Holocaust Centre*, Newark: Quill.

Sodaro, A. (2011) 'Politics of the Past: Remembering the Rwandan Genocide at the Kigali Memorial Centre', in E.T. Lehrer, C.E. Milton and M.E. Patterson (eds) *Curating Difficult Knowledge: Violent Pasts in Public Places*, Basingstoke: Palgrave Macmillan.

Stefansson, A.H. (2010) 'Coffee after Cleansing? Co-existence, Co-operation, and Communication in Post-Conflict Bosnia and Herzegovina', *Focaal*, 57: 62–76.

Stoll, D. (1999) *Rigoberta Menchú and the Story of All Poor Guatemalans*, Boulder: Westview Press.

Straus, S. and L. Waldorf (eds). (2011) *Remaking Rwanda: State Building and Human Rights after Mass Violence*. Madison: University of Wisconsin Press.

Strejilevich, N. (2006) 'Testimony: Beyond the Language of Truth', *Human Rights Quarterly*, 28.3: 701–713.

Summerfield, D. (1999) 'A Critique of Seven Assumptions behind Psychological Trauma Programmes in War-Affected Areas', *Social Science and Medicine*, 48.10: 1449–1462.

Tal, K. (1996) *Worlds of Hurt: Reading the Literatures of Trauma*, Cambridge: Cambridge University Press.

Theriault, H.C. (2012) 'Against the Grain: Critical Reflections on the State and Future of Genocide Scholarship', *Genocide Studies and Prevention*, 7.1: 123–144.

Truth and Reconciliation Commission (TRC). (1998) *Truth and Reconciliation Commission of South Africa Report*, Vol. 1., Johannesburg: Palgrave Macmillan.

Umutesi, M.B. (2004) *Surviving the Slaughter: The Ordeal of a Rwandan Refugee in Zaire*, Madison: University of Wisconsin Press.

United Nations. (2008) *Address to the United Nations General Assembly by the President of the International Criminal Tribunal for Rwanda, 13th Annual Report of the International Criminal Tribunal for Rwanda*, United Nations General Assembly.

Vansina, J. (1980) 'Memory and Oral Tradition', in J.C. Miller (ed.) *The African Past Speaks: Essays on Oral Tradition and History*, Folkestone: Dawson.

——. (2006 [1961]) *Oral Tradition: A Study in Historical Methodology*, New Brunswick: Transaction Publishers.

Wajnryb, R. (1999) 'The Holocaust as Unspeakable: Public Ritual versus Private Hell', *Journal of Intercultural Studies*, 20.1: 81–93.

Weinberg, W. (1985) *Self-Portrait of a Holocaust Survivor*, Jefferson: McFarland & Co.

Williams, P. (2004) 'Witnessing Genocide: Vigilance and Remembrance at Tuol Sleng and Choeung Ek', *Holocaust and Genocide Studies*, 18.2: 234–254.

Wilson, R. (1997) 'Representing Human Rights Violations: Social Contexts and Subjectivities', in R. Wilson (ed.) *Human Rights, Culture and Context: Anthropological Perspectives*, London: Pluto Press.

——. (2001) *The Politics of Truth and Reconciliation in South Africa: Legitimizing the Post-Apartheid State*, Cambridge: Cambridge University Press.

Wilson, K.M. and T.F. Crowder-Taraborrelli (eds). (2012) *Film and Genocide*, Madison: University of Wisconsin Press.

Young, J.E. (1993) *The Texture of Memory: Holocaust Memorials and Meaning*, New Haven: Yale University Press.

——. (2000) *At Memory's Edge: After-Images of the Holocaust in Contemporary Art and Architecture*, New Haven: Yale University Press.

Zorbas, E. (2009) *Reconciliation in Post-Genocide Rwanda: Discourse and Practice, Dissertation*, Development Studies, London School of Economics and Political Science.

1 'No man's land' and the creation of partitioned histories in India/Pakistan

Pippa Virdee

The point of departure by Britain from its most prized colony, India, resulted in one of the most violent episodes of the twentieth century, subsequently uprooting an estimated fifteen million people. This was the result of unprecedented levels of communal violence, which contained elements of both spontaneity and planned ethnic cleansing. The dislocation was at its peak in the Punjab between August and December 1947. The majority of the migrants came from the Punjab, Sind, North West Frontier Province and Bahawalpur State on the Pakistani side, and from the East Punjab, the East Punjab States, Delhi and the United Provinces on the Indian side. Bengal, on India's eastern border, was also partitioned with the creation of East Pakistan (contemporary Bangladesh), but levels of violence were lower. Forced migration in Bengal was on a much smaller scale, although it was drawn out for many years (Chatterji 2007; Talbot and Singh 1999). The violence, which prompted this mass forced migration, resulted in an estimated death of one million people, mostly during the immediate weeks following independence in August 1947. But as Pandey in *Remembering Partition* points out, the debates on the levels of violence and casualties are bound by 'rumour' rather than verifiable truths (2001: 91). The longer-term legacies of this violent beginning in the form of strained relations between India and Pakistan have in many ways overshadowed the trauma and dislocation felt by millions of innocent people, who were forced to flee their homes. The loss of ancestral homelands for millions of people continues to resonate even today for the communally reconfigured Punjabi nation in West (Pakistan) and East (India) Punjab and among the diaspora.

This chapter first contextualizes the background to the violence and migration that accompanied independence and Britain's departure from its 'jewel in the crown'. It then discusses remembrance of these events as reflected in the main controversies among scholars surrounding the nature of the violence, the number of casualties and, more recently, to what extent partition-related violence should be considered genocide and/or a form of ethnic cleansing. Next, it considers the ways in which literature and film have represented partition and debates over a peace museum and a memorial. Finally, this chapter considers the ways in which oral testimonies have been increasingly used to delve into the human cost of partition and considers the legacy of partition in conserving a re-imagined Punjabi community in the subcontinent and among the diaspora.

Introduction

As independence from British colonial rule drew closer and the idea of a separate homeland for India's Muslims became a reality, Punjab, a province which the leader of the Muslim League, Mohammad Ali Jinnah, termed the 'cornerstone' of Pakistan, effectively became the battleground. The British government put forward the 3 June Plan (Indian Independence Act 1947) that accepted the partition of Punjab and favoured a two-state solution to independence. Punjab was unusual because it comprised three main communities: Hindus, Sikhs and Muslims. Table 1.1 provides an overview of the religious composition in pre- and post-partition Punjab. While the 1941 census shows that Muslims were the majority community, in reality this varied across the province, and areas in central Punjab were the most mixed. Moreover, the 1941 census was unreliable because it was done under wartime conditions. It subsequently became a source of tension when minorities put forward their claims to the Boundary Commission (Chester 2009). Historically, Punjab had always had a strong pluralist and composite cultural tradition that statistical data and simple religious categorization do not reveal (Bhasin-Malik 2007). It was also – quite significantly – the spiritual homeland of a small but significant Sikh community, which added further complexity at the time of partition.

Based on outdated maps and census material, the barrister Cyril Radcliffe, who had no previous experience with South Asia or cartography, was given the responsibility of drawing the partition line in six weeks. Radcliffe arrived in India in July 1947, and although he complained of the short timeframe,

Table 1.1 Religious composition of population in Punjab, 1941 and 1951

	1941 United Punjab	*1951 West Punjab*[a]	*1951 East Punjab*[b]
Total population	34,309,861	20,651,140	17,244,356
Hindus	29.1%	0%	66%
Muslims	53.2%	98%	2%
Sikhs	14.9%	0%	30%
Christians	1.5%	0%	1%
Others	1.3%	2%	0%

Sources: Census of India (1941 and 1951), Government of India and Census of Pakistan (1951), Government of Pakistan

[a] According to the 1951 Census of Pakistan, in West Punjab there were 33,052 Hindus and 402,856 Others; no Sikhs or Christians were recorded.

[b] 68,712 Others were recorded, but the percentages are rounded off: this group is therefore recorded as being 0 per cent of the population.

the Boundary Commission reached its decision just days before independence and determined the fate of millions of people. To make matters worse, even though India gained independence on 14 August 1947 and Pakistan was created on 15 August 1947, the actual boundary between the two countries was not announced until 17 August 1947 (Chester 2009; Yong 1997). No prior notice was provided to the people who were still uncertain about which side of the border they would be on. During the months between August and December 1947, almost all the Sikhs and Hindus of West Punjab left Pakistan to create new homes in India and similarly nearly all the Muslims of East Punjab (and many from adjoining areas) left India to create new homes in the Dominion of Pakistan.

There was evidently a lack of foresight and leadership as British rule came to an end. The British administration was keen to exit as soon as possible to avoid being embroiled in a prolonged civil conflict, while the newly created states of India and Pakistan were too focused on the endgame to foresee the repercussions of partition, especially in terms of migrations, but also in terms of the economic consequences of division. The engulfing violence in the province forced many people to flee their homes, which in turn meant more people were forced out to make space for the incoming refugees. It was clear to the leadership that events had spiralled out of control; they forced the leaders of India and Pakistan, Jawaharlal Nehru and Liaquat Ali Khan, respectively, to issue a joint statement at the end of August 1947:

> The Punjab was peaceful and prosperous only a short while ago. It is now witnessing scenes of horror and destruction and men have become worse than beasts. They have murdered their fellow beings with savage brutality and have spared neither women nor children. They have burnt houses and looted property. Even people fleeing in terror have been butchered. ... Both Government (sic) are thus devoting all their energies to the task of restoring peaceful conditions and protecting the life, honour and property of the people. They are determined to rid the Punjab of the present nightmare and make it at (sic) once again the peaceful and happy land it was.
>
> (Singh 2006: 508)

The full statement is aimed at restoring order and giving the impression that the respective governments are in control of the situation. However, even when law and order was restored by early 1948, the official, state-sponsored history of this period has tended to celebrate the achievement of independence and play down the dislocation surrounding partition, displacing blame for the violence. The new states could hardly admit to failing to be able to protect minority citizens at the outset of their existence. Hence, they played down the violence and later trumpeted successful refugee rehabilitation to boost state legitimacy. The Indian nationalist approach led by individuals like V. P. Menon (a political insider and constitutional adviser to the last

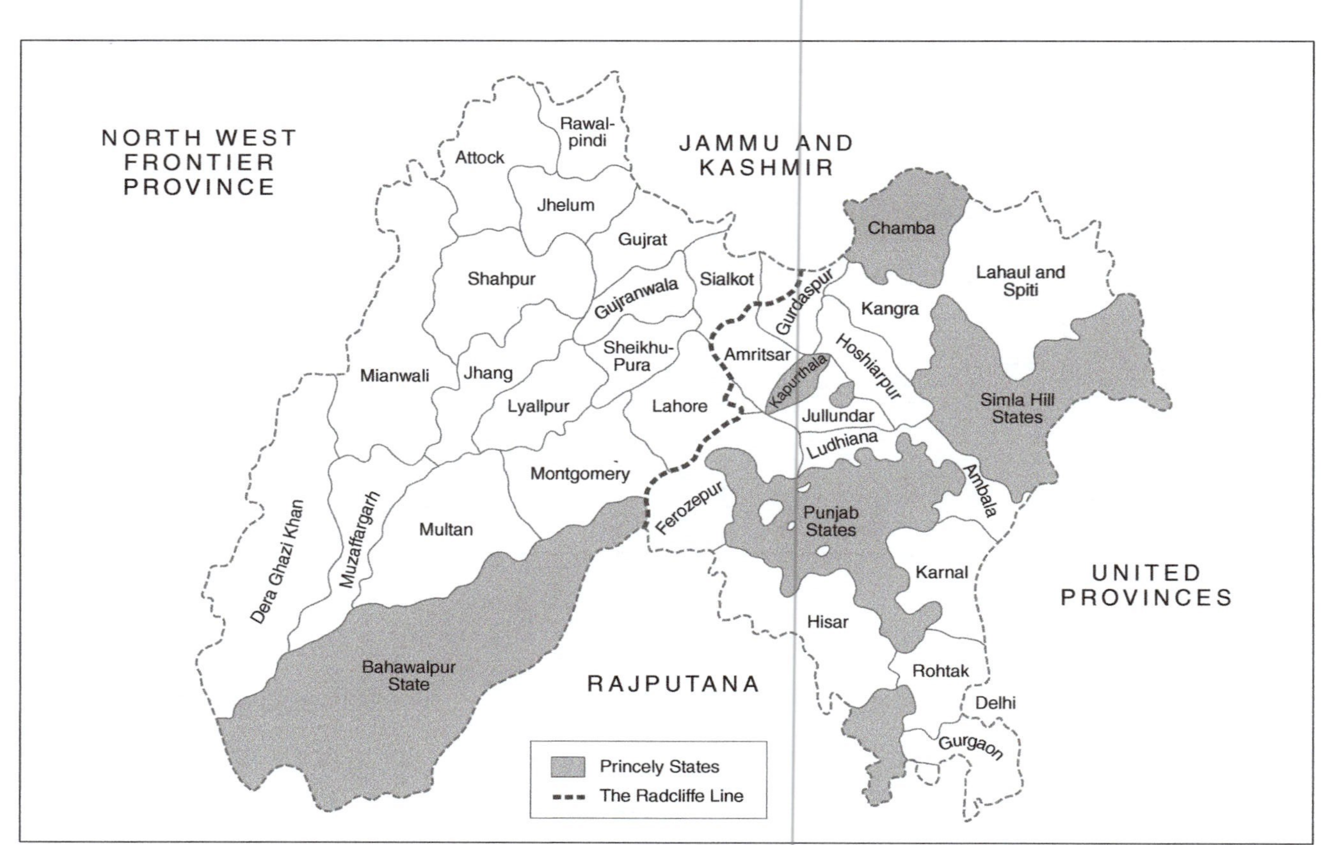

Map 1.1 The Radcliffe Boundary Line
Source: Pippa Virdee.

three Viceroys during British rule in India) was to interpret partition as the net result of years of divisive policies adopted by the colonial power, which undermined pre-existing cultural unities and social interaction that had cut across religious identity (Menon 1985). The Pakistani perspective is epitomized by politicians like Chaudhry Khaliquzzaman (Governor of East Pakistan, 1953–1954), who in his memoir, *Pathway to Pakistan* (1961), argues that the creation of a separate homeland was necessary in order to safeguard Muslim rights and interests. The ideologically incompatible discourses arising from the Indian 'divide and rule' and the Pakistani 'two-nation theory' understandings of partition following independence have often obstructed the remembrance of partition.

Scholarly divisions, debates and controversies

There are a number of problems associated with the study of partition-related violence. These concern the extent to which it was spontaneous or planned, the degree to which any localized case studies can form part of a broader historical narrative, and the extent to which partition violence differed from 'traditional' communal violence (Das and Nandy 1986).[1] These issues also raise the question of the extent to which the concepts of 'ethnic cleansing' and 'genocide' are useful in understanding the events that took place in Punjab. These concepts are still relatively new in the study of partition, but they are important in the wider historiographical context. In recent research, writers such as Talbot (2007), Hansen (2002) and Brass (2003a) have attempted to bring the Punjabi experience into the main literature on genocide, which has been largely dominated by the Holocaust partly perhaps because the contemporaneous events in Europe overshadowed those in Asia. More controversially, it could be argued that there is even a 'hierarchy of suffering': when we consider the vision of 'the emaciated women and men liberated from concentration camps' (Lal n.d.), anything else would become invisible in comparison with these shocking and disturbing images.

At the most basic level, there is a dispute concerning the number of casualties arising from the partition-related violence; estimations vary considerably. It is in reality an impossible task to ascertain precise figures, and hence numbers have varied to suit political objectives. Indian nationalist writers have tended to lean towards the higher end of the spectrum while British writers have tilted towards the lower end. In Pakistan, the casualties represent the price of demanding a separate state from the domineering Hindu majority. This is hardly surprising as successive governments in both India and Pakistan have emphasized the problems their new states were able to surmount, while British governments have wished to preserve a legacy not marred by scenes of disorder.

The debate surrounding the number of casualties is longstanding. It was still a concern to Lord Mountbatten, even years after he had relinquished the office of Viceroy of India. In a letter to Penderel Moon (a British civil servant), written on 2 March 1962, he declared that he was 'keen that an authoritative record should be left for the historians long after I am dead ... ' even though he was neither particularly keen on defending himself at this stage 'nor [on] joining in the argument' (Letters on Divide and Quit). The following extract from a letter sent by Mountbatten to Moon on 2 March 1962 highlights the inconsistency surrounding the casualties.

> My estimate has always been not more than 250,000 dead; and the fact that your [Moon] estimate is not more than 200,000 is the first realistic estimate I have seen. I have often wondered how the greatly inflated figures which one still hears were first arrived at, and I think that they were due largely to the wild guesses which were made in those emotional days after the transfer of power. That they still persist is very clear; for example, Mr Leonard Mosley's latest book[2] gives, I understand, the figure of 600,000, and only the other day a backbench conservative MP told one of my staff that the figures were [sic] three million!
>
> (Letters on Divide and Quit)

In 1948, G.D. Khosla, who became Chief Justice of the East Punjab High Court in 1959, led the Fact Finding Commission by the Government of India to refute the Pakistani charge of genocide against Muslims emerging from United Nations debates over the Kashmir conflict (Tan and Kudaisya 2000: 253). Khosla wrote *Stern Reckoning* shortly after this, in which he estimates the number of casualties to be around 200,000 to 250,000 non-Muslims and probably an equal number of Muslims, bringing the total to nearly 500,000 (1989 [1949]: 299). The historian Patrick French (1997) contends that deaths numbered closer to one million. In a recent interview, the Indo-Canadian writer Shauna Singh Baldwin suggested the figure of five million (Rajan 2011). Many of the police records were destroyed during the disturbances, and due to the lawlessness of the state at the time, the records that do exist are unreliable in providing a comprehensive picture. Furthermore, it is difficult to calculate and differentiate between those who died directly due to the violence and those who died during the mass exodus, through starvation and disease. The truth in reality will never be known because it is an impossible task; as Pandey (2001: 91) suggests, casualty numbers are based on rumour and repetition, both of which continue to reverberate.

Anders Bjorn Hansen has argued that the intentions, intensity and degree of organization of the violence by communal groupings warrant the violence in the Punjab to be understood as a manifestation of genocide (2002). Interestingly, partition violence has not traditionally been incorporated into broader accounts of genocide or ethnic cleansing as we understand these terms today. Recent literature such as *Centuries of Genocide* (Totten and Parsons 2013) continues to overlook the massacres that took place in Punjab in 1947, as does Mann's analysis (*The Dark Side of Democracy*, 2005) of ethnic cleansing. One explanation for this omission is that the term has been deployed in relation to the Holocaust and the post-Cold War violence in the Balkans and Rwanda. This raises the question of whether it is appropriate to apply this term retrospectively to events that took place in Punjab. However, individual case studies do point to organized and systematic acts. For example, Copland refers to the Muslim expulsion in 1947 from Alwar and Bharatpur as not just a communal episode, but also a case of systematic 'ethnic cleansing' (1998: 216), frequently a precursor to genocide.

The 1948 United Nations Convention for the Prevention and Punishment of the Crime of Genocide defines genocide as 'acts committed with intent to destroy, in whole or in part, a national, ethnical, racial or religious group' (Art. 2). Not all scholars, however, subscribe to this view, partly due to the omission of other persecuted groups within this limited definition. Hansen interestingly points out that during the partition of Punjab, there was not a well-defined category of victim and perpetrator; in fact there was a civil war-like conflict escalating during the handover of power. Furthermore, there were primarily three groups (Muslims, Hindus and Sikhs), and each group was 'capable of being the perpetrator and the victims depending on their power and influence in given areas' (Hansen 2002:3). One of the other problems is that genocide is itself associated – and sometimes used synonymously – with the term 'ethnic cleansing'. Ishtiaq Ahmed, who has been considering this dilemma vis-à-vis partition violence, suggests that 'ethnic cleansing is a generic term that covers removal of a distinct population on the basis of ethnic, religious, sectarian and other such factors from a specific territory' (2012: 1). Ahmed argues that while genocide results in destruction of a nation or people in whole or in part, ethnic cleansing can lead to the same result using less severe methods. There is, however, a distinction in 'whether the intention was to rid unwanted people from a territory or to destroy them physically' (2012: 6). The former was certainly evident in Punjab and was further exacerbated by the refugees fleeing from the fear of reprisal killings.

Paul Brass has nevertheless referred to the Punjab violence as 'retributive genocide' which becomes enveloped in a 'cycle of revenge and retribution' (2003b: 72): the boundaries between victim and perpetrator become completely blurred. As an alternative to genocide, other scholars have suggested that perhaps what happened in Punjab could be 'termed fratricide rather than genocide' (Kabir 2002: 248). This could include not only assaults on the 'other', but also the murder of women of one's own family to spare them from the 'dishonour' associated with rape and abduction. Jason Francisco shares this view and argues that 'the partition stands as the archetype of what I would call nationalist fratricide, the conflict between people of a common cultural heritage' (2000: 372). He contends that this is distinct from ethnic conflict or nationalist genocide, which are characterized by state-sponsored persecution or slaughter of cultural or religious minorities, such as the European Jews. Even Khosla's book, which was first published in 1949, describes the magnitude of the horrors of 1947 with the comment that 'history has not known a fratricidal war of such dimensions' (1989: 4).

Furthermore, the notion of a hierarchy of suffering can also be applied to the partition violence itself. Leaving aside the global perspective, one only has to look to the 'chief sufferers' (Major 1995) of partition violence and migration. The plight of women, low castes and children has only recently begun to be addressed by scholars. In the 1990s, a new generation of feminist writers (Butalia 1998; Menon and Bhasin 1998) willing to challenge taboo subjects such as violence, rape and the abduction of women allowed some barriers to be broken. Interestingly, there was an ongoing debate about ethnic cleansing, genocide and war crimes against women in Bosnia-Herzegovina going on in Europe at the same time. In this case, 'feminist activists made a concerted effort to affect the statute establishing the International Criminal Tribunal for the Former Yugoslavia, the rules of evidence under which rape and other crimes of sexual violence would be prosecuted' (Engle 2005: 778). Thus there was now a wider discussion about the use of mass rape against women in conflicts; indeed Menon and Bhasin note the similarities with the accounts of violence against women in Bosnia-Herzegovina with the partition violence in Punjab (1998: 63). In both these cases, women are the upholders of community honour and are then tainted by the 'other' and forced to take on the burden of dishonouring the community.

It is estimated that 75,000 women were raped and abducted during this time on both sides of the border. Women were brutalized and dishonoured in order to inflict collective wounds on the 'other'. This also triggered 'pre-emptive' sacrifices by women to prevent 'dishonour' in the family. The most quoted episode is of the Sikh women in Thoha Khasla (a town now in contemporary Pakistan), which has been immortalized since Urvashi Butalia recovered this account (1998) during the March 1947 massacres in Rawalpindi. The account begins with Sant Raja Singh, who took the life of his daughter and martyred her after praying and asking for forgiveness. This is then followed by the actions of Sardarni Gulab Kaur, who plunged into the well and committed suicide rather than be dishonoured. In total, around 90 women, all of one lineage, perished. The account has been used to show the bravery and courage of the women. Further, Rameshwari Nehru, who was a social worker and head of the Women's Section in the Ministry of Relief and Rehabilitation, likened the 'pre-emptive' sacrifices to the old Rajput tradition of self-immolation (Pandey 2001: 88) in which women sacrificed themselves on the funeral pyres of their husbands. Baldwin (2000), however, questions the patriarchal discourse associated with this, which terms it as 'bravery', 'duty' and 'martyrdom'. By doing so, the violent act performed by the male head is justified. The fact that some women did not die and that others were not so forthcoming for this 'sacrifice' is less visible, and what is remembered is the 'heroic' act. The emotional turmoil of the dilemmas facing women at the time and subsequently has been most evocatively captured in the 2003 film *Khamosh Pani* (*Silent Waters*), which is discussed later in this chapter.

Regardless of whether the terms 'genocide' or 'ethnic cleansing' are deployed, a debate still rages regarding the 'spontaneity' or 'planning' of the violence. The role of the local state is important here. For writers such as Brass (2003b) who see links between partition and post-independence communal violence, the complicity of the local law enforcement agencies and the political motivations of the 'producers' of violence are crucial factors. Those who regard the violence as unplanned either ignore the role of the state, or maintain that its collapse in 1947 was a crucial factor in explaining the outbreaks. The main difference between the violence in the years preceding partition and partition violence itself is that the former was carried out while there was still a functioning government, admittedly a weak one on occasions. The collapse of state authority during the transitory period of transferring power is probably one reason why the violence was so widespread and horrific during the months following partition. As I found during my research on Malerkotla, a small Muslim princely state in the Indian Punjab, the role of the state was crucial in maintaining law and order; consequently, Malerkotla remained a haven of peace for Muslims while surrounded by the partition violence in neighbouring British India (Virdee 2007). Conversely, the riots that occurred in Rawalpindi in March 1947 followed the resignation of the minority government formed after the election of 1946 by Unionist Khizar Hayat Tiwana (see Kamran 2007). Arguably then, the vacuum created by the absence of a functioning authority was a prerequisite for any violence to occur.

Literature, film and remembering partition

> A future student of history would wonder how hundreds of thousands of people suddenly made up their mind to abandon their homes and belongings forever without even hope of crossing the border, let alone the certainty of rehabilitation later. The woeful tale of the stampede and orgy that followed in the wake of the partition of the country would be forgotten in the course of time, but while memory serves, tears would always burst whenever the tragedy is recalled.
>
> (Dhiman 1962: 24–25)

I start with the above quote, which is taken from a small publication detailing the Punjab industries following partition because it encapsulates so much that is tragic about the partition. It highlights the human suffering, the violent (and as some argue genocidal) forced migration, and although the pain may eventually subside, this quote also touches upon the individual's capacity to recall those painful memories. Mustaq Soofi, in a recent article in *Dawn* (2013), quoted the title of Brecht's poem 'When the Wound Stops Hurting What Hurts is the Scar', and it is this 'scar' that continues to haunt Punjab: it is the spectre of a violent beginning which continues to loom over a divided home. But what happens once survivors pass away with the passage of time? Does that mean we forget about it? Is it no longer necessary to remember the event? Or does it become even more important to ensure that these memories are not lost with that generation? Many in the past have questioned why, surprisingly, there has not been a meaningful partition memorial of some sort to commemorate those who lost their lives and those who survived, and to promote peace between India and Pakistan.

There already exist some memorials: there is the Martyrs Monument in the purpose-built capital of Indian Punjab, Chandigarh, which commemorates the people lost during the freedom struggle and the partition of Punjab. In Pakistan, there is Bab-e-Pakistan in Lahore, which was developed on the Walton Camp site, which was one of the largest refugee camps in Punjab, and which commemorates the millions who were made homeless and destitute. There is also a small privately built peace memorial on the Indian side of the Attari-Wagah border, but these initiatives barely receive widespread coverage, and most of the general public are unaware of their existence. The push for a meaningful peace museum or memorial has been mooted for some time, it has largely been driven by peace activists, online campaigns and occasional endorsements by the political leadership on both sides of the border. These initiatives include Aman ki Asha, Friends without Borders, Indo Pak Bangla Friendship (one of the many Facebook forums) and Asiapeace, which was started by the Association for Communal Harmony in Asia in 2001 as part of a sustained and coordinated campaign to promote peace and harmony in South Asia. But these initiatives still remain marginal even though, rather importantly, they continue to maintain and encourage dialogue across borders.

There has obviously been some urgency to establish a memorial because those who witnessed these events first-hand are a fading generation. Personal testimonies of first-hand accounts have been collected by a number of historians (Talbot and Tatla 2006; Virdee 2009), and now increasingly by oral history projects within diaspora communities. The 1947 Partition Archive based in the United States is one example of the latter, but other smaller projects have also been conducted in the United Kingdom and oral testimony collections are preserved in Leicester, Cambridge and London (among other locations).[3] Some initiatives also exist in the subcontinent, such as the Citizens Archive of Pakistan (CAP), a repository for partition oral histories (and other projects) and the brainchild of the Academy Award-winning documentary maker, Sharmeen Obaid-Chinoy. In India, CAP worked closely with the Delhi-based NGO Routes2Roots on the 'Exchange for Change' project that encouraged interaction between children in order to demystify the 'other' by learning about their shared history and culture.[4] The Nehru Memorial Museum and Library in New Delhi also has a collection of interviews related to the freedom movement. But there is a vigour with which these projects are currently being conducted in the diaspora that is not found in either India or Pakistan. This may be partly explained through the exposure that the diaspora community has to other memorials, museums and commemorations, especially with respect to the Holocaust. There is evidently some cultural transfer taking place. Furthermore, there has been an increased interest in documenting 'hidden histories', in multicultural Britain at least; I have personally worked on two such projects with The Herbert Art Gallery and Museum (Coming to Coventry, 2006) and the Royal Geographical Society (The Punjab: Moving Journeys, 2008), respectively. Both of these projects were about incorporating minorities into mainstream history in public spaces. Projects such as these provide the impetus needed to explore and document partition narratives from a people's perspective.

Anindya Raychaudhuri argues that a partition museum would certainly help in healing and educating while at the same time 'helping in the project of nation-building by promoting an informed citizenry' (2012: 175). But Raychaudhuri's article is also titled 'Demanding the Impossible', which highlights how difficult the task of developing a memorial for partition has been. The natural place for a memorial or museum has always been at the Attari-Wagah border in Punjab. Thousands of people used this space to travel across the newly created Radcliffe boundary; special scheduled trains crossed the border carrying fleeing refugees, though some of those trains arrived at their destination in a charred and lifeless state. After the snake-like foot convoys, the trains were the most popular form for transporting the refugees, yet the history of partition is replete with horrific stories of planned attacks on trains, trains filled with corpses stripped of their former identities. The burning trains would arrive at platforms and motivate further reprisal killings. Some were lucky enough to survive:

> They [Sikhs] blocked the way of our train – halting our journey for three days. It seemed that the Sikhs were preparing for a big attack. There were four to five military men of Baloch regiment with us. With great effort of these soldiers our train set off again. On going a little ahead, we found scores of Sikhs lying on the ground, who were ready to attack our train. Our military men opened fire on them and the entrenchments of Sikhs became their graves.
>
> (Interview with Haji S., 2002)

Khuswant Singh's fictional account, *Train to Pakistan*, written in 1956, is perhaps the most widely quoted reference point for memories of partition atrocity. It captures all the absurdities of partition with its portrayal of Mano Majra, once a sleepy village, but now on the newly created border between India and Pakistan. The book poignantly ends with the dilemma facing the main protagonist over what action the villagers, as individuals, should take regarding a planned attack on a train headed for Pakistan with Muslim refugees. Singh's novel was important because it brought out the human dimension of partition; rather than focusing on the decision-makers, Singh told the story of how those decisions affected ordinary villages like Mano Majra and how villagers' lives were thrown into turmoil by decisions made far away.

It is indeed these ordinary voices that get trapped in the space that became two new nations after independence. The acclaimed short story writer Saadat Hasan Manto most poignantly touches upon the space that became 'no man's land' in his Urdu short story, *Toba Tek Singh*, first published in 1955. The story is set in a lunatic asylum, whose existence was overshadowed by the looming partition. Its inmates had little knowledge of how this would impact them. The madness of partition is set against the madness in the lunatic asylum and the story of Bishan Singh, more popularly known as Toba Tek Singh, an old town in what would become Pakistan. The exchange of population ultimately meant the exchange of the inmates in the asylum, and it is during this moment that Manto concludes his story:

> Before the sun rose, a piercing cry arose from Bishan Singh, who had been quiet and moving all this time. Several officers and the guards ran towards him; they saw that the man who, for fifteen years, had stood on his feet day and night, now lay on the ground, prostrate. Beyond a wired fence on one side of him was Hindustan and on the other side was Pakistan. In the middle, on a stretch of land which had no name, lay Toba Tek Singh.
> (Bhalla 1999: 573)

Manto, a migrant from India, was never completely at ease in Lahore and died in 1955, shortly after his arrival. The confusion of identity and citizenship is a theme which resonates in his work, and as the ending of *Toba Tek Singh* unfolds, we find the remnants of the many migrants that were torn between two spaces in no man's land. To mark Manto's birth centenary in 2012, Ajoka Theatre in Lahore developed a new play based on his writings, *Kaun hai Yeh Gustakh? (Who is this recalcitrant?)* This recent tribute to Manto testifies to the importance that literature continues to play in bridging the divisions between the people of India and Pakistan. Shahid Nadeem, the writer of *Kaun hai Yeh Gustakh?* has spoken about the importance of cultural exchanges as he prepared for the play's performance in Delhi (Interview with Shahid Nadeem, 2013).

Fiction was perhaps the only way in which the emotive, traumatic and religiously sensitive material could be depicted in countries that were divided on the basis of religion. It was also the ideal medium for capturing the ambiguities and the shades of grey of that divided ordinary people. Authors such as Intizar Hussain, Bhisham Sahni, Saadat Hasan Manto and Amrita Pritam (Bhalla 1999; Hasan 1997) wrote from their own personal experiences of dislocation and captured the human drama of partition. The universal suffering, psychological scars, violent realties, painful misery of brutalizing women's bodies and disillusionment of the new states are themes which could be explored through the medium of fiction. The trauma associated with the partition and displacement is something that both the states of India and Pakistan have shied away from because this became the necessary price of freedom and separation. Additionally, fiction was an ideal medium because there was also a deep nostalgia for a happier undivided land.

The nostalgia for the past can also play out more dramatically. This is most poignantly captured in the film *Khamosh Pani* (2003), which depicts the human drama and trauma of 1947 through the rise of Mohammad Zia-ul-Haq's military dictatorship (1978–1988) in Pakistan. Set during his rise to power in

1979, the two narratives are interwoven, and gradually we begin to see the narrative threads unravelling; however, we also see the parallels between the two narratives become clear. The main protagonist of the film is Ayesha, and as the film progresses, we see through flashbacks how she decided not to jump into the well to save her 'honour'. Dishonoured in her family's eyes, she was captured by Muslims, raped and ultimately married to one of her captors before converting to Islam. Through the unfolding narrative, we see the scars of that painful period which is depicted by her fear of the village well and her refusal to go near it. The elders in the community are aware of this traumatic past, but remain silent throughout, until one day Ayesha learns that her brother is visiting a Sikh *gurdwara* (place of worship) with other pilgrims from India. Through this turning point, Ayesha's son, Saleem, learns of his mother's past. But a radicalized Saleem is unforgiving, and Ayesha ultimately jumps into that well. The violence depicted is not always actual, it is sometimes psychological, and this manifests itself in a number of ways. We see the violence from her family, her refusal to make that pre-emptive sacrifice, the enveloping political violence which targeted women like Ayesha, and the silent trauma that haunted her throughout her life. We then finally see her son disowning his own mother and his own past. Saleem's gradual affinity with Zia-ul-Haq's form of Islam and rejection of his more moderate upbringing is the parallel narrative that shows the darker side of religious fervour.

Remembering to forget

Since the publication of Butalia's groundbreaking book, *The Other Side of Silence* (1998), in which she places ordinary people at the centre of this great tragedy, there has been a significant shift in collecting oral testimonies from survivors of the partition violence and those who were forced to migrate as a result of partition. It has allowed the researcher to delve into the human story and the everyday lived experience. This stands in contrast to earlier accounts, which were predominately concerned with 'high politics' and which relied on documentary sources. Thus, by weaving in fictional, autobiographical and first-hand accounts we can try to make some sense of a violent past. The quote below from Ahmed (2012) highlights how, as an individual, Mujahid Taj Din tries to justify his own actions during 1947. He was a member of the Khaksar movement[5] and was involved in a group attack on a Gurdwara in the Mozang area of Lahore. While he talks about his actions, he is at the same time providing legitimacy and justification for his actions. The local sub-inspector invokes religious duty to gather Din, amongst others, to attack the Sikhs in Mozang in order to ultimately clear space for incoming Muslim refugees:

> He [sub-inspector] told us that if we died fighting against non-Muslims we will be shaheeds (martyrs) and if we survived we will be ghazis (soldiers of Allah). He told us that our Muslim brothers and sisters were being

> killed in India ... When we attacked there were not more than 20 to 30 Sikh men and women in the temple. All of them perished in the inferno ... We were told that Pakistan would be an Islamic state ... To achieve that, Hindus and Sikhs, who were Kafirs (infidels), had to be killed or kicked out of Pakistan. However, we never got our Islamic state ... then why were we asked to do what we did? ... I pray to God to give me mafi (pardon) for the murder of those Sikhs and Hindus ... We were misguided and used by our politicians.
>
> (Ahmed 2012: 291–292)

While it is possible that Mujahid Taj Din is remorseful and that he wants to apologize for his actions, there are also numerous questions about the motives leading to this possibility: his remorse is based on memories created retrospectively, which are malleable and pragmatic, and, perhaps in Din's case, influenced by the warm reception he had when he visited Delhi in 1968 as part of a delegation.

But the need to forget and move away from the place of trauma is a useful tool to erase those painful memories. The account below with a migrant who came to England in 1965 'attests to the power of the need to forget, to erase history or memory as a basis for identity' (Raj 1997: 108). Raphael Samuel and Paul Thompson, referring to Freud, assert that 'memory is inherently revisionist, an exercise in selective amnesia. What is forgotten may be as important as what is remembered' (quoted in Raj 1997: 108):

> Yes, our family was first in Punjab, then we went to Bihar, then we came here ... We were in West Pakistan, in Rawalpindi. Then we were in East Ham, now we are in Leyton so how many places you want to remember? For what? ... So I am from nowhere, because connections are just like footsteps, you move your foot and erase the previous mark. The step is gone.
>
> (Raj 1997: 107)

Thus, erasing those former memories alleviates the fractures – though the problem for many of the partition refugees is that there has been no closure. The forced displacement following the violent and traumatic start led to permanent fractures because of the strained relations between India and Pakistan since 1947. Furthermore, there are cultural pressures which meant that, in the case of what happened to women, there has been almost complete silence. When I interviewed Farkhanda Lodi, a Punjabi writer, she expressed her sadness at the suffering that women are subjected to, suggesting that women are forced to remain weak due to their social and cultural conditioning. In her interview, she reflected on the plight of women in Pakistan:

> As you see our respectable culture does not allow us to speak about such things. That is why she never discusses this issue [referring to

> abduction] ... She is weak, helpless and vulnerable. She has been forced to remain weak. It is the training; she gets this from her parents, culture and the social environment that develop in her a pitiable pathetic soul. Our system and society do not allow her to progress. So she is in pain, for me her life is a constant misery ... .
>
> (Interview with Farkhanda Lodi, 2007)

While Lodi touched on the issue of silence surrounding the discussion of this painful past, especially in relation to women, others often internalized those childhood memories. Having spent many years interviewing partition refugees, one theme that resonates constantly is how many people felt that it was a temporary measure and that once the law and order situation was brought under control, they would return to their homes. But increasingly, the new nations of India and Pakistan were defined by difference that added permanence to the border and more importantly to the division amongst the people. As Amitav Ghosh says, 'If there is no difference, both sides will be the same; it will be just like it used to be before ... what was it all for then? Partition and all the killing and everything?' (quoted in Mukherjee 2009: 448). Many of the refugees I spoke to harboured hope of returning, but as the following extract highlights, this hope faded with time, especially for Abdul. Abdul was 19 at the time of partition and was originally from the Chaura Bazaar area of Ludhiana, India. His family had a small hosiery business in Ludhiana, but left in August 1947 due to the increased tension in the town. He was one of the many who left in a train escorted by the military to Lahore; from there, he moved around and eventually settled in Lyallpur:

> Many people thought about going back to Ludhiana in few years ... We knew partition occurred on a national level and not on provincial levels. We were right because nobody could go back and partition could not be undone. This discussion has refreshed my memories, and a stream has taken me back to my city, my street, bazaars and the mosque.
>
> (Interview with Abdul, 2003)

Abdul was certainly moved by the discussion of 1947, but interestingly he still uses the possessive to indicate that it (although not within his physical reach) is *his* city and *his* street. In this sense, oral histories and memories narrate a different story to the official national discourse. While the official public testimonies talk about the freedom movement and the creation of Pakistan, the unofficial private testimonies still hark back to the undivided land; there is then still much nostalgia for the pre-partitioned homeland. But there is no celebration, only vague diminishing memories of ancestral homelands; silences reverberate because there is limited public discourse about this very human tragedy. But while these accounts remain, they will always evoke a bleak period in the subcontinent's history. Interestingly, in a recent trilogy, documentary film-maker Ajay Bhardwaj has been attempting to capture this hazy space that is the shared and composite culture of Punjab. In his film, *Milange Babey Ratan De Mele Te* (*Let's Meet at Baba Ratan's Fair*), he captures the voices of a marginalized idea of Punjabiyat ('Punjabiness', especially through language; see Ayres 2008), which becomes replaced by contending identities through the establishment of two new nation-states. In this film, Bhardwaj takes you through a journey that pieces together remnants of a pre-partitioned Punjab in which identities were fluid and people blended together in fairs and Sufi shrines. While Bhardwaj attempts to 'recover' these lost traditions and bring them into the mainstream, others content themselves with nostalgia.

Conclusion

It has to be remembered that the violence that erupted in August 1947 was not a unique event as such; it was the culmination of a chain reaction. It followed months, indeed years, of political tension and was partially reactive in retaliation for the riots that took place in March 1947 in Rawalpindi. However, the riots in March were intrinsically linked to the partition period, and the increasing prevalence of violence as a political tool in that period is an element that requires further analysis. What is also apparent in the case of Punjab is how the boundaries between the perpetrator and victim are blurred. The academic discussion about to what extent we can consider 1947 to be a genocide continues; the longer-term legacy has been that people cannot forget (though they may want to) that they are shaped by the spectre of partition. This is true for the lands that were partitioned more so than the whole nation-state, which in its vastness can conveniently forget partition.

The demographic changes resulting from the population exchange after 1947 are important in understanding the mindset of the two new nations. Gyan Pandey notes how the violence of 1947 created new subjects and new positions. He argues that after partition, individuals and families had to remake themselves and 'had to struggle to overcome new fears, to gradually rebuild faith and trust and hope and to conceive new histories – and new "memories" that are, in some reckonings – "best forgotten"' (2001: 16). By creating new subjects, memories are not only different from the official voices, but they are also re-imagined to accommodate the new landscape, a territory which was plural, but now speaks the language of homogeneity. Remembering the violent beginnings would mean unearthing 'hidden histories' of pre-1947 which attest to a different history and one that conflicts with the politics of the present. But generations have now grown up with distorted histories and a curriculum of hatred (Kumar 2002) that try to erase the other – partitioned histories that encourage and reflect perceived differences. Oral testimonies play a vital role in documenting this period from a human perspective while challenging nationalist discourse. Yet even these memories can be selective in recalling the past: shaped by retrospective authenticity, they can emulate nationalist discourse too.

This raises the question of whether we can ever have a lasting memorial that represents the victims of the partition. How can the grief and pain suffered by millions of people during this great upheaval be recognized and acknowledged? Memorials in India and Pakistan are likely to consider only one side; it is unlikely they will acknowledge the butchering of the 'other'. And so the legacy of partition continues. It is here that the numerous fictional accounts, poems and some visual representations are useful in capturing those nuanced emotions. The greys of historical truths are captured in these cultural representations of partition.

Notes

1 Veena Das and Ashis Nandy see 'traditional' violence in terms of a feud in which communities continue to live together afterwards (177–190).
2 Mountbatten is discussing Leonard Mosley's *The Last Days of the British Raj*, which was published in 1961 and which was very much pro-British in its consideration of the final days in India.
3 The 1947 Partition Archive: http://www.1947partitionarchive.org/; East Midlands Oral History Archive, Leicester; Centre of South Asian Studies, The Oral History Collection, Cambridge. Andrew Whitehead has deposited his partition interviews at the School of Oriental and African Studies, University of London.
4 The Citizens Archive of Pakistan's official website: http://www.citizensarchive.org/projects/; Routes2Roots's website: http://www.routes2roots.com/home.php.
5 The Khaksar movement established by Allama Mashriqi was based in Lahore and concerned with uplifting of the masses and with freeing them from British rule. In 1940, there was a violent confrontation between the Khaksars and the colonial government.

Bibliography

Ahmed, I. (2012) *The Punjab Bloodied, Partitioned and Cleansed*, Oxford and Karachi: Oxford University Press.

Ayres, A. (2008) 'Language, the Nation, and Symbolic Capital: The Case of Punjab', *The Journal of Asian Studies*, 67.3: 917–946.

Baldwin, S.S. (2000) *What the Body Remembers*, London: Anchor.

Bhalla, A. (1999) *Stories about the Partition of India*, New Delhi: HarperCollins.

Bhasin-Malik, K. (2007) *In the Making: Identity Formation in South Asia*, Gurgaon: Three Essays Collective.

Brass, P. (2003a) *The Production of Hindu-Muslim Violence in Contemporary India*, Seattle: University of Washington Press.

——. (2003b) 'The Partition of India and Retributive Genocide in the Punjab 1946–1947: Means, Methods and Purposes', *Journal of Genocide Research*, 5.1: 71–101.

Butalia, U. (1998) *The Other Side of Silence: Voices from the Partition of India*, New Delhi: Penguin Books.

Chatterji, J. (2007) *The Spoils of Partition: Bengal and India 1947–1967*, Cambridge: Cambridge University Press.

Chester, L. (2009) *Borders and Conflict in South Asia: The Radcliffe Boundary Commission and the Partition of Punjab*, Manchester: Manchester University Press.

Copland, I. (1998) 'The Further Shores of Partition: Ethnic Cleansing in Rajasthan in 1947', *Past and Present*, 160: 203–239.

Das, V. and A. Nandy. (1986) 'Violence, Victimhood and the Language of Silence', in V. Das (ed.) *The Word and the World: Fantasy, Symbol and Record*, New Delhi: Sage Publications.

Dhiman, R. (1962) *Punjab Industries*, Ludhiana: Dhiman Press of India.

Engle, K. (2005) 'Feminism and its (Dis)contents: Criminalizing Wartime Rape in Bosnia and Herzegovina', *The American Journal of International Law*, 99.4: 778–816.

Francisco, J. (2000) 'In the Heat of Fratricide: The Literature of India's Partition Burning Freshly', in M. Hasan (ed.) *Inventing Boundaries: Gender, Politics and the Partition of India*, New Delhi: Oxford University Press.

French, P. (1997) *Liberty or Death: India's Journey to Independence and Division*, London: HarperCollins.

Hansen, A.B. (2002) *Partition and Genocide: Manifestation of Violence in Punjab, 1937–1947*, New Delhi: India Research Press.

Hasan, M. (1997) *India Partitioned: The Other Face of Freedom*, Vol. 1, New Delhi: Roli Books.

Kabir, A.J. (2002) 'Subjectivities, Memories, Loss of Pigskin Bags, Silver Spittoons and the Partition of India', *Interventions: International Journal of Postcolonial Studies*, 4.2: 245–264.

Kamran, T. (2007) 'The Unfolding Crisis in Punjab, March–August 1947: Key Turning Points and British Responses', *Journal of Punjab Studies*, 14.2: 187–210.

Keller, S. (1975) *Uprooting and Social Change: The Role of Refugees in Development*, Delhi: Manohar Book Service.

Khaliquzzaman, C. (1961) *Pathway to Pakistan*, Lahore: Longmans.

Khamosh Pani (Silent Waters). (2003). Film. Directed by Sabiha Sumar. New York: First Run/Icarus Films.

Khosla, G.D. (1989 [1949]) *Stern Reckoning: A Survey of Events Leading Up to and Following the Partition of India*, New Delhi: Oxford University Press.

Kumar, K. (2002) 'Partition in School Textbooks: A Comparative Look at India and Pakistan', in S. Settar and I. B. Gupta (eds) *Pangs of Partition*, Vol. 2, New Delhi: Manohar Book Service.

Lal, V. (n.d.) 'Partitioned Selves, Partitioned Pasts: A Commentary on Ashis Nandy's "The Death of an Empire"', Available at: http://www.sscnet.ucla.edu/southasia/History/Independent/Partitionselves.html. Accessed: 17 July 2013.

Letters on Divide and Quit. (1962) Letter from Mountbatten of Burma, 2 March 1962. Mss Eur F230/34, India Office Records and Private Papers, British Library.

Major, A. (1995) 'The Chief Sufferers: The Abduction of Women during the Partition of the Punjab', *South Asia: Journal of South Asian Studies*, 18 (Suppl. 1): 57–72.

Mann, M. (2005) *The Dark Side of Democracy: Explaining Ethnic Cleansing*, Cambridge: Cambridge University Press.

Menon, R. and K. Bhasin. (1998) *Borders and Boundaries: Women in India's Partition*, New Delhi: Kali for Women.

Menon, V.P. (1985) *The Transfer of Power in India*, New Delhi: Sangam Books.

Milange Babey Ratan De Mele Te (Let's Meet at Baba Ratan's Fair). (2012). Film. Directed by Ajay Bhardwaj. Delhi: Mainstay Production.

Misri, D. (2011) 'The Violence of Memory: Renarrating Partition Violence in Shauna Singh Baldwin's What the Body Remembers', *Meridians: Feminism, Race, Transnationalism*, 11.1: 1–25.

Mosley, L. (1961) *The Last Days of the British Raj*, London: Weidenfeld and Nicolson.

Mukherjee, M. (2009) 'Dissimilar Twins: Residue of 1947 in the Twenty-First Century', *Social Semiotics*, 19.4: 441–451.

Pandey, G. (2001) *Remembering Partition: Violence, Nationalism and History in India*, Cambridge: Cambridge University Press.

Raj, D.S. (1997) 'Partition and Diaspora: Memories and Identities of Punjabi Hindus in London', *International Journal of Punjab Studies*, 4.1: 100–127.

Rajan, A. (2011) 'Memory's Harvest', *The Hindu*. 14 May 2011. Available at: http://www.thehindu.com/todays-paper/tp-features/tp-metroplus/article2017464.ece. Accessed: 17 July 2013.

Raychaudhuri, A. (2012) 'Demanding the Impossible: Exploring the Possibilities of a National Partition Museum in India', *Social Semiotics, 22.2: 173–186.*

Singh, K. (1956) *Train to Pakistan*, New York: Grove Press.

Singh, K. (ed.). (2006) *Select Documents on Partition of Punjab – 1947*, Delhi: National Book Shop.

Soofi, M. (2013) 'A Spectre Haunts Punjab!', *Dawn*. Available at: http://x.dawn.com/2013/06/21/a-spectre-haunts-punjab/. Accessed: 17 July 2013.

Talbot, I. (ed.). (2007) *The Deadly Embrace: Religion, Violence and Politics in India and Pakistan 1947–2002*, Karachi: Oxford University Press.

Talbot, I. and G. Singh. (1999) *Region and Partition: Bengal, Punjab and the Partition of the Subcontinent*, Karachi: Oxford University Press.

——. (2009) *The Partition of India*, Cambridge: Cambridge University Press.

Talbot, I. and D.S. Tatla. (eds). (2006) *Epicentre of Violence: Partition Voices and Memories from Amritsar*, Delhi: Permanent Black.

Tan, T. and G. Kudaisya. (2000) *The Aftermath of Partition in South Asia*, London: Routledge.

Totten, S. and W. Parsons. (eds). (2013) *Centuries of Genocide: Essays and Eyewitness Accounts*, London: Routledge.

United Nations High Commissioner for Human Rights. (1948) Article 2 of the *Convention on the Prevention and Punishment of the Crime of Genocide*. Approved by the United Nations General Assembly Resolution 260 A (III) of 9 December 1948. Available at: http://www.genocidewatch.org/genocide/whatisit.html. Accessed: 17 July 2013.

Virdee, P. (2007) 'Partition and the Absence of Communal Violence in Malerkotla', in I. Talbot (ed.) *The Deadly Embrace: Religion, Politics and Violence in the Indian Subcontinent 1947–2002*, Karachi: Oxford University Press.

——. (2009) 'Negotiating the Past: Journey through Muslim Women's Experience of Partition and Resettlement in Pakistan', *Cultural and Social History*, 6.4: 467–484.

Yong, T.T. (1997) '"Sir Cyril Goes to India": Partition Boundary-Making and Disruptions in the Punjab', *International Journal of Punjab Studies*, 4.1: 1–20.

Interviews

Interview with Farkhanda Lodi, Lahore, April 2007.

Interview with Abdul, Montgomery Bazaar, Faisalabad, January 2003.

Interview with Haji S., who migrated from Ludhiana, December 2002.

Interview with Shahid Nadeem, Lahore, January 2013.

2 Three films, one genocide

Remembering the Armenian Genocide through *Ravished Armenia*(s)

Donna-Lee Frieze

Introduction

When *Ravished Armenia* – an eight-reel, eighty-five-minute, silent dramatized film based on actual events – first screened in New York City in 1919, it was primarily for the purposes of fundraising. Aurora Mardiganian, a survivor of the Armenian Genocide, played the lead role in this film. However, the entire full-length feature film was thought lost until recently, when a twenty-minute segment of the film was found in Armenia. Following the separate discovery in Yerevan (the capital of Armenia) in 1994 by Eduardo Kozanlian and Zareh Tjeknavorian, respectively, the twenty-minute segment was incorporated into two new films (although both used the same footage), one by Tjeknavorian, the other by Richard Kloian. Both films are distinct in their notions of filmic representation, memory and the sacred memorialization of the Genocide. It is no oversight that one rendering is titled *Ravished Armenia* in order to pay homage to the original film and the Genocide. The second rendering, titled *Credo*, aims to separate itself from the initial film. The two versions illuminate notions of memorialization and reflection, and yet the new *Ravished Armenia* and *Credo* utilize different editing and audio techniques – the former with pedagogical motives and the latter with an emphasis on aesthetics and affect – in order to produce two disparate ways of remembering the Genocide.

Despite being lost for over ninety years, the original *Ravished Armenia* remains a revered text among generations of Armenians as demonstrated by the present-day reactions to the two subsequent twenty-minute versions of the film. The two current versions speak exclusively, and yet distinctly, to the memorialization and the remembering of the Genocide. As the 1919 film no longer exists, *Ravished Armenia's* function as a tool of remembering has ceased. The new *Ravished Armenia* and *Credo* function as ghosts of the original film and as tributes to the original film's status in the Armenian diaspora. In order to explain the origins of the two new films, this chapter provides a brief history of the events of 1915 and outlines the purpose behind the making of the original film, including Mardiganian's tortured re-enactment of the Genocide. It then explores the significance of the new

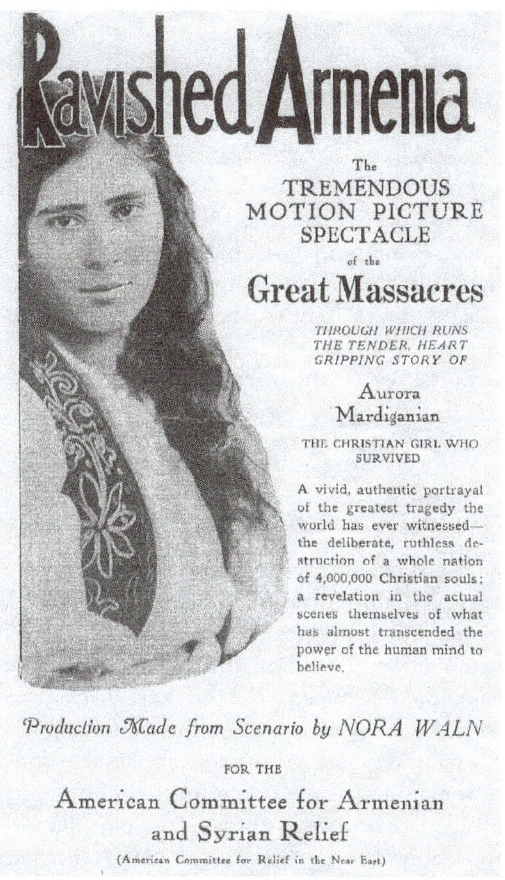

Figure 2.1 American Committee for Armenian and Syrian Relief poster for *Ravished Armenia*. Reproduced with permission of the Armenian Genocide Museum-Institute.

versions and how film is used in the transformation of the memory of the Genocide.

There have been many films produced on genocide; they primarily began being made in the 1980s, but their frequency increased in the 1990s and into the twenty-first century due to the increased awareness of genocidal activity across the globe. Most, but by no means all, films about genocide have been documentaries which focused on the plight of victims, lack of political global will, testimony from various global and regional actors, and survivor testimony. Most commonly, fiction films are centred around the circumstances of an individual, with the hope of capturing viewer identification, if not with the victim's predicament, then at least with the emotions of the protagonist victim. Few films on genocide, whether documentary or fiction, speak specifically to the notion of the group. Thus, although film has, on occasion, been an effective way of communicating group destruction, it can be a powerful medium for understanding and provoking empathy for an individual portrayed on the screen who has been the victim of group destruction. With a plethora of films about genocide that focus on individual suffering within group chaos (for example, see *No Man's Land*, *Savior*, *Rabbit-Proof Fence*, *The Grey Zone*, *Life is Beautiful*, *The Pianist* and *Sometimes in April*), cinema audiences are arguably conditioned to understand and remember past genocides as personal tragedies. A defining and unique feature of *Ravished Armenia* is its hybridized genres, blending a fictional account of Mardiganian's genocide experience with documentary 'truth', presenting the film to its audience in 1919 as a 'frank story' (*Ravished Armenia* 2009). As outlined below, the new *Ravished Armenia* capitalizes on the documentary effect of the original, while *Credo*, less concerned with defining itself as either a documentary or drama, is more engaged with the affect of remembering.

The Armenian Genocide and *Ravished Armenia*

On 24 April 1915 in Constantinople, Ottoman authorities – the Committee of Union and Progress (CUP), a political organization that began as a revolutionary party – rounded up approximately 250 prominent Armenian intellectuals, professionals, and political and cultural figures, and exterminated them. As the genocide developed, the targeting of important Armenian cultural leaders became a pattern throughout Ottoman Turkey (Balakian 2003: 211). Such executions are common genocidal techniques, as perpetrators believe the remainder of the community will be reluctant to revolt if their leaders are killed. Moreover, these acts may demonstrate intent to destroy the remainder of the group. Shortly after their arrest, Armenian men in the Ottoman army were disarmed and then executed in order to destabilize the remaining Armenian population (Balakian 2003: 176; 178). Ostensibly, the CUP was punishing the Armenians (who numbered approximately two million) living in Ottoman Turkey for colluding with the Russians against the Ottomans during the First World War. Despite this perceived treachery, the Armenians had been a persecuted Christian minority living loyally under Ottoman rule for hundreds of years. The disintegration of said rule in the late-nineteenth and early-twentieth centuries coincided with the emergence of Turkish nationalism and discrimination against 'the non-Muslim subjects of the empire', who 'rendered that empire ripe for perennial conflicts' (Dadrian and Akçam 2011:13). In the context of war and determined not to repeat the Balkan Syndrome – autonomy and equal economic and human rights, in this case for the Armenians, resulting in political destabilization – the CUP prepared the 'ground for a radical solution' against the background of the allied invasion of the Dardanelles Peninsula in 1915 (Dadrian and Akçam 2011:14). According to Jay Winter, the British Allied landing at Gallipoli 'clearly aimed to knock Turkey out of the war ... [and] precipitated elements of the genocide, evidently planned before the assault on the peninsula' (Winter 2003:40). From April 1915, the Armenian population was subjected to forced deportations without food, water or shelter; mass killings; rape; sexual slavery and mandatory conversion. In short, the Ottomans committed intended group destruction of the Armenians, a deft description of what was later to be termed 'genocide'. This occurred all over Ottoman Turkey, intensifying in 1915 when up to one million Armenians were massacred. After gruelling death marches into the northern part of the Syrian Desert in 1916, Armenians were again massacred. The genocide continued, with less intensity, until 1922. It is estimated that 1.5 million Armenians were killed (Balakian 2003: 179–180). The genocide destroyed part of the group not only through massacres, but through slavery, conversions, and deportations as well. Women and children were the principal victims of the latter, since most of the men had already been murdered. The Armenian Genocide was not a consequence of the war; the CUP used the war to justify the Genocide. Many missionaries and ambassadors witnessed the genocide, but perhaps the most reliable eyewitness in the English-speaking world was Henry Morgenthau Sr, the American ambassador to the Ottoman Empire beginning in 1913 (Morgenthau 1918). Because the United States was still neutral in the war, Morgenthau held his post until 1916 and thus witnessed massacres and tortures, which he described in detail in his memoir (Morgenthau 1918: 306–308). Morgenthau's account was considered highly authoritative: he even had an acting role in *Ravished Armenia*, giving the stamp of authenticity to the Mardiganian story (Kozanlian 1999: 2).

The Ottoman regime had disintegrated by the time Mustafa Kemal (Atatürk) – with his 'master-narrative of modern Turkish history' (Ulgen 2010: 369) – became modern-day Turkey's first president in 1923. Atatürk's desire to court the modern European world coincided with his eagerness to forget *and* deny the past, accentuating his 'master-narrative' of Ottoman history and Turkish nationalism. Historian Taner Akçam claims that Atatürk may have displayed contrition regarding the treatment of the Armenians – calling the events 'a shameful act' (Akçam 2006); however, there is stronger historical evidence that suggests Atatürk combined 'the myth of "murderous Armenians"' with the victimization narrative of the Turks 'as an "oppressed nation"'(Ulgen 2010: 371), versions of history that would establish official Turkish nationalism and ideology. The rise of Atatürk may have coincided with the beginning of the vicious denial campaign of the genocide that continues vigorously in Turkey today, and which is why the original *Ravished Armenia*, released four years before Atatürk's presidency, marks a time of remembering.

With no homeland to return to (Armenia became a short-lived republic from 1918 to 1920), survivors of the Genocide spread into the diaspora, from the Middle East to the United States. Aurora Mardiganian, an orphaned survivor of the Armenian Genocide, found her way to the United States, arriving on 5 November 1917, searching for her only surviving family member, a brother (Bay Area Armenian National Committee 2009). Film historian Anthony Slide is credited with bringing Mardiganian's story and surviving intertitles from the original film to print, allowing a historical investigation into *Ravished Armenia* (Slide 1997). According to Slide, Mardiganian's adopted Armenian-American parents placed advertisements in the paper searching for the lost brother when the notifications caught the eye of newspaper journalists, who interviewed her regarding her experiences of the Genocide. As a result of these interviews, screenwriter Harvey Gates and his wife were quick to see the 'commercial potential' of Mardiganian's story, and eventually the Gates's 'became her legal guardians'. Mardiganian wrote her memoir in Armenian in 1918, which Gates interpreted into English through a translator (Slide 1997: 6–7). Because Mardiganian's English was poor, she had no means with which to verify Gates's reconstruction of her story. The book, titled *Ravished Armenia* and published in 1918, was widely read by the American and British community, as was the same memoir published in the United Kingdom the following year. In 1919, at the prompting of Gates, Mardiganian signed papers authorizing her to appear in a 'picture', which she understood to mean a still photograph. Gates then rushed her to Los Angeles to star in a film about her experiences in the Genocide (Slide 1997: 7).

Ravished Armenia directed by Oscar Apfel was the creation of the American Committee for Armenian and Syrian Relief, a missionary organization developed in 1915 to help victims of the Armenian Genocide. One of the screenwriters was Nora Waln, who was the publicity secretary for the Committee (Armenian Genocide Museum-Institute 2011; Torchin 2006: 214). Proceeds from the film, which eventually reached thirty million US dollars, went to the charity Near East Relief and provided food and shelter for thousands of Armenian orphans (Armenian Genocide Museum-Institute 2011). It also helped to mobilize support for the League of Nations' 'protection of persecuted minorities' (Aldgate and Robertson 2005: 38). It was not unusual for Hollywood in its formative years to produce films on 'distant places and eras … as part of a broader attempt to elevate the cultural legitimacy of the motion picture industry' (Brégent-Heald 2010:146). It was a favourable outcome for everyone – for everyone except Mardiganian.

The apparent 'goodwill' and 'benevolence' behind the making of the film proved traumatic for Mardiganian. She was not prepared in any way for acting or acting out her genocidal narrative, nor was she equipped to cope with the publicity. For instance, after she stepped out of her dressing room and was confronted with men wearing fezzes and swords she thought: 'they fooled me. I thought they were going to give me to these Turks to finish my life' (quoted in Slide 1997: 9). During the production, she fell off a high set and broke her ankle, but she was still required to act in the film and walk on her foot in spite of the pain. Slide pointedly remarks that audiences would believe that the bandages around her ankle 'covered wounds inflicted by the Turks rather than the barbarians of Hollywood' (Slide 1997: 9). Mardiganian had to endure this after she witnessed the horror that many other Armenian

Figure 2.2 American Committee for Relief in the Near East fundraising campaign for *Ravished Armenia*, January 1919. Reproduced with permission of the Armenian Genocide Museum-Institute.

Genocide survivors experienced: the murder of her parents and siblings (Balakian 2003: 314). Mardiganian's story (as a survivor of the Genocide – and Hollywood) has turned her into a powerful symbol and an agent of remembrance. In some contemporary Armenian circles, she is known as the 'predecessor of Anne Frank' (Sánchez 1996: 10), which elevates her status as a genocide victim and as the ultimate martyr in remembering the Armenian Genocide.

Ravished Armenia was, as Slide puts it, an 'eyewitness report ... presented as popular entertainment for the masses ... of an oppressed minority – a minority that just happened to be white and Christian and with which most Americans could empathize' (Slide 1997: 3). In other words, the film claimed dramatized documentary truth, sought missionary aims through aid to orphaned Armenian children and had a fair dose of cynicism behind it (McLagan 2006: 191). *Ravished Armenia* was a sensation, not because it was highly crafted – indeed it received only a few lukewarm reviews (Torchin 2006: 214) – but because the publicity focused on rape, redemption, religion and race. As Meg McLagan points out, *Ravished Armenia* 'was a coproduction of commercial and quasi-Christian-quasi-humanitarian human rights interests' (2006: 193). How the Genocide is remembered is influenced by the rediscovered film; the navigation between human rights movements in the early twentieth century; the 'affect-intensive images and narratives' (McLagan 2006: 194); and, more controversially, the film's focus on sexual violence.

The emphasis on the sexual violence on women in the film cannot be overlooked, particularly as this genocide is more widely associated with its deportations (as gas chambers are associated with the Holocaust). The poster for the New York City opening insists that this film will make 'the blood of American women boil', and the advertising for the film 'enticed' audiences to see 'girls impaled on soldiers' swords' (Bay Area Armenian National Committee 2009), promising that '*Ravished Armenia* ... [will] show real harems' (Apfel quoted in Slide 1997: 10). Sequences focusing on old men with

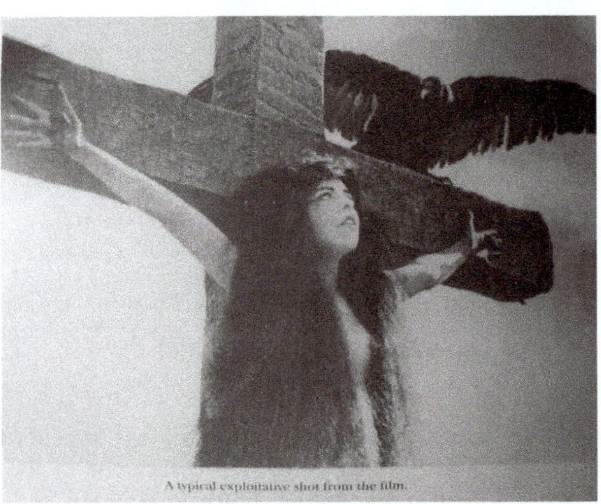
A typical exploitative shot from the film.

Figure 2.3 Still from the last frames of *Ravished Armenia*. Reproduced with permission of the Armenian Genocide Museum-Institute.

their nails ripped out were deemed 'too horrible for public use', but images of impalement through the anus or vagina were considered appropriate.

What attracted Gates and the others in early Hollywood were Mardiganian's syncretic qualities – a white but exotic child-woman, Christian female who is raped by the savage, dark-skinned, Muslim Turk. Indeed, it was not uncommon for women to be portrayed by Hollywood at the time as 'youthful, beautiful, mysterious, strong-willed, and exotic orphans, who are nonetheless marked as asexual child-women' (Brégent-Heald 2010: 147), nor was it unusual for audiences in the 1910s and 1920s to have their stereotypes reinforced: the uncouth, dark-skinned male (especially from Europe) who 'lacked the ability to exercise [sexual] self-control' (Shrock 1997: 72) would have helped fuel compassion for the innocent white, Christian female. Despite the shocking images that *Ravished Armenia* must have portrayed and the remakes/recreations that contain traces of these sequences, the film validates the genocide and shows that parts of the Western world cared enough to incorporate a narrative of the events into their popular culture.

Because the original film was created during a period of outside acknowledgement of the events, it is understandable that it is considered sacred and that it is an ideal vehicle for remembering the Genocide. First, it is the earliest film made on the Genocide and possibly the first film produced on *any* genocide. *Ravished Armenia* was produced and screened at a time when the events of the Genocide were not officially questioned or debated by the Western world. In addition, the 'images ... are of the same time period as the historic events they tell' (Sánchez 1996: 10). Hence, for some in the diaspora, *Ravished Armenia* (while not of course believed to be a documentary) takes on a 'notable documentary *effect*' (Sánchez 1996: 10, my emphasis) in much the same way it did on its release. This effect ensures that Mardiganian's film is perceived by viewers as a raw slice of testimony, validating the truth of the Genocide. Seen in this way, *Ravished Armenia* is 'one of the biggest pillars standing against the Turkish denial almost a century later' (Moraitis 2011). Finally, it was produced while Armenia was an independent nation-state (before it was incorporated into the Soviet Union), albeit, a troubled and short-lived one: the film represented a wholeness of a period that was soon to be fractured. Thus, Mardiganian's ephemeral fame coincided with the brief existence of the Democratic Republic of Armenia (Ulgen 2010: 376–377; Bloxham 2005: 99–100). The four-year period is a crucial time in history for the Armenian diaspora, an almost mythological period, when the Genocide was remembered, mourned and acknowledged by the Western world and its 'cause' embraced by the United States and, in particular, by President Woodrow Wilson's Fourteen Points (Wilson's attempt to end the war and create peace in Europe), which, in its twelfth point, implied the protection of Armenians (Wilson 1918).

The blurring of the distinction between factual documentary and fictional account extends to the life of the film in which the tropes of fracturing, dispossession and manipulated identity were curiously mimicked. To begin with, Harvey Gates changed Arshaluys Mardigian's Armenian name to (an only slightly less Armenian-sounding name) Aurora Mardiganian (Slide 1997: 7). The film was interchangeably titled *Ravished Armenia* and *Rape of Armenia*, and at some point it was called *Memorial of Truth* and even *Armenia Crucified* (American Film Institute Catalogue n.d.). Even though the film opened uncensored in New York to packed audiences, in Britain, where it was given the more ghostly title, *Auction of Souls*, the film was censored. However, with the permission of Scotland Yard, it opened three weeks before the book (upon which it was based) was banned in libraries across Britain and the United States in 1920 due to its graphic material (Armenian Genocide Museum-Institute 2011). Released in cinemas across the world, *Ravished Armenia* was a reminder that the Genocide forced many survivors to live in the diaspora. *Ravished Armenia* is very much the product of the diaspora: for example, the sequences of the iconic Mount Ararat were filmed at Mount Baldy in California, and Santa Monica Beach was chosen to represent the Syrian Desert (Bay Area Armenian National Committee 2009).

If only to deepen the identity problems of *Ravished Armenia*, its life after its brief existence is, from 1920 onwards, cloaked in mystery and rumour. Some contemporary Armenians living in the diaspora say the film went missing, while others claim it was destroyed. Others still are convinced that, with the exception of a few reels, the film 'disappeared under Turkish influence' (Sánchez 1996: 10–11). Some argue that the original nitrate film was lost at sea on a journey to Georgia or was 'stolen by thieves' (Armenian Genocide Museum-Institute 2011). The sacredness of *Ravished Armenia* contributes to the romantic image of the film lost at sea, still alive on its waves, and it reinforces the notion that the 'documentary effect' meant as much to the Turks as to the Armenians. In many ways, it would seem that the life and the attempted deaths of the film – through censorship and its virtual disappearance – is an engaging metaphor for the diaspora and the entire politicization of the Genocide (McLagan 2006: 194) in the early 1920s and today, cementing the Genocide's footprints in concepts of identity, memory, displacement and dispossession.

Remaking *Ravished Armenia* as a response to 'genocide'

The issue of recreating a film on the Armenian Genocide that was made thirty years prior to the word 'genocide' entered the lexicon (the Genocide Convention was adopted by the United Nations in 1948) is problematic. The filmmakers and Mardiganian did not interpret what had happened to the Armenians as 'genocide', at least not in the way Raphael Lemkin, who formulated and conceptualized the word, understood the crime. However, this does not imply that the sequences from the recovered film are difficult to recognize as acts of genocide. *Ravished Armenia* was centred around Mardiganian's experiences in the Genocide, and thus it focused on the individual's endeavour to escape torture, rape and attempted forced conversion to Islam.

Coincidentally and serendipitously, the remaining surviving reels predominantly show sequences of group destruction. While the 1948 Universal Declaration of Human Rights was a statement on individual rights, the 1948 Genocide Convention (adopted by the UN General Assembly the day before it adopted the Universal Declaration) was designed to protect groups. It is remarkable, then, that the surviving frames of the film speak more to the Convention's articulation of acts of genocide against groups, than does, in all likelihood, the original full feature film, which emphasized individual experience. The remakes of *Ravished Armenia* present an understanding and remembering of the Armenian Genocide as a genocide, even though the film-makers had no control over the surviving sequences of the original film. Had the original film survived in its full-length form, it is possible that Mardiganian's personal story would have been more prominent and the intentional group destruction of the Armenians less so. In addition, a remake allows those living in an era of 'postmemory' – a term developed by Marianne Hirsch to describe the traces of traumatic memory inscribed on and retold to younger generations by their parents and grandparents (Hirsch 2012: 1) – to explore an unravelling of what it means to remember the Genocide and the legacy of postmemory during the current denial.

Because the ongoing denial of the genocide by the Turkish government today dominates counter-statements from Armenians and genocide studies scholars, the emphasis on memorial and remembering reinforces the reality of the Genocide. Despite the plethora of eyewitness testimonials from ambassadors and missionaries (Balakian 2003), and the photographs and writings from the First World War German lieutenant and medic Armin T. Wegner (Armenian National Institute 2013), there has been little filmic representation of the Genocide. Before Atom Egoyan's 2002 fiction film *Ararat* (an independent Canadian production that targeted a select 'art house' audience), very few fiction or documentary films were produced on the Genocide. This is perhaps why memorials organized on 24 April each year by the Armenian National Committee (a grassroots organization, which has chapters around the United States and affiliations throughout the wider diaspora) that commemorate the beginning of the Genocide are keen to show current filmic documentaries about the Genocide.

Such memorial events are deeply solemn, but also include passionate speeches against the denial from politicians, scholars and third-generation survivors, and commemorate the loss (of people and land) through the rejuvenation of culture: dance and music. At one recent commemoration in Melbourne, Australia, a dramatic dance was performed by young Armenian women, who theatrically recreated a slow-moving, but impassioned, death march. Black and white moving images were projected on to the wall behind them. Later, when asked by an Armenian member of the audience where these images were from, I answered, *Ravished Armenia*, instantly recognizing the images studied in preparation for this chapter. 'Of course', he responded. 'That's all we have'. Such comments reinforce the centrality of the original lost film and its two remakes as visual tropes for remembering. The two remakes, *Credo* and the new *Ravished Armenia*, capitalize on the traces of the original film: remaking *Ravished Armenia* meant revitalizing and preserving the memory of the Western world that did not forget.

Despite rumours surrounding the afterlife of *Ravished Armenia*, Kozanlian is certain that all prints of the film have vanished, except one held by Yervand Setian, a French-Armenian film-maker. According to Kozanlian, Setian lost major portions of the reels, apart from the twenty-minute segment that was later discovered in 1994, on his journey from France back to Armenia in the 1940s (Sánchez 1996: 11; Tjeknavorian 2012; Armenian Genocide Museum-Institute 2011). However, it is uncertain whether the discovered reels are out-takes of the film left on the cutting room floor, an intact twenty-minute sequence or different segments of the larger lost film (Bay Area Armenian National Committee 2009; Armenian Genocide Museum-Institute 2011). In 2009, Kozanlian gave the surviving reels to Richard Kloian to edit. Kloian was not a film-maker, but a dedicated Armenian Genocide researcher who was eager to be part of the remaking.

Credo

In 2005, two film-makers, Zareh and Alina Tjeknavorian made the film *Credo*, a lesser-known film than its cousin, the new *Ravished Armenia*, which was produced four years after *Credo*. Based on the same footage as the new *Ravished Armenia, Credo*, even before its successor, challenges the pedagogical and historical accuracy-demands of the new *Ravished Armenia*. Even though it uses identical footage, *Credo* is a remarkably different film from the new *Ravished Armenia*, creating inventive ways of remembering the Armenian Genocide by challenging the dogmatic and instructional nature of some documentary films on genocide. *Credo* gives the impression that the music carries the images and dictates them and divides the film into three parts, one of which is *Ravished Armenia*. The next one incorporates evidence of massacres from the photographs by Armin T. Wegner and the final part consists of footage from a contemporary documentary made about a memorial in Yerevan. *Credo* does not seek to reincarnate the original *Ravished Armenia*; rather, it is its own, unique film.

Credo's music does not accompany the images; it is the footage that supports the music. Loris Tjeknavorian, a composer and an Iranian of Armenian descent, recorded his 'Symphony No. 2 Credo' in 1980 on the 65th anniversary of the Armenian Genocide, capturing the Armenian chant, prayer or credo from the third century. The symphony represents three movements, including 'the life of the people … [and] a reoccurring death motif carried by the bass drum' (Tjeknavorian 2012). In 2010, on the 90th anniversary of the Genocide, Tjeknavorian's son Zareh and his wife Alina, both film-makers, wanted to commemorate the event and the symphony by adding the surviving twenty minutes of footage from the original *Ravished Armenia* to the music.

To tie in with the three symphonic movements, Zareh and Alina Tjeknavorian first used the recovered footage, then took still photographs and then, finally, inserted footage from a 1995 genocide commemoration in Yerevan taken from Carlo Messa's film *Destination: Nowhere*. In this third section of *Credo*, Tjeknavorian, the composer, can be seen conducting the orchestra, and Mischa Wegner, son of Armin T. Wegner, leads the masses to the memorial. Thus, even though *Credo* is divided into three sections, it seamlessly melds them through the movement of the symphony, creating a mnemonic connection between dramatic representation, unembellished still images and mourning and memorialization through documentary. It is as moving as it is uplifting. As Zareh Tjeknavorian has written, 'the fragments of ... [*Ravished Armenia*] and the Credo symphony took to each other like earth and water' (Tjeknavorian 2012). It is this very organic description, coupled with a finale in Yerevan, that pieces together, no matter how metaphorically, Armenia's ancestral home for its people. *Credo* focuses on the Genocide, but the movements of the symphony drive the images into fusions of historical and present notions of vitality and creativity. Zareh and Alina Tjeknavorian's film is, in Zareh's words, 'a testament to both the transcendent power of art and to the survival, and vitality, of Armenian life' (Tjeknavorian 2012). It is about remembering *and* it is a testament to creativity and life.

Although *Credo* uses almost exactly the same footage as the new *Ravished Armenia*, it challenges the 'documentary effect' and authority of the original film by changing the title to reflect the importance of the soundtrack, rather than the images. Indeed, *Credo*'s symphony grounds the Genocide and its aftermath, and yet Tjeknavorian's abstract Armenian score (J. Tjeknavorian in Tjeknavorian 2012) points to a ruptured aftermath, a Sisyphean nightmare struggling against the ongoing denial.

The new Ravished Armenia

In 1994, the year that Mardiganian died, Argentine-Armenian researcher Eduardo Kozanlian found remnants of *Ravished Armenia* in Yerevan around the same time that Zareh and Alina Tjeknavorian discovered the reels. Kloian saw the potential pedagogical effects of the surviving reels and edited them accordingly. The new *Ravished Armenia* aims to teach its audience generally about genocide and specifically about the Armenian Genocide. It uses the footage as a tool to counter denial, and, as an homage to the original film's use of intertitles, it inserts subtitles to explain the Genocide as a means of educating its viewers. The new *Ravished Armenia* is assembled like a quasi-documentary, where Kloian's subtitles 'authenticate' the provocative images (The Armenian Weekly Online 2010). Perhaps Kloian was aware of one 1919 review which claimed there would be no doubt that the film would be 'handed down as a historical manuscript in picture' (Judson quoted in Slide 1997: 13). The subtitles before the beginning of the footage ask the viewer to note how many instances of genocide can be found in the film, stimulating activists' notions of images 'as transparent mirrors of reality … [that] conflate them with proof' (McLagan 2006: 192). The subtitles help validate the images, guiding the viewer through each sequence. The genocide remembered here is restorative; the subtitles are designed to make the audience believe this is Arshaluys Mardigian's real genocide, not Aurora Mardiganian's Hollywood experience. By re-editing the fragments, overlaying the specific subtitles that 'teach' details of the Genocide, the new *Ravished Armenia* (and, in turn, the memory of the Genocide) is steered by the descendants of survivors. This is particularly pertinent, as denial, by its very nature, seeks to manipulate the (de)remembering of the Genocide. Like *Credo*, the new *Ravished Armenia* also inserts a unique soundtrack over the footage; however, the music is chosen to underline the seriousness of the history lesson.

The new *Ravished Armenia* uses music as a servant to the images: the images in the film are at the forefront. The overlaid music of Samuel Barber's 'Adagio for Strings' conveys a desire to repair, restore and renew all that the Genocide removed and displaced. In other words, the music does not *inform* the images. The music only complements and enhances the affect and emotion one *should* feel for such dramatic and devastating images that are emphasized by the pathos of the soundtrack. Barber's 'Adagio' was chosen as the musical score for melodramatic and emotional effect in films such as *The Elephant Man* (1980) and *Platoon* (1986). The use of the familiar dramatic and majestic score re-emphasizes the substance of the film. The music's status within the classical canon gives the film further authority.

Despite the wide acceptance by the Armenian diaspora of the new film as authentic, Matilde Sánchez has argued that it is difficult to ascertain if the remaining fragments of the film belong to the original because, as indicated above, 'there are no traces of Aurora' (Sánchez 1996: 11). Perhaps this is why, on my visit to the Armenian Genocide Museum-Institute in Yerevan in 2010, the director of the museum pointed to Aurora when her face appeared on the screen as I viewed the new *Ravished Armenia* as it played on a loop. His aim was not to prove that Aurora was in the film, but, more specifically, to confirm that these were fragments from the original film. To believe otherwise is to deny the remembering and to legitimize the 'documentary effect', an effect that lives on in the images of the two remakes.

Although *Credo* and the new *Ravished Armenia* are recreated and edited differently from each other, both contain similar images. Because Mardiganian experienced unimaginable sexual horror, the images in the recreations enhance the authenticity of her experience and the Genocide. Apart from the emphasis on sexuality, the films focus on the 'religious dimension of Turkish atrocities … by connecting to a visual tradition of suffering in Christian iconography' (Torchin 2006: 215). The symbols of martyrdom, the Bible and Christianity, virtue and endurance proliferate throughout the films (McLagan 2006: 194). If the Genocide were not enough, the tropes of religion and sexuality were given a strong focus, for example in the images of the 'sexually … cruel' (Torchin 2006: 217) Turk, who is no more strongly actualized in the film than in the last image of the crucified Armenian women vulnerable to a black raven (or Turk). These images, as Torchin points out, 'draw on a tradition of representation, producing a recognizable form of suffering that merits outrage and compassion' (Torchin 2006: 217). Indeed, the biblical iconography extends beyond the images to the subtitles in the new *Ravished Armenia*, noting that Armenia was the first country to adopt Christianity and laying claim to Mount Ararat – the momentous icon – and the Garden of Eden, both of which are on Armenia's ancestral land (Slide 1997: 207). In the aftermath of the Genocide, the focus on biblical and sexual elements in the films means that the rape of Armenian women and the attempt to destroy Christianity are never to be forgotten.

The new *Ravished Armenia* and *Credo* focus on women who are auctioned and mothers who have to comfort their teenage daughters who are raped, abducted and tortured. These are not normative images of this genocide (usually portrayed as mass deportations alone). *Ravished Armenia*, it seems, induced many notions of genocide. However, what is of importance here is that the Genocide is remembered through images of non-stereotypical acts of genocide. Mass rape of the victim group in order to impregnate women with babies from the perpetrator's 'race' or ethnicity is a common way to intentionally destroy a group in acts of genocide. However, it is not a popular representation of *this* genocide, nor is it a widespread interpretation, outside of international criminal law, of what genocide is or could be.

Conclusion

Should the new *Ravished Armenia* be condemned for using Aurora as 'a patriotic myth … [who] in moments seem[s] to have only existed in the melancholy of those exiled' (Sánchez 1996: 10)? Why does a film, which speaks more to the exploitation of a traumatized girl who had experienced genocide, be considered such a sacred text? Should *Credo* be criticized for de-emphasizing the original film?

It is wiser to take a cautious approach to the ways in which the two subsequent films remember the Genocide. The pedagogical method of the new *Ravished Armenia* plays an important role in presenting nuanced images of intended group destruction, specifically rape, torture and mass abduction. *Ravished Armenia* was filmed in 1919 while the Genocide was ongoing (albeit, most of the destruction had been committed years earlier). The closeness of the original film to the Genocide clouds the distance between the horrendous reality of the events and its representation. If we can imagine an American feature film, made in 1944, with a survivor of the Nazi *Einsatzgruppen* as the star protagonist, we can grasp the impact *Ravished Armenia* had on the minds of New Yorkers in 1919. The creators of the new *Ravished Armenia* should be admired for sanctioning 'raw' images. And through its documentary usage of the footage, the film helps foster the memory of the original production, which, despite the film-maker's obtuse regard for Mardiganian's trauma, could not predict the power its images would have and how those images would speak to a then unnamed crime.

Perhaps the new *Ravished Armenia* and *Credo* are reflections of generational memory; the former produced by second- or third-generation survivors and the latter made by third- or fourth-generation survivors. Both allude to the importance of remembering, but are methodologically dissimilar. Both are restorations: the former raises the status of the ultimate Armenian Genocide survivor, Arshaluys Mardigian and her embodiment in memory of the Genocide. *Credo* represents a reinvention of life (music and community) and place (Armenia).

Both films seek to remember the Genocide as a denied act that has gnawed at the survivors and their descendants since Atatürk's stubborn 'master-narrative' in 1923. While Turkey has Atatürk's metamorphic tropes to transform Turkey 'from empire to republic, [and reinvent] the Ottoman past, and eventually Turkish national identity' (Ulgen 2010: 384), Armenian descendants have two films, templates of a lost (and imagined) film, both loaded with their own mythological underpinnings; and yet both are also powerful tools of remembering a genocide in the struggle against the denial.

By attempting a recreation of the original film, the new *Ravished Armenia* captures the period before the rise of Atatürk – on the brink of the modern Turkish state – and with it the ongoing denial. Its faithfulness to the original film may seem at first sentimental and pandering to melodrama that actually obfuscates the historical events, but when seen as an homage to a period where the atrocities were publicized without fear of deniers skewing the historical facts, then the new *Ravished Armenia* and *Credo* can be celebrated and respected for their chosen, and effective, ways of remembering the Armenian Genocide.

Bibliography

Akçam, T. (2006) *A Shameful Act: The Armenian Genocide and the Question of Turkish Responsibility*, New York: Metropolitan Books.

Aldgate, A. and J.C. Robertson. (2005) *Censorship in Theatre and Cinema*, Edinburgh: Edinburgh University Press.

American Film Institute Catalogue. (n.d.) 'Auction of Souls'. Available at: http://www.afi.com/members/catalog/AbbrView.aspx?s=&Movie=2105. Accessed: 20 June 2011.

Armenian Genocide Museum-Institute. (2011) '"Auction of Souls" or "Memorial of Truth"'. Available at: http://www.genocide-museum.am/eng/online_exhibition_6.php. Accessed: 30 March 2013.

Armenian National Institute. (2013) 'Armenian Deportees: 1915–1916'. Available at: http://www.armenian-genocide.org/photo_wegner.html. Accessed: 5 May 2013.

The Armenian Weekly Online. (2010) 'Obituary: Richard Kloian (1937–2010)'. Available at: http://www.armenianweekly.com/2010/05/12/richard-kloian-1937-2010/. Accessed: 19 June 2011.

Balakian, P. (2003) *The Burning Tigress: The Armenian Genocide and America's Response*, New York: HarperCollins.

Bay Area Armenian National Committee. (2009) '"Ravished Armenia" Screened at San Francisco Library'. Available at: http://www.anca.org/press_releases/press_releases.php?prid=1715. Accessed: 30 May 2011.

Bloxham, D. (2005) *The Great Game of Genocide: Imperialism, Nationalism, and the Destruction of the Ottoman Armenians*, Oxford: Oxford University Press.

Brégent-Heald, D. (2010) 'Women in between: Filmic Representations of Gender, Race, and Nation in *Ramona* (1910) and *The Barrier* (1917) during the Progressive Era', *Frontiers: A Journal of Women Studies*, 31.2: 145–176.

Credo. (2005). DVD. Directed by Z. Tjeknavorian and A. Tjeknavorian. United States: Aralez Pictures.

Dadrian, V. and Akçam, T. (2011) *Judgment at Istanbul: The Armenian Genocide Trials*, New York and Oxford: Berghahn Books.

Hirsch, M. (2012) *The Generation of Postmemory: Writing and Visual Culture after the Holocaust*, New York: Columbia University Press.

Kozanlian, Y. (1999) 'About the *Auction of Souls*', *Harach*, trans. V. Maeossian and H. Mayissian.

McLagan, M. (2006) 'Introduction: Making Human Rights Claims Public', *American Anthropologist*, 108.1: 191–195.

Moraitis, S. (2011) 'Remembering "Ravished Armenia": Arshaluys (Aurora) Mardiganian's Take on Genocide', *The Globe Times*. 23 December. Available at: http://www.theglobetimes.com/2011/12/23/ravished-armenia-genocide/. Accessed: 5 March 2012.

Morgenthau, H. (1918) *Ambassador Morgenthau's Story*, New York: Doubleday.

Ravished Armenia. (2009). DVD. Directed by R. Kloian. Richmond: Heritage Publishing.

Sánchez, M. (1996) 'Imágenes mudas de Armenia' ('Mute Images of Armenia'), trans. J. McLeod, *Clarin*, 10–11.

Shrock, J. (1997) 'Desperate Men, Desperate Deeds: Gender, Race, and Rape in Silent Feature Films, 1915–1927', *The Journal of Men's Studies*, 6.1: 69–89.

Slide, A. (1997) *Ravished Armenia and the Story of Aurora Mardiganian*, Lanham and London: Scarecrow Press.

Tjeknavorian, Z. (2012) 'Credo'. E-mail. 29 May 2012.

Torchin, L. (2006) '*Ravished Armenia*: Visual Media, Humanitarian Advocacy, and the Formation of Witnessing Publics', *American Anthropologist*, 108.1: 214–220.

Ulgen, F. (2010) 'Reading Mustafa Kemal Atatürk on the Armenian Genocide of 1915', *Patterns of Prejudice*, 44.4: 369–391.

Wilson, W. (1918) 'President Woodrow Wilson's Fourteen Points', *The Avalon Project*, Yale Law School. Available at: http://avalon.law.yale.edu/20th_century/wilson14.asp. Accessed: 4 May 2013.

Winter, J. (2003) 'The Armenian Genocide in the Context of Total War', in J. Winter (ed.) *America and the Armenian Genocide of 1915*, New York: Cambridge University Press.

3 Memorial stories

Commemorating the Rwanda Genocide through fiction

Nicki Hitchcott

Over one hundred days between April and July 1994, as many as one million Tutsi and moderate Hutu were brutally massacred in Rwanda (Des Forges 1999; Prunier 1995). Such was the extent and range of the horrific brutalities inflicted on the victims during these months in 1994, that they are often described as being beyond our imagination. As Rwandan novelist Gilbert Gatore's narrator warns us in a fictionalized description of genocidal killing, what happened in Rwanda 'surpasses any horror or cruelty that even the most depraved mind might picture' (Gatore 2012: 84). Genocide fiction, then, is a paradoxical genre insofar as it attempts to imagine that which it is impossible to imagine. Yet, despite what is generally acknowledged as the unimaginable nature of the Rwanda Genocide, a growing number of creative writers have attempted to construct their own, imagined versions of what happened in 1994 through commemorative works of fiction. This chapter will discuss the ways in which a fictional text can capture the painful memories of the Rwanda Genocide and, in so doing, implicate the reader in the ambiguous processes of imagining and remembering. Focusing on Boubacar Boris Diop's novel *Murambi, the Book of Bones*, it will compare the act of commemorating genocide through fiction with the memorials that have been erected in Rwanda since 1994, particularly South-African sculptor Bruce Clarke's Garden of Memory, which was inaugurated in 2000 at Nyanza-Kicukiro near the Rwandan capital of Kigali. Although memorials clearly have different social functions from literary texts, this chapter will suggest that the two forms of commemoration are not as distinct as they might at first seem. Works of fiction have an important role to play not only in helping us to remember crimes against humanity, but also in furthering our understanding of the complexities of genocide.

Rwanda Genocide fiction

Before 1994, there was very little literary production from or about Rwanda. After the Genocide, a number of written testimonies have been produced by survivors, mostly women now living in Europe, who write about their personal experiences of the horror (Kayitesi 2004; Kayitesi 2009; Mukagasana 1997, 1999; Mukasonga 2006, 2008; Mujawayo and Belhaddad 2004, 2006). A very small number of fictional works by Rwandans has also begun to appear, but none by authors who were actually living in the country at the time of the genocide. US-based Rwandan academic Aimable Twagilimana's 1996 novel, *Manifold Annihilation* is, to my knowledge, one of the first works of post-genocide fiction by a Rwandan author writing in English. Another early work in English is returnee John Rusimbi's novel, *By the Time She Returned* (1999). Rusimbi's second novel, *The Hyena's Wedding*, appeared in 2007. In French, one of the first post-genocide works of fiction by a Rwandan author was exiled writer Benjamin Sehene's 2005 novel, *Le Feu sous la soutane* (*The Fire Beneath the Cassock*), based on the true story of Father Wenceslas Munyeshyaka, a Catholic priest who, having fled to France in 1994, was subsequently indicted by the International Criminal Tribunal for Rwanda for crimes against humanity, including genocide and rape (Hitchcott 2012). Following *Le Feu sous la soutane*, two further novels were published by Rwandan writers in exile in 2006: Joseph Ndwaniye's autobiographical novel, *La Promesse faite à ma soeur* (*The Promise I Made my Sister*), based on the author's return to Rwanda after the Genocide, and Jean-Marie Rurangwa's *Au sortir de l'enfer* (*Leaving Hell*). Although *Au sortir de l'enfer* is marketed by Rurangwa's publisher, L'Harmattan, as a novel, the author writes in his postscript that he wants his text to be read as a testimony, based as it is on historical truth (Rurangwa 2006: 197). From this brief survey of Rwandan fictional production after 1994, it can be seen that, until 2008, all the post-genocide literary texts fall into the category of testimonial fiction insofar as they are invented stories based ostensibly on witness accounts of the Genocide. None of the authors, however, actually experienced the Genocide first-hand.

Indeed, between 1999 and 2008, all the Rwanda Genocide novels published in French and in English share a marked preoccupation with recording and remembering 'the truth', albeit through the accounts of fictional witnesses. Unfortunately, none of these novels has had a great deal of commercial success, nor have any of them received much attention in the academic world. Even prolific Rwandan author Scholastique Mukasonga's first novel, *Notre-Dame du Nil* (*Our Lady of the Nile*), which, like her other testimonial texts, is published by prestigious French publisher Gallimard in its high-profile 'Continents noirs' series, was barely acknowledged before it unexpectedly appeared on the final shortlist for the Prix Renaudot, which it then won in 2012. Ironically, the first commercially successful work of fiction by a Rwandan author who was actually living in Rwanda in April 1994 is a novel that deliberately resists and challenges being read as a 'true' story by making Rwanda invisible and alluding to the Genocide in non-specific terms. First published in French in 2008, Gilbert Gatore's *The Past Ahead* refuses to explicitly name the author's birth country while at the same time it provides the reader with a series of textual clues that point to the Rwanda

Genocide (Hitchcott 2013). Although commercially successful, Gatore's novel has generated some controversy and has led some critics to challenge the status of both the text and its author. In particular, the novel has been criticized for encouraging readers to sympathize with a fictional member of the militia who brutally kills many people, including his own father. The text has also been controversial because it was reported that its author, Gatore, is the son of an alleged Hutu perpetrator exiled in France and wanted for crimes against humanity (Coquio 2010: 262–265; Lacoste 2010: 347–348).

In fact, the most successful works of fiction on the 1994 Genocide have not been written by Rwandans at all, but rather by what we might call 'historic onlookers' (Felman and Laub 1993: 96) or 'tourists with typewriters' (Holland and Huggan 2000). The best known of these is French-Canadian journalist Gil Courtemanche's novel, *Un dimanche à la piscine à Kigali*, which has been translated into English as *A Sunday at the Pool in Kigali* (Courtemanche 2004) and was adapted into a feature film directed by Robert Favreau in 2006. In the academic world, the fictional works that have generated the most interest are those produced by the 1998 Fest' Africa project, 'Rwanda: Écrire par devoir de mémoire' ('Rwanda: Writing with a Duty to Remember'). Coordinated by Chadian author Nocky Djedanoum, organizer of the annual Lille-based festival of African literature and culture, the project involved sending a group of ten African writers to Kigali for a two-month period of residence where they were invited to reflect on and write about the 1994 genocide (Hitchcott 2009a). Nine texts were published as a result of this initiative, including four novels (Diop 2001; Lamko 2002; Monénembo 2000; Ilboudo 2000), two travel narratives (Tadjo 2000; Waberi 2000) and a collection of poetry (Djedanoum 2000). The authors were then invited, along with artists, performers and academics, to a Rwandan meeting of Fest' Africa in Kigali and the Rwandan university city of Butare in the summer of 2000. This high-profile event included the performance of a piece by a member of the group, Chadian dramatist Koulsy Lamko, whose unpublished play, *Corps et voix, paroles rhizome* (*Bodies and Voices, Rhizome Words*), consisted of excerpts from several of the 'Writing with a Duty to Remember' texts, adapted for the stage (Semujanga 2008: 14).

Explicitly presented as commemorative works of fiction by writers who visited Kigali after the Genocide had ended, the Fest' Africa novels might appear to be less grounded in 'truth' than the first decade of testimonial novels by authors from Rwanda. Yet, the very nature of the project nevertheless suggests a similar emphasis on recording and remembering the events of 1994 in what is generally a fictional form. In particular, the novels are dominated by witnesses, real or imagined, and each of these witnesses refers explicitly to named events and places connected with the Genocide, notably memorial sites such as Nyamata, Ntarama and Murambi, which were visited by the authors during their stay. Three of the Fest' Africa novels have now been translated into English, two of them by North American university presses (Diop 2006, Monénembo 2004) and one in the Heinemann Africa Writers Series (Tadjo 2002). This chapter will now focus on one of these novels, *Murambi, the Book of Bones* by Senegalese author Boubacar Boris Diop, first published in French in 2000 and then in English translation in 2006 by Indiana University Press. The novel tells the story of Cornelius Uvimana, a Rwandan who, having spent twenty-five years in exile, goes back to his birthplace, Murambi, in July 1998, in order to find out what had happened to his family in 1994. Before he arrives in Rwanda, Cornelius believes that almost his entire family has been slaughtered, leaving only his uncle, Siméon Habineza, still alive. However, Cornelius eventually learns that his father, Dr Joseph Karekezi, is not, in fact, dead, but was actually the engineer of a genocidal massacre at Murambi. This novel has been chosen, as it explicitly links the role of fiction with the physical memorials that have been constructed in Rwanda in memory of the Genocide, in this case the Murambi memorial museum in Gikongoro Province. Listed as one of Africa's 100 Best Books of the Twentieth Century, *Murambi* is a brilliant example of the ways in which an African author tackles the difficulties of commemorating genocide through fiction.[1]

Fictional commemoration

Diop's novel is based on the massacre, in April 1994, of an estimated 50,000 men, women and children on the site of the Murambi Technical School in southern Rwanda. Fearing for their lives, the Rwandans had taken refuge in the classrooms of the school, where they remained for two weeks without food or water before eventually being brutally murdered by interahamwe militia (African Rights 2007). The bodies were thrown into mass graves, where they were later discovered by United Nations investigators. The school buildings now house a memorial museum, where the bodies of some of the victims, exhumed from mass graves and preserved in lime, are displayed in memory of the Genocide. When Diop visited the Murambi memorial with the Fest' Africa group in 1998, it was a makeshift museum with former classrooms filled with piles of skeletons, skulls and clothing of the victims of the massacre. In May 2011, the Rwandan National Commission for the Fight against Genocide (CNLG), in association with the Aegis Trust, a UK-based NGO, opened a more formal memorial museum on the site, but the corpses still remain. Forever trapped in the horror of experiencing their own deaths, the skeletons of the victims appear to continuously re-enact the atrocities of April 1994. Writing in *The Guardian*, Aegis's founder and chief executive, James Smith (2006), explains that 'by stopping them turning to dust and by keeping their memory alive, we aim to prevent this scene from recurring in Rwanda or elsewhere in the world'. Smith's emphasis on the importance of preserving the bones suggests that, without the material evidence, the victims' stories will be forgotten; they will turn to dust.

Of course, the difficulty with the materialization of memory through the display of bodies lies precisely in the way in which it attempts to objectify a quintessentially subjective process. As Susan Crane reminds us, 'memory is not static, but it can be made to seem so through the creation of forms of representation that attempt to solidify memories' meanings, and it is through this realm of preservation that memories interact with museums' (Crane 2000: 1–2). Memories can become fixed through preservation and display, and so the decision about what and how to preserve and display can also determine what and how we remember. For this reason, it can be argued that commemoration always has an agenda. This is certainly Kenneth Harrow's view of the Rwandan government's decision to build memorials on sites like Murambi. Such memorials, Harrow argues, serve to construct a reductive version of the complex history of the Genocide: 'with or without the guides the shrines function to canalize our reactions and understandings into a fixed narrative of the genocide – one that seems almost to write itself' (Harrow 2005: 41). For Harrow, genocide memorials fail to include the visitor in their attempts to objectify and institutionalize memory. In his view, the only useful account of genocide is 'the account that refuses to leave the reader out of it: the account where the past is not distanced from our lives, and where the consequences are not over for us or for them; the account that refuses the comfortable position of distance and mere observation' (Harrow 2005: 40). Shrines and testimonials, he suggests, fail to generate such a painful proximity; works of fiction, on the other hand, can – and sometimes do – achieve this aim. To accept such a view is to make an important distinction between memorial sites like Murambi and fictional commemorations. While it is indisputable that works of fiction and museums perform different social functions, often in very different ways, my reading of Diop's memorial text in relation to the memorial museum will highlight a number of interesting similarities and raise some important questions about how we remember genocide.

Like the other texts produced by the 'Writing with a Duty to Remember' mission, *Murambi* can be read as an individual act of commemoration, but it can also be argued that, as a collection, the nine texts that emerged from the project form a commemorative site in their own right. Indeed, Harrow quotes a web statement from the 'Writing with a Duty to Remember' project that appears to identify these texts as such: 'the collection will represent a kind of monument raised in memory of the victims of genocide … a kind of matching piece to the very material monument that Bruce Clark [*sic*], a South African sculptor, has started working on in Rwanda' (Harrow 2005: 44).[2] What is interesting here is the suggestion that the Fest' Africa collection of texts and Bruce Clarke's ongoing sculptural project, the Garden of Memory (see Figure 3.1), are both types of genocide monuments, a comparison that appears to blur the distinction between what are generally recognized as two very different forms of commemoration.

Figure 3.1 Commemoration Ceremony at the Garden of Memory. With permission of © Bruce Clarke.

In fact, what connects the 'Writing with a Duty to Remember' texts with the Garden of Memory is an emphasis on encouraging the continuing processes of memory rather than on recording and fixing memories in the past. In this respect, both memorials begin to resist what Pierre Nora describes as a fundamental opposition between history and memory (Nora 1997: 24), and so might lend themselves to interpretation as sites invested with collective memories and emotions – what Nora calls 'lieux de mémoire'. However, despite alluding in its title to debates in France over the 'duty to remember', the Fest' Africa project demonstrates what the historians in *Histoire d'Afrique*, Chrétien and Triaud's important collection, identify as 'the stakes of memory'.[3] In his introduction to the volume, Jean-Louis Triaud emphasizes the complex networks of memories on the African continent. Through successive acts of power, Triaud writes, memories in Africa have become institutionalized such that memory work is now required not only to record, but also to revisit and reconstruct histories (Chrétien and Triaud 1999: 10–11). While the Fest' Africa initiative responded to what the participating authors saw as a duty to record and remember, the very varied collection of texts produced resists a single narrative version of the Genocide. Sculptor Bruce Clarke also emphasizes the multiplicity of memories of genocide in his Garden of Memory project. Officially opened in 2000, Clarke's garden hopes to eventually contain one million individually marked stones in memory of each of the people who died in Rwanda between April and July 1994 (see Figure 3.2). Clarke has attempted to represent the Genocide in a tangible way by inviting visitors to the garden to lay stones themselves and so to participate actively in the process of remembering. Each visitor will, of course, remember the Genocide differently, and it is the clash of different memories that Clarke's project hopes to encourage.

Figure 3.2 Laying Stones at the Garden of Memory. With permission of © Bruce Clarke.

On the website for the Garden of Memory, the project is described in the following terms:

> There is thus a multiple challenge facing us. How is it possible that a memorial, a 'work of art', render justice to the enormity of the event – genocide of the Tutsi population and the extermination of Hutu democrats? Secondly, how can the form of the 'memorial sculpture' be dignified and yet communicate the enormity of the event to as many people as possible? Lastly, how can we integrate into its very creation a commemorative ceremony, a cathartic and pedagogic process involving as many people as possible, perhaps even the killers too?

Further down the page, Clarke places the familiar Murambi photograph of skeletons laid out on tables, explaining that, in his Garden of Memory:

> There will be no 'depiction' in the artistic sense of the word. Normally depiction is limited to the field of what can be depicted. It often lacks reverence for the victims and their families. It can make images of horror look banal and thus 'normalise' the horror itself. We need memorials that encourage reflection and contemplation, which involve the onlooker. An abstract depiction transcends conventional forms and encourages reflection, respect, and humanity.

By juxtaposing a documentary photograph with an emphasis on artistic abstraction, Clarke seems to be suggesting that, in this case, the two types of memorial (museum and artwork) are not so distinct after all. Each provides a space for individuals to create their own commemorative narratives of the Genocide.

Implicating the reader

What seems to characterize discussions of how to commemorate the Rwanda Genocide is a strong desire to implicate the audience in the process of remembering. The invitation to lay memorial stones marks the Garden of Memory as an ongoing process of memorialization rather than a static object. The act of participation is of paramount importance here. Such an emphasis on the role of the visitor and his or her memory is not, of course, exclusive to the creation of memorials, but informs contemporary museum theory at all levels of conception and reception. Crane notes that:

> Remembering as a personal and cultural experience as well as a social process figures into the museum visit, museum design and theorizing about museums. Collections and individual objects, in their relation to each other and their relations to anyone who encounters them, are used to create meaningful messages about us, them, and the museum.
>
> (Crane 2000: 5)

Just as the curator creates meaning by suggesting ways of reading a display, so the visitor also generates new meaning by choosing to read the display in a particular way. In other words, the visitor's response is individual and often unpredictable. Similarly, an author can only guide the reader to interpret a memorial text in a certain way. This makes the commemoration of genocide in fiction a particularly difficult task; those who experienced the events first-hand will experience the process of remembering very differently from those who observed it from a safe distance through the (often distorted) eyes of the Western media.

In an interview about *Murambi*, Diop explains his attempt to control his readers' reactions to the text:

> So as not to give the reader the opportunity to close his or her eyes again, I chose carefully the scenes I wanted to describe ... Each time events seemed too cruel or unbelievable, I avoided talking about them ... The reader likes to believe that what is said in a particular novel about a genocide is totally invented. That helps him feel okay and to have the impression that our world is not so terrible.
>
> (Di Genio 2006)[4]

Here Diop clearly identifies his intended readership as located outside Rwanda. The reader's gaze, like Diop's own, is an external gaze on the events commemorated. As an outsider himself – a tourist in Rwanda – Diop is careful not to sensationalize the horrors of 1994. Although the novel does contain many graphic descriptions of violence, Diop's claim, that he deliberately chose to write a work of fiction that is less horrifying than the reality it represents, adds another layer to the issue of the role of memory in commemorating genocide and raises a number of questions. Does the fact that the stories of Rwanda are so far removed from the experience of most people in the world make it more difficult to implicate the reader in a text about the Genocide? Will a memorial story only function if it makes a direct connection with each reader's memory? Paradoxically, for Diop, telling too much of the truth risks undermining the story's believability. In other words, what Audrey Small rightly identifies as the 'distress of the writer' (Small 2006: 202) in the Fest' Africa texts seems to translate into an attempt to minimize the distress of the reader. Diop wants to make his text believable precisely because the truth is so difficult to believe. This emphasis on the importance of being believed is expressed openly in the novel when survivor Gérard Nayinzira tells Cornelius his story of witnessing an interahamwe militiaman raping a dead woman:

> I saw that with my own eyes. Do you believe me, Cornelius? It's important that you believe me. I'm not making it up, for once that's not necessary. If you prefer to think that I imagined these horrors your mind will be at peace and that's not good. The pain will get lost in opaque words and everything will be forgotten until the next massacre. They really did incredible things. It happened in Rwanda only four years ago, when the entire world was playing soccer in America.
>
> (Diop 2006: 175–176)

As the main protagonist, Cornelius represents the visitor or reader upon whose individual memory the commemoration of the Murambi massacre depends. Cornelius must not only believe the story, but he must also be troubled by it, and so remember it. As visitor, the figure of Cornelius also mirrors Diop's own experience when he, along with the other Fest' Africa writers, travelled to Rwanda in July 1998. Alexandre Dauge-Roth reads the parallels between Diop and Cornelius as part of what he describes as a 'self-reflexive work of remembering' in which the character reflects the author's need to position himself in relation to events that he himself has not experienced (Dauge-Roth 2010: 104). As the story of his father's involvement begins to unfold, Cornelius becomes a participant – rather than an observer – in the history he discovers.

Cornelius's attempt to come to terms with what has happened and his personal relationship with the massacre eventually leads the reader to examine his or her own relationship with the Genocide. A history teacher, Cornelius had already read a lot about the Genocide, but it is not until he returns to Rwanda that he really begins to understand. Here, Diop's novel begins to point to the limitations of history as a source of understanding as well as to the importance of memory. As he travels from Kigali to Murambi, Cornelius remembers such events from his childhood as the 1973 massacres that led him to flee Rwanda twenty-five years earlier. The central question driving the narrative – what really happened at Murambi? – encourages the reader to follow Cornelius's attempts to piece together these memories in order to build up a picture of the Genocide. Furthermore, Cornelius's many questions prompt the reader to interrogate the memories as they are revealed. In this way, the reader accompanies Cornelius on his journey to try to understand the horror. This process of implicating the reader becomes particularly acute when Cornelius finally visits the site at Murambi. At this point, as Eileen Julien notes in her foreword to the English translation, 'the novel opens a space of reckoning, calling on us readers, like Cornelius, to reflect and weigh the question of responsibility, to imagine a new future' (Julien 2006: x).

Although the reader is drawn into a space of painful proximity with the events commemorated in the text, the decentred structure of the novel prevents the reader from identifying too closely with Cornelius. Although he is ostensibly the main protagonist, Cornelius's journey is related in the third person. In addition to Cornelius's story, the Genocide is remembered through eight fictional first-person testimonies, including those of two members of the interahamwe, an army colonel and Dr Joseph Karekezi himself. This means that, unlike Cornelius, the reader hears the voices of the fictional perpetrators at first hand and so in a way becomes a more objective witness than Cornelius is ever able to be. The effect of these multiple narrators is to encourage the reader to view the Genocide from a variety of different angles and to resist a reductive interpretation of the events. The same technique is used by Tadjo in her travel narrative *L'Ombre d'Imana*, also produced after the Fest' Africa mission (Hitchcott 2009b). In both of these texts, the decision to present the genocide from multiple points of view suggests a desire to let readers come to their own conclusions and, in so doing, create their own narratives of genocide. What such polyvocal narrations also demonstrate is the instability of historical discourse on Rwanda. Cornelius's journey causes him to rewrite the story of his family's death, exposing the unreliability of official versions of 'the truth'. Inevitably, Diop has chosen to privilege certain 'facts' about the Genocide over others, but his decision to present a multiplicity of genocide narratives in the novel implicitly challenges any reading that claims to be a final version of events.

Initially, Cornelius positions himself and his family as victims in the shared memory of genocide. However, when he finally hears the truth about his father's role in the killings, he is forced to re-evaluate his own position: 'from that day on his life would not be the same. He was the son of a monster … He had suddenly discovered that he had become the perfect Rwandan: both guilty and a victim' (Diop 2006: 78). Similarly, the reader's horror and surprise on learning that a seemingly liberal Hutu man should now be guilty of complicity in genocide forces a re-evaluation of the history of Rwanda. Having previously been tortured in prison as a Tutsi sympathizer, Dr Karekezi justified ordering the death of his own Tutsi wife (Cornelius's mother) and two of their children with the words, 'It's just history that wants blood. And why would I only spill other people's? Theirs is just as rotten' (Diop 2006: 107). The actions of Dr Karekezi exemplify the essential incomprehensibility of genocide. What happened in Rwanda was not, as the Western media repeatedly suggested, a case of ethnic conflict; it was an organized attempt to eliminate an entire group of people.

Forcing the reader to re-evaluate history is particularly important in the context of events that were either misrepresented or, at worst, ignored by the rest of the world. What the mass graves at sites like Murambi clearly show is that this was a carefully planned series of killings, which the perpetrators then attempted to conceal by burying the bodies. Despite such evidence, Western reactions to the Rwanda Genocide – both during and after the events of 1994 – have been characterized by a sustained attempt to present the events in terms of ethnic conflict or civil war rather than genocide (Melvern 2007). The world's failure to recognize what was really happening in Rwanda is the target of ironic criticism in Diop's novel, as can be seen in the following remark made by video store proprietor, Michel Serumondo:

> The World Cup was about to begin in the United States. The planet was interested in nothing else. And, in any case, whatever happened in Rwanda, it would always be the same old story of blacks beating up on each other. Even Africans would say, during half-time of every match, 'They're embarrassing us, they should stop killing each other like that.'
>
> (Diop 2006: 9–10)

This powerful image of the world watching football during the genocide in Rwanda highlights just how little attention was paid to the events of 1994. A similar point is made by Diop in his earlier novel, *Le Cavalier et son ombre* (*The Knight and his Shadow*), when Lat-Sukabé, the narrator, recalls a Rwandan friend telling him that the death of Brazilian Formula One racing driver Ayrton Senna was given thirteen minutes' coverage on the television news, while the death of one million Rwandans was reported in a single minute (Diop 1999: 71). Moreover, as Michel's sardonic comment in *Murambi* reveals, the reduction of the Rwanda Genocide to 'tribal warfare' was not an exclusively Western phenomenon; other African nations were also guilty of failing to recognize the Genocide and of condemning the Rwandan people as uncivilized.

One nation is singled out for particular criticism in the novel: France. Diop even quotes former French president, François Mitterrand's infamous statement, made in 1994, that, 'In those countries a genocide doesn't mean much' (Diop 2006: 177). France's long and well-documented support of Hutu Power – which included supplying arms and military training to the interahamwe militia – has received a great deal of criticism because, as Melvern notes, France 'possessed the most detailed knowledge of what was going on in Rwanda' (Melvern 2000: 234). Another important exposé of France's role in the Genocide is found in the testimony, *France–Rwanda: les coulisses du génocide* (*France–Rwanda: Behind the Scenes of Genocide*) by Vénuste Kayimahe, a Rwandan Genocide survivor and another member of the Fest' Africa group. Having worked for twenty years at the Centre Culturel Français in Kigali,

Kayimahe was betrayed by the French authorities when, a few days into the Genocide, they chose to evacuate all the French staff at the centre, leaving him behind. Fortunately, Kayimahe was saved from certain death by some Belgian soldiers and eventually managed to escape with some of his family to Kenya. In *Murambi*, Diop uses the fictive first-person narrative of French army colonel Etienne Perrin to condemn the actions of French troops during the Genocide. During a conversation with Dr Joseph Karekezi, Perrin struggles to justify his own and France's involvement: he is not guilty, he insists, because the French did not actually kill people. However, as Karekezi reminds him, the French built barbecues and volleyball courts on top of the mass graves at Murambi. They also evacuated war criminals to places of safety, having looked the other way while hundreds of thousands of people died. In a momentary acknowledgement, Perrin tells a colleague, 'We did nothing to prevent the massacres. We were the only ones in the world who could have done it' (Diop 2006: 124).

In his non-fiction essay 'Kigali–Paris: le monstre à deux têtes' ('Kigali–Paris: The Two-headed Monster), Diop gives a well-researched and compelling analysis of France's role in the Genocide (Diop 2007: 51–85). However, as a work of fiction with a wider readership, it is Diop's novel that may well prove more effective in drawing attention to France's guilt. According to Williams, 'ideas about victim status, inherited guilt and moral responsibility … are both shaped by, and interpreted within, memorial museums' (2007: 22). The same is true of memorial fiction. First published in Paris in 2000, *Murambi* invites French readers in particular to participate in the acknowledgement of France's responsibility for what happened in Rwanda. This is not to claim that all readers will read the text in the same way, nor indeed that Diop's readership is restricted to France, but rather to emphasize the potential in novels like *Murambi* for articulating and imagining that which is absent or suppressed in official versions of the Genocide. Furthermore, Fiona Mc Laughlin's English translation of *Murambi* brings the text to the attention of readers in Britain and the USA, two nations that, like France, were also guilty of aiding and abetting the Genocide (Dallaire 2003: 323).

In *Murambi*, Diop's fictive visitor to the Murambi memorial experiences guilt by association. As the son of the man who orchestrated the massacre, Cornelius feels responsible, but worries that to tell his guide this would be meaningless (Diop 2001: 175; 2006: 145). In fact, Cornelius's guilt makes perfect sense in the context of a story that makes no sense at all: 'All that is absolutely unbelievable … Even words don't know any more what to say' (Diop 2006: 96). Despite the struggle for meaning, most of the questions that Cornelius asks are not answered in the novel because, as the text reveals, there is no rational explanation for genocide. If the perpetrators have a motive, then it is greed and power, a point reinforced in the novel by the haunting parallel between the perfectly preserved skeletons of the victims and the untouched, dust-covered interior of Dr Karekezi's luxury mansion.

Imagining the unimaginable

What is common to all the different views on genocide memorials discussed above is an emphasis on the real and the tangible, rather than on symbolic abstraction. The same is true of *Murambi*. This emphasis on the real is what inspired Diop to create a reasonably straightforward narrative; compared with Diop's previous novels, *Murambi* is an easy read. In an interview about the Fest' Africa mission, he explains: 'The great novel on the Rwanda Genocide will be written in fifteen years. What we wanted was to act. Taking a purely political stance, I wrote a fairly loose plot that I filled with facts to generate debate' (in Moncel 2000).[5] Similarly, in the novel, when Cornelius's uncle, Siméon Habineza, tells him about the dogs drinking from the pools of blood that seeped from the graves where the victims were buried, Cornelius interprets the story as a metaphor for Rwanda. Siméon, however, is quick to correct him: 'It's not a symbol … Our eyes saw it' (Diop 2006: 153). Indeed, like all the Genocide novelists, Diop's decision to base his novel on a real historical event prevents the reader from interpreting the novel as simply a work of fiction. This explains Gérard's comment in the novel on the limitations of metaphor in representing genocide: 'All the beautiful words of the poets, Cornelius, can say nothing, I swear to you, of the fifty thousand ways to die like a dog within a few hours' (Diop 2006: 175). Fictionalizing Africa is, as Catherine Kroll notes, always problematic given that the continent has been 'close to existential erasure' by self-serving Western colonialist discourse for centuries (2007: 655–656). Fictionalizing the genocide in Rwanda is more difficult still, since, throughout its history Rwanda has been successively defined by a series of mythologies created by colonial and neo-colonial powers, including the infamous Hamitic Hypothesis that led to the classification of the Rwandan people on so-called ethnic grounds and that became one of the motives for genocide.[6]

To emphasize the difficulties in fictionalizing genocide is not to diminish the role of fiction in commemoration, but rather to recognize the difficulty of imagining the unimaginable, particularly if, as *Murambi*'s narrator suggests, 'every chronicler could at least learn [from the genocide] – something essential to his art – to call a monster by its name' (Diop 2006: 179). Indeed, Diop has been openly critical of his own decision to create a fictional imagining of Rwanda in his earlier novel, *Le Cavalier et son ombre*, written before he had set foot in the country. Writing this text, he explains, was a purely literary experience born out of his own ignorance of the Genocide combined with authorial vanity (Diop 2007: 25–27). After the Fest' Africa trip, Diop and the other writers agreed, he writes, that 'the only way to reconstruct this distress in all its depths was to take a chance on simplicity' (Diop 2007: 28).[7] In *Murambi*, Diop's fictional writer Cornelius has a similar change of heart in relation to writing about Rwanda. Having initially thought that he might write an absurd play about the events of 1994, he leaves Murambi having changed his mind. A symbolic representation no longer seems appropriate;

instead, Cornelius 'would tirelessly recount the horror. With machete words, club words, words studded with nails, naked words and ... words covered with blood and shit' (Diop 2006: 179). Paradoxically, Cornelius's commitment to realist descriptions of the Genocide is precisely expressed through metaphor: he will use machete words to hack into the silence around what happened in Rwanda. Through such apparent contradictions, Diop's text reveals the limitations of language in memorializing genocide and demonstrates the tension between a desire to tell 'the truth' and the constructedness of the memory narrative. On the one hand, the genocide writer is concerned with the transmission of facts; on the other hand texts like *Murambi* rely on our imagination for understanding and commemoration. Moreover, despite an emphasis on realism, poetic language is still useful here since, as James Young notes, 'the language and metaphors by which we come to events tell us as much about how the events have been grasped and organized as they do about the events themselves' (Young 1988: 91).

Conclusion

As a documentary novel, *Murambi* fills two important functions in the commemoration of genocide: the text leaves material traces of what happened in 1994, and, at the same time, through its construction, it implicates the reader in the very complex process of remembering. In Kigali, Cornelius is shocked that the Genocide appears to have left no visible trace on the city: 'Only the city herself could have answered these questions he still couldn't ask anyone. But the city refused to show her wounds' (Diop 2006: 49). Although the majority of his questions remain unanswered because there can be no rational explanation for what happened, Cornelius does find some of his answers at Murambi, where the wounds are still visible on the bones of the dead. It is the physical space of Murambi that binds together the many different players in this story of genocide; and for each of them, the place will hold different memories and different meanings. Murambi thus acts as both a repository of memory and a trigger for the fictional reconstruction of memory. In the same way, the Murambi memorial museum itself invites participation – that of the visitor's imagination – particularly as the many thousands of bones on display will remain unidentified. Visits to the site have generated – and will no doubt continue to generate – a range of different narratives, including that generated in US director Sam Kauffman's short film *Massacre at Murambi* (2007), which uses the story of the massacre to interrogate events in Darfur. Kauffman's text extends the symbol of Murambi beyond the nation-space of Rwanda to a global reflection on genocide and inhumanity. In other words, the memorial site at Murambi provokes different acts of commemoration that will be performed differently by different people in different places at different times. Memories of genocide are multiple and complex, as the polyphonic narrative of Diop's novel shows. Such multiplicity cannot be encapsulated in a single monument or shrine, but rather in the multidirectional nature of the acts of remembering evoked by an effective memorial or text. Readers of genocide novels like *Murambi* are invited to perform their own acts of commemoration: to remember the Rwanda Genocide of 1994 and to interpret it for themselves.

Notes

1 What follows has been adapted from my earlier article, 'Writing on Bones: Commemorating Genocide in Boubacar Boris Diop's *Murambi*' (Hitchcott 2009c).
2 'l'ensemble [de textes] constitutera une manière de monument élevé à la mémoire des victimes du génocide ... comme un pendant au monument, bien matériel celui-ci, sur lequel un sculpteur sud-africain, Bruce Clark [*sic*], a commencé à travailler au Rwanda'.
3 'les enjeux de mémoire'.
4 'Pour ne pas donner au lecteur l'occasion de refermer les yeux, j'ai soigneusement sélectionné les scènes à décrire ... Chaque fois que les événements m'ont paru trop cruels et incroyables, je me suis gardé d'en parler ... Le lecteur aime croire que ce qui est dit dans tel roman sur un génocide est totalement inventé, ça l'aide à se sentir bien et à ne pas avoir l'impression que notre univers est si épouvantable.'
5 'Le grand roman sur le génocide rwandais sera écrit dans quinze ans. Nous, nous voulions agir. Dans une position purement politique, j'ai écrit une intrigue assez molle où j'ai logé des faits, afin de susciter un débat'.
6 The Hamitic Hypothesis, which was introduced in Rwanda by the former Belgian colonial powers, identifies the Tutsi as a different race, which originated from outside sub-Saharan Africa and which was therefore closer to Europeans than the Bantu Hutu (see Mamdani 2001: 79–87).
7 'la seule façon de restituer cette détresse dans sa profondeur était de faire le pari de la simplicité'.

Bibliography

African Rights. (2007) '*Go. If You Die, Perhaps I Will Live': A Collective Account of Genocide and Survival in Murambi, Gikongoro, April–July 1994*, Kigali: African Rights.

Chrétien, J.-P. and J.-L. Triaud. (1999) *Histoire d'Afrique: les enjeux de la mémoire*, Paris: Karthala.

Cook, S.E. (2007) 'The Politics of Preservation in Rwanda', in S.E. Cook (ed.) *Genocide in Cambodia and Rwanda: New Perspectives*, New Brunswick: Transaction Publishers: 281–299.

Coquio, C. (2010) 'Poétiser l'enfant tueur: questions sur *Le Passé devant soi* de G. Gatore', in D. Lévy-Bertherat and P. Schoentjes (eds) *'J'ai tué'. Violence guerrière et fiction*, Geneva: Droz: 231–265.

Courtemanche, G. (2003) *Un dimanche à la piscine à Kigali*, Paris: Denoël.

——. (2004) *A Sunday at the Pool in Kigali*, Edinburgh: Canongate Books.

Crane, S.A. (2000) 'Introduction: Of Museums and Memory', in S.A. Crane (ed.) *Museums and Memory*, Stanford: Stanford University Press: 1–13.

Dallaire, Lt.-Gen. R. (2003) *Shake Hands with the Devil*, London: Random House.

Dauge-Roth, A. (2010) *Writing and Filming the Genocide of the Tutsis in Rwanda: Dismembering and Remembering Traumatic History*, Lanham: Lexington Books.

Des Forges, A. (1999) *'Leave None to Tell the Story': Genocide in Rwanda*, New York: Human Rights Watch.

Di Genio, L. (2006) 'Interview with Boubacar Boris Diop', in *Fiera Lingue*. 24 May. Available at: http://www.fieralingue.it/modules.php?name=News&file=article&sid=303. Accessed: 22 February 2013.

Diop, B.B. (1999) *Le Cavalier et son ombre*, Abidjan: Nouvelles éditions ivoiriennes.

——. (2001) *Murambi, le livre des ossements*, Abidjan: Nouvelles éditions ivoiriennes.

——. (2006) *Murambi, the Book of Bones*, trans. F. Mc Laughlin, Bloomington: Indiana University Press.

——. (2007) *L'Afrique au-delà du miroir*, Paris: Philippe Rey.

Djedanoum, N. (2000) *Nyamirambo!*, Bamako: Le Figuier and Lille: Fest Africa.

Felman, S. and D. Laub. (1993) *Testimony: Crises of Witnessing in Psychoanalysis and History*, London: Routledge.

'Garden of Memory' website (n.d.). Available at: http://www.bruce-clarke.com/pages/le-jardin-de-la-memoire. Accessed: 18 November 2013.

Gatore, G. (2008) *Le Passé devant soi*, Paris: Phébus.

——. (2012) *The Past Ahead*, trans. M. de Jager, Bloomington: Indiana University Press.

Harrow, K.W. (2005) '"Ancient Tribal Warfare": Foundational Fantasies of Ethnicity and History', *Research in African Literatures*, 36.2: 34–45.

Hitchcott, N. (2009a) 'A Global African Commemoration – "Rwanda: Ecrire par devoir de mémoire"', *Forum for Modern Language Studies*, 45.2: 151–161.

——. (2009b) 'Travels in Inhumanity: Véronique Tadjo's Tourism in Rwanda', *French Cultural Studies*, 20.2: 149–164.

——. (2009c) 'Writing on Bones: Commemorating Genocide in Boubacar Boris Diop's *Murambi*', *Research in African Literatures*, 40.3: 48–61.

——. (2012) 'Benjamin Sehene vs Father Wenceslas Munyeshyaka: The Fictional Trial of a Genocide Priest', *Journal of African Cultural Studies*, 24.1: 21–34.

——. (2013) 'Between Remembering and Forgetting: (In)Visible Rwanda in Gilbert Gatore's *Le Passé devant soi*', *Research in African Literatures* 44.2: 76–90.

Holland, P. and G. Huggan. (2000) *Tourists with Typewriters: Critical Reflections on Travel Writing*, Ann Arbor: University of Michigan Press.

Ilboudo, M. (2000) *Murekatete*, Bamako: Le Figuier and Lille: Fest Africa.

Julien, E. (2006) 'Foreword: An Urn for the Dead, an Hourglass for the Living', in B.B. Diop, *Murambi, the Book of Bones*, trans. F. Mc Lauglin, Bloomington: Indiana University Press: ix–xii.

Kayitesi, A. (2004) *Nous existons encore*, Paris: Michel Lafon.

Kayitesi, B. (2009) *Demain ma vie: enfants chefs de famille dans le Rwanda d'après*, Paris: Laurence Teper.

Kroll, C. (2007) 'Rwanda's Speaking Subjects: The Inescapable Affiliations of Boubacar Boris Diop's *Murambi*', *Third World Quarterly*. 28.3: 655–663.

Lacoste, C. (2010) *Séductions du bourreau. Négation des victimes*, Paris: Presses Universitaires de France.

Lamko, K. (2002) *La Phalène des collines*, Paris: Le Serpent à Plumes.

Laville, S. (2006) 'Two Years Late and Mired in Controversy: The British Memorial to Rwanda's Past', *The Guardian*, 13 November. Also available at: http://www.theguardian.com/world/2006/nov/13/rwanda.sandralaville.

Mamdani, M. (2001) *When Victims Become Killers: Colonialism, Nativism and the Genocide in Rwanda*, Princeton: Princeton University Press.

Massacre at Murambi. (2007). Short Film. Directed by Sam Kauffman. Rwanda and United States: PBS POV.

Melvern, L.R. (2000) *A People Betrayed: The Role of the West in Rwanda's Genocide*, London: Zed Books.
——. (2006) *Conspiracy to Murder: The Rwandan Genocide*, Second Edition, London: Verso Books.
——. (2007) 'Missing the Story: The Media and the Rwanda Genocide', in Allan Thompson (ed.) *The Media and the Rwanda Genocide*, London: Pluto Press: 198–211.
Moncel, C. (2000) 'Rwanda: écrits contre l'oubli', *L'Humanité*. 3 June. Available at: http://www.humanite.fr/node/419003. Accessed: 23 February 2013.
Monénembo, T. (2000) *L'Aîné des orphelins*, Paris: Seuil.
——. (2004) *The Oldest Orphan*, trans. M. F. Nagem, Lincoln: University of Nebraska Press.
Mujawayo, E. and S. Belhaddad. (2004) *SurVivantes: Rwanda dix ans après le génocide*, La Tour d'Aigues: Éditions de l'Aube.
——. (2006) *La Fleur de Stéphanie: Rwanda entre réconciliation et déni*, Paris: Groupe Flammarion.
Mukagasana, Y. (1997) *La Mort ne veut pas de moi*, Paris: Fixot.
——. (1999) *N'aie pas peur de savoir*, Paris: Robert Laffont.
Mukasonga, S. (2006) *Inyenzi ou les Cafards*, Paris: Gallimard.
——. (2008) *La Femme aux pieds nus*, Paris: Gallimard.
——. (2012) *Notre-Dame du Nil*, Paris: Gallimard.
Ndwaniye, J. (2006) *La Promesse faite à ma soeur*, Liège: Les Impressions Nouvelles.
Nora, P. (1997) *Les Lieux de mémoire*, Vol. I, Paris: Gallimard.
Prunier, G. (1995) *The Rwanda Crisis: History of a Genocide, 1959–1994*, London: Hurst & Co.
Rurangwa, J.-M.V. (2000) *Rwanda: le génocide des Tutsi expliqué à un étranger*. Bamako: Le Figuier and Lille: Fest Africa.
——. (2006) *Au sortir de l'enfer*, Paris: L'Harmattan.
Rusimbi, J. (1999) *By the Time She Returned: A Refugee's Tale*, London: Janus Publishing.
——. (2007) *The Hyena's Wedding: The Untold Horrors of Genocide*, London: Janus Publishing.
Sehene, B. (2005) *Le Feu sous la soutane: un prêtre au coeur du génocide rwandais*, Paris: L'Esprit Frappeur.
Semujanga, J. (2008) *Le Génocide, sujet de fiction? Analyse des récits du massacre des Tutsi dans la littérature africaine*, Montreal: Éditions Nota Bene.
Small, A. (2006) 'Tierno Monénembo: Morality, Mockery and the Rwandan Genocide', *Forum for Modern Language Studies*, 42.2: 200–211.
Smith, J. (2006) 'Our Memorial to 50,000 Dead is No Empty Historic Exercise', *The Guardian*, 21 November. Also available at: http://www.theguardian.com/commentisfree/2006/nov/21/comment.rwanda.
Tadjo, V. (2000) *L'Ombre d'Imana: voyages jusqu'au bout du Rwanda*, Arles: Actes Sud.
——. (2002) *The Shadow of Imana: Travels in the Heart of Rwanda*, trans. Véronique Wakerley, Oxford: Heinemann.
Twagilimana, A. (1996) *Manifold Annihilation*, New York: Rivercross Publishing Inc.
Waberi, A.A. (2000) *Moisson de crânes*, Paris: Le Serpent à Plumes.
Williams, P. (2007) *Memorial Museums: The Global Rush to Commemorate Atrocities*, Oxford: Berg.
Young, J.E. (1988) *Writing and Rewriting the Holocaust: Narrative and the Consequences of Interpretation*. Bloomington: Indiana University Press.

4 To be hunted like animals

Samuel and Joseph Chanesman remember their survival in the Polish countryside during the Holocaust

Pam Maclean

> We run away on the field on the (on the) haystacks in the morning (you know). And we grab out a piece from the haystacks from the (from the) straw (you know) and we try get in both together and we sit and me and my father (aah) together. And I covered up all the holes with the straw and about ten o'clock in the morning the machine guns start to kill – to kill people – the whole lot.
>
> (Chanesman 1996)

Reflecting the triumph of genocidal criminality over economic logic, by late 1942, the Nazi occupiers of the Lublin region in eastern Poland had decided to 'liquidate' remaining Jewish work camps. One such camp was located near the town of Kurow, north-west of Lublin, which, prior to the war, was home to a substantial Jewish population, including Samuel Chanesman and his son Joseph, who was fifteen years old in 1939 at the time of the German invasion. By being conscripted for forced labour and relocated to a work camp near Kurow, Samuel and Joseph had escaped the March 1942 deportation from the Kurow Ghetto that had claimed Joseph's mother and two brothers. Forced labour was only a temporary reprieve from death, of course, and when in November 1942 Samuel was told by 'a Pole' that the thirty-two Jews in the camp would be shot the following day, he realized immediate escape represented the only chance for him and his son to survive. The following morning, they somehow achieved this, and Joseph's account of hiding in the haystack describes their first precarious night on the run – a forewarning of another year and a half of the terror the two experienced as they resisted falling prey to the *Judenjagd* – the 'Jew hunt'.

According to Christopher Browning, the term *Judenjagd* was coined in late 1942 by members of Police Battalion 101, then situated in the northern Lublin area. In the wake of the campaign to 'cleanse' this region of Jews through 'ghetto clearing', the Battalion was given the task of locating and summarily shooting any Jews who attempted to hide in the surrounding fields and forests, as well as those found hiding in the villages – a process that continued until the end of the German occupation (Browning 1992: 122–127). Browning observes that these relatively disorganized and individualistic

Judenjägde, belonging to the latter phase of the Holocaust, have escaped adequate scholarly attention, partly because such 'personal' and non-mechanized forms of killing do not fit comfortably into the standard paradigm of Holocaust as 'systematic' genocide on a mass scale, but also because of an absence of documentation for these events (Browning 2006).

And so we come to Samuel and Joseph Chanesman, survivors of, and witnesses to, the *Judenjägde* in the Lublin region. The parallel accounts of their ordeal – produced some forty years apart in two different languages, Yiddish and English, and, significantly, in fundamentally different testimonial genres – document the traumatic experience of the hunted. Not surprisingly, despite understandable discrepancies in detail due in part to the effects of the passage of time on Joseph's memory, these accounts agree on the stark reality of their time evading capture: their acute physical deprivation through starvation, exposure to the elements and living for extended periods in darkness; their continual relocation from one precarious hiding place to another; their total reliance on a minority of 'friendly' Poles for protection, coupled with a constant fear of betrayal from hostile locals; and, finally, the trauma of witnessing the fate of fellow Jews in hiding who were murdered on the spot (including finding the remains of Jews killed by grenades thrown directly into bunkers).[1]

Notwithstanding these similarities, the contrast between how Samuel conveys and understands what occurred and how Joseph presents his story is striking. On the one hand, Samuel's contribution consists of a series of letters written to a friend in Yiddish in 1948 and reproduced in the Kurow *yizkor* (memorial) book, published in Israel in 1955 (Hanisman 1955).[2] (As will be discussed in greater detail later in the chapter, *yizkor* books were conceived of as a form of communal commemoration of Jewish cities and towns destroyed in the Holocaust.) The letters were based on the diary entries Samuel made every day he was in hiding. Samuel also mentions that at various times he had access to newspapers. This helps to explain how he was able to create such a clear, chronologically well-organized and, with a few exceptions, clinical account of his experiences under Nazi persecution. The expression of personal emotion is remarkably restrained given the horror of what is told.

On the other hand, in his 1996 videotestimony given in the Jewish Holocaust Centre in Melbourne, Australia, Joseph, speaking in heavily accented English, presents a powerful but chaotic account of personal trauma. As is evident in the opening quotation, his testimony is, to use Wendy Hesford's term, 'rhetorically ungovernable' (Hesford 2004: 106).

Arguably, the differences between these two testimonial discourses are illustrative of the paradigmatic shift in Holocaust remembrance that Annette Wieviorka contends reflects changing ideological contexts:

> Testimonies, particularly when they are produced as part of a larger cultural movement, express the discourse or discourses valued by society at the moment the witnesses tell their stories as much as they render an

> individual experience. In principle, testimonies demonstrate that every individual, every life, every experience of the Holocaust is irreducibly unique. But they demonstrate this uniqueness using the language of the time in which they are delivered and in response to questions and experiences motivated by political and ideological concerns. Consequently, despite their uniqueness, testimonies come to participate in a collective memory – or collective memories – that vary in their form, function, and in the implicit or explicit aims they set for themselves.
>
> (Wieviorka 2006: xii. See also Waxman 2006)

Whereas Samuel's account is constrained within the rhetorical conventions of the *yizkor* book, with its orientation towards the written documentation of cultural destruction and collective remembrance and mourning (Wieviorka 2006: 25–28), Joseph's late-twentieth-century testimony is firmly located within 'The Era of the Witness' that privileges individual experience and creates a sense of 'intimacy' between speaker and viewer (Wieviorka 2006: 107–108). Under these circumstances, viewers are so emotionally affected by the individual's testimony that their focus is primarily on the psychological and emotional trauma of the testifier at the expense of engagement with the broad 'political' (and here she includes historical) factors shaping the events themselves (Wieviorka 2006: 141–143).

Nonetheless, the following discussion of Samuel and Joseph's accounts suggests that, despite the heuristic value of identifying distinctive testimonial categories, in reality it may be too simplistic to assume that the different rhetorical tropes shaping memorial books and electronic media hermetically seal the two memorial genres from each other. To take one example, individual despair does at times break through Samuel's attempts to convey a chronologically structured narrative of events as part of the broader story of the destruction of his community, and Joseph punctuates the fractured narration of his personal trauma with concern for the suffering of his fellow Jews. Intriguingly, the tension between collective and individual remembrance that is evident at this micro level of analysis resonates in broader debates about what it means to remember genocide. Samuel and Joseph's struggle to reconcile their experience of personal violation (which is not inherently genocidal) with violation of the collectivity (which is) lies at the core of what it means to remember genocide.

Recalling personal experiences? Recalling the community's experiences? Samuel's contribution to the Kurow *yizkor* book

The Kurow *yizkor* book was one of hundreds of volumes dedicated to the memory of specific eastern European Jewish communities that appeared after the war.[3] In keeping with this memorial genre, the Kurow *yizkor* book comprised an edited anthology of contributions, mainly from survivors or expatriates who had left before the Nazi invasion. Most contributions, including Samuel's, are written in Yiddish, the language spoken by the majority of eastern European Jews prior to the Holocaust. Although based on a mediaeval German dialect, Yiddish is written in a Hebrew script.

The introductory chapters to the Kurow *yizkor* book encapsulate the dual function performed by the anthology. It fulfilled an obligation to Jewish religious memorial and martyrological traditions, and it was driven by an imperative to preserve the secular history of the town's Jewish community, including the documentation of the Nazi onslaught. Chapters listed in the introductory section, like 'A Burial Place and a Memorial' and 'Our Cemetery List of the Holy Dead Sons of Kurow' are thus juxtaposed to chapters with titles such as, 'Official Documents about the Holocaust'. In an attempt to counter the erasure of memory of the town's extensive Jewish existence, considerable space is devoted in the body of the book to articles describing religious and community organizations, key moments in Kurow's pre-Holocaust history, as well as amusing anecdotes of life in the town and biographical sketches of notable personalities. Samuel's contribution is included in a section devoted to local memories of the Holocaust in Kurow. The section's title, 'In the Bunkers, Caves, Stalls, Fields and Forests (September 1939–May 1945): Memories from the Survivors', encompasses virtually all the settings in which the Chanesmans found themselves following their escape from the work camp and highlights the precariousness of life on the run for Jews.[4] The grouping together of survival stories also underlines the editor's perception that what was being remembered was a common set of experiences shared by Kurow survivors.

A letter to his best friend written in July 1948, and incorporated into Samuel's chapter in the Kurow *yizkor* book, reveals that Samuel may have understood his task somewhat differently from the editor:

> Now about Chaim Rochelman's [unidentified contact of Samuel] idea to call the brochure [sic] 'Hurbn Kurow' ('The destruction of Kurow'), I have to tell you that it does not please me. I don't feel that you appreciate the pain and suffering we went through. To voice such an opinion about the title is very easy. I believe the writing should go by the title of 'The experiences of Samuel Chanesman and his son Joseph during the destruction of Kurow'.
>
> (Hanisman 1955: 261)

Possibly Samuel has confused the title of the *yizkor* book with that of his own contribution, but even so, it is worth noting that in his proposed title Samuel places his and his son's experiences before that of the town. The final title of Samuel's chapter as published in the *yizkor* book, 'Kurow's suffering and the survival of Samuel Chanesman', both reverses Samuel's suggested order and transfers the Chanesmans' suffering to the town (while deleting his son's name altogether).

Samuel's letter helps to explain how one of the most striking and seemingly deviant passages – in the sense that it strays from the path of objective observation of communal suffering – came to be included in his account. In a description, replete with emotion and personal terror, Samuel recalls how, for three weeks in June and July 1943, more than half a year after their initial escape from the work camp, when other possible hiding places in farmers' sheds and bunkers were no longer available, he and his son were once again forced to seek refuge in the fields.

By the summer of 1943 Samuel's almost laconic portrayal of events as evidenced in his depiction of the first day of hiding in the haystacks that so horrified his son a year previously: 'My son Joseph and I looked out on the fields surrounding us. We climbed into a stack of hay that lay out in the field, and that was how we spent our nights' (Hanisman 1955: 247), became increasingly emotional.

As they again ventured into the fields, Samuel and Joseph were assisted by a non-Jewish Pole, Antoni Kordowski, a cobbler with whom Samuel had done business prior to the war and who, at great personal risk, continued to help Jews during the war:

> Life in the open field was a nightmare. We were acutely aware of the farmers' movements around us and did not dare to utter a word the entire day. You could hear any movement from a far distance. If the Poles realized that we were hiding there, our lives would be in great danger. There now existed a new law that stated that if you discover, or hear of a Jew in hiding, you have to pass the information on to the closest police. If you were found to have withheld information, your possessions could be confiscated or you could be sentenced to death. It was very difficult to get used to the brightness of the day, for the first few days. We were not used to the rays of the sun, as we had been hidden in underground darkness. We had to spend our days in the field, lying on the wet earth. It was forbidden to stand or sit up, in case someone would notice us. The worst part was when the rains came, sometimes it would rain for six to eight days straight, we would spend the whole day lying in water, waiting desperately for the God-sent moment, when the sun would set and we would allow ourselves to stand up. We were completely soaked to the skin, lying there, without even a little bread. But when night fell, we started freezing, crawling around in the open field. We could hear the sound of our own footsteps in the night, and we sometimes even came across some other miserable people, who found themselves in the same situation, such as Hersh Kotlash, Rina Ritzer, Yehoshua Cukerman, who was also crawling around in the darkness, looking for some sustenance for his wife and two children. After walking around for a short time, refreshing ourselves, we returned to our same patch of corn, to our same wet plot of earth, and went to sleep. Then the sun would rise and we would continue to lie absolutely still, no noise, no movement, as if we were barely alive.

> Antoni Kordowski was confident of this hiding spot. He checked it out carefully and assured us that it would be just as good as a bunker. He brought us food and the Polish papers every three days. He was, however, unable to supply us with drinking water. That we had to find ourselves. I would like to mention that on 1 July 1943, it began raining and rain continued to fall for the next five days. My son was already sick by the fourth day. He just lay on the soaked earth, crying and crying. He said he envied his mother and brothers who were no longer alive.
>
> They had already left this world, and their suffering had stopped. The rain kept on pouring and he got paler and paler. I saw that I had to save him from the rain. I lay myself down on top of him. I lay on my hands and on my knees, protecting him from the rain with my body, until he came to himself. We had to crawl to the nearby farms to try and get some water to drink. Sometimes we managed to get a piece of bread or a potato from some friendly farmer. When the rains stopped, we were burnt to a crisp during the day and eaten up by mosquitoes every night.
>
> (Hanisman 1955: 256–258)

Whereas Joseph remembered protecting his father on the first night in the haystack, now their roles were reversed and it was Samuel who shielded his son. Physical deprivation and suffering were made worse by the realization that immediate family members had been murdered. Samuel felt increasingly powerless to prevent a similar fate befalling him and his son.

Reference to a specific date, the precise enumeration of days elapsed and the listing of the names of fellow Jews hiding in the fields indicate, however, that even when recalling unimaginable trauma, Samuel did not lose sight of his broader responsibility to contribute to the historical knowledge of what had occurred. Take, for instance, this description of how his Polish protector warned him in early February 1943 to escape from the bunker where he was hiding:

> The Germans had learnt that sixteen Jews were hiding in this bunker, and we had to escape and save ourselves any way we could. His [the Polish helper's] men had told him that the Germans were planning to come and kill us the next day. The sixteen hidden Jews were:
>
> I and my son, Avramche Goldberg with two children, Chaim Tevel Okun, his wife and two children, Chaya Tzimmerman (Sholem Raav's daughter) with three children, there was Ruzia from Lublin, with two children.
>
> The next day, the German soldiers surrounded the bunker and threw in a few hand grenades, thinking that we were inside. However, we had escaped. The other fourteen Jews were killed elsewhere during the war, each of them in a different place.
>
> (Hanisman 1955: 249)

Another example of Samuel's matter-of-fact style is evident as he recounts his last two months spent in yet another bunker, this time buried beneath the dirt floor of a farmer's barn: 'After lying for two months in the dark bunker, we didn't see any light for the whole two months and I became ill and lay with a high fever until 27 February 1944' (Hanisman 1955: 264). Such attention to documenting precise dates underlines the role *yizkor* books played in archiving evidence of the Holocaust. That it was important to Samuel to keep abreast of what was happening around him is apparent in his references to helpers who not only supplied him with food and drink, but also with newspapers, which provided reference points for dates and, significantly, information about the latest German decrees relating to the occupation. No matter how nightmarish his circumstances, Samuel kept in touch with external events.

An earlier part of the July 1948 letter quoted on p. 74 (Hanisman 1955: 261) documents Samuel's commitment to contributing to the post-war historical record. In the letter, Samuel mentions that he had contacted a representative of the Central Jewish Historical Commission (CJHC), an organization formed in 1944 by surviving Jewish historians following eastern Poland's liberation by Soviet forces. In the immediate post-war period, the CJHC was actively engaged in gathering evidence from survivors that documented their experiences. At one of its earliest meetings, it resolved that 'any kind of printed and handwritten materials, photographs, illustrations, documents, material proofs, as well as the documentation of any oral testimonies of victims and witnesses of the Nazi terror who remained [alive]' should be collected as a matter of urgency (quoted in Aleksiun 2008: 78). Where possible, such material was to be gathered in one place; Lublin was, in fact, the first community visited by a CJHC historian, and until the liberation of western Poland in1945, the CJHC had its headquarters in Lublin.[5] According to Natalia Aleksiun (2008), this collection process served multiple objectives. Not only did the CJHC see itself as engaged in the conventional historical practice of presenting 'objectively' verifiable evidence to establish historical fact, but it also believed its work performed a vital commemorative role in relation to 'murdered communities'. For the CJHC, preservation of communal memory constituted a moral duty to future generations that transcended simple narrative. The CJHC further hoped that its activities would serve to counter anti-Semitism and would be used to identify Nazi criminals and assist in their prosecution. Thus, in the case of the post-war historians and the contributors to *yizkor* books, the boundary between professional and commemorative writing appears somewhat blurred, with Jewish historians, albeit without compromising their professional standards, embracing commemoration and grassroots contributors, like Samuel, recognizing that they played an important role as historical witnesses.

In a chapter that investigates the neglected contribution of professional Jewish historians in the immediate aftermath of the Holocaust, Mark Smith also explores the relationship between the work of the professional historians and the writing of *yizkor* books, a relationship whose importance, he argues, has been underestimated. A key feature of post-Holocaust *yizkor* book compilation was the formation of a 'lay-professional partnership' between community writers and professional historians:

> They [the professional historians] assumed the interrelated functions of documenting the popular urge for self-expression, giving exposure to the testaments of those who had perished, supporting commemorative efforts by survivors, incorporating the voices of both survivors and victims into their works, and making available the results of their research to the Yiddish-speaking public.
>
> (Smith 2012: 55–56)

Despite concerns being raised about the reliability of survivor testimony, professional historians regarded eyewitness accounts published in the *yizkor* books as invaluable sources for their own research. As founding member of the CJHC and pioneering Holocaust historian Philip Friedman commented in 1948, 'Apart from official sources (archives) there are – and these are the very most important – living sources, quivering reality with traces of the "historical process" on their bodies and in their hearts' (quoted in Smith 2012: 63).[6] Professional historians' recognition of the significance of *yizkor* books is reflected in their own contributions to *yizkor* books, as well as their reviews of some *yizkor* books in professional journals (Smith 2012: 61).

There is a risk that the shared communal focus of both historians and the compilers of *yizkor* books may, nonetheless, paper over the tension between the urge to express personal suffering and the imperative to document and remember the community. David Roskies recognizes this danger when he identifies the transformative role *yizkor* books play in converting 'private' memories into 'community' memories, with the observation that '(w)ithout political or institutional memory backing, no Holocaust testimony or text got published' (Roskies 2012: 89).[7] An alternative approach to the effect of communal/institutional framing on private Holocaust narrative is suggested by Adina Cimet (2011). She points out that the peculiar function served by *yizkor* books as vehicles of mourning created possibilities for private grief to be given a wider public meaning without downplaying or trivializing individual pain. Cimet – who, like Roskies, recognizes that *yizkor* books changed their objectives over time in response to changing contexts – argues that by the 1950s, compilers of *yizkor* books increasingly acknowledged that their expressions of grief had to be heard beyond their survivor community. In other words, they 'realized that the mourning process, especially as unique a mourning as theirs, could ensure a future with continuity of meanings and purposes for their own surviving children' (Cimet 2011: 129). Mourning the dead was not simply an exercise in recovering the past for those who had survived: it became critical that future generations shared an obligation to remember so as to reaffirm the failure of the Nazis to destroy the community.

The following poem, published in a 1956 *yizkor* book, with its invocation to the bridal couple to remember the Jewish destruction, powerfully underlines the imperative of transmitting memory across generations, even at a time of celebration:

> Remember the *churbn* [destruction];
> May the memory of it all be there while you eat and in your blood.
> Clasp your teeth and remember;
> When you eat, remember;
> When you drink, remember;
> When you hear a song, remember;
> When the sun is shining, remember;
> When the night arrives, remember;
> When you build a house, break a wall in it and remember;
> If you plant a field, make a mountain of stones, let them be a witness and memorial for those that did not get a burial;
> When you walk your child to the *chuppah* [the canopy under which Jews are married], remember;
> May the dead and the living be one, as are united those that were murdered with the remnants of Israel.
> Listen … and say,
> Amen.
>
> (quoted in Cimet 2011: 131)

Like the Jewish historians discussed earlier, contributors to later *yizkor* books became increasingly aware of the role *yizkor* books could play in the intergenerational transmission of Holocaust memory. Cimet also suggests that later *yizkor* books further mobilized memory with the explicit goal of providing evidence to the international community for the prosecution of Nazi crimes (Cimet 2011: 128–129).

For Samuel, however, mourning appears to be more about fulfilling a sense of immediate obligation to the collective memory of the Kurow victims of what he terms the 'German bandits' than intergenerational transfer of memory. Interspersed through his narrative are lists of the names of fellow Kurow Jews murdered in the 'Jew hunts', together with the details of how they were murdered. Although depicted as victims of a common fate, considerable care is taken to personalize each individual's death. For instance, in the case of married women, their maiden names are listed, familiar given names are provided, as are children's ages. Such naming strategies are fundamental to the *yizkor* book becoming 'a burial place and a memorial' so that (to quote the Kurow volume's editor) 'the lost and slain may find their final resting-place' (Grosman 1955: n.p.).

The metaphor of the *yizkor* book as a 'substitute gravestone' (Kugelmass and Boyarin 1983:12) is reinforced in Samuel's horrifying description of the murder of religious Jews during an *Aktion* (round up) for deportation to extermination camps:

> The *Judenrat* [Jewish council responsible for administering the local Jewish community] and the Jewish police force were told that they had fifteen minutes to round up all the men, women and children in the town and assembled them in a certain spot, in the middle of the marketplace. Whoever did not reach the market place in the fifteen minutes that were assigned to them would be shot. The SS soon began shooting at the crowd; terrified women, with tiny children in their hands, began running on the spot in the middle of the marketplace, carrying bundles of bedding, valises stuffed with things that had been lying ready for this terrible day. As Meir Zalcman [the ritual slaughterer], was standing in line with his family, a nasty *Volksdeutscher* [ethnic German Pole] came up with a knife and cut off half of his beard, together with half of his cheek. We heard a gunshot, and Boruch Zalcberg fell on the ground; he was a young man, twenty-two years old. He was unwell and could not run fast enough … The crowd started to panic. There was screaming amongst the young and the old. People were screaming *Shema Israel* – ['Hear O Israel', the last words that a Jew must utter before he dies] …
>
> (Hanisman 1955: 241)

> After the Jewish populace of Kurow was sent out, their belongings were thrown about the square. They were given out to the Poles who were watching the scene, and enjoying this with much glee. Gedi [an ethnic Pole] gave a new order to the *Judenrat* that they had to accompany him to all the Jewish homes, where he was to finish off the rest of the Jews, who were too sick to come to the marketplace. Wherever he came across a sick person, they were shot. These are the people who were shot:
>
> Alter Yosef Goldberg, Chaim Shia Niderberg, Tuvia Weiss, Alter Yavitz, Avraham Hersh Kartsman, Esther Shildkroit, with some ten children.
>
> As all the Jews were being led to Konskewolia, they would shoot randomly into the crowd. Those who were shot just fell on the road; they were Nemi Hanisman, Sheva Asfis, Wolf Oberklaid, Dovid Tenenboim.
>
> (Hanisman 1955: 242)

> Pious Jews took off their clothing in order to die in white. They remained in their white underwear. That was what Shloime Tevel Vachenhauser did, as well as Moshe Kave Lekis.
>
> (Hanisman 1955: 243)

Samuel and his son survived this *Aktion* by refusing to report and remaining in hiding until their incarceration in the work camp. Samuel recalls how their work unit was then ordered to:

> collect all the victims who had been killed in the *Aktion*, and bury them in the Jewish cemetery.
>
> We also found pieces of torn Torah scrolls.[8] I buried them with my own hands, together with our brothers who had been shot. Apart from finding our murdered brothers, we also found the down of our feather bedding that rained down like a winter storm. The Poles scoured any of the houses that had remained standing, and took from them all that their hearts desired. Soon thereafter, we saw Polish women wearing skirts made of our prayer shawls.
>
> (Hanisman 1955: 245)

The violent scene that Samuel, an observant Jew, describes is appalling, but what makes it even worse is the wanton desecration that occurs on multiple

Figure 4.1 Frontispiece Kurow *yizkor* book showing the Old Kurow synagogue ark that contains torah scrolls. The photograph was taken in 1937.

Source: M. Grosman (ed.) *Izkor book. In Memoriam of our Home-town Kurow*, Tel Aviv and New York: Residents of Kurow in Israel.

levels, whether through the mutilation of a religious Jew's beard, the destruction of sacred texts or the transgressive act of women wearing prayer shawls that are otherwise used exclusively by men in a religious context. By naming the victims and providing specific details of how they died, Samuel's words construct a metaphorical gravestone for the anonymous dead whom he was forced to bury.

Not only do Samuel's specific references to his coreligionists' adherence to religious practice in the face of mistreatment act to restore their dignity in the face of Nazi humiliation, they also illustrate a further function performed by Holocaust *yizkor* books, the characterization and commemoration of the dead as martyrs, whose lives were sacrificed for the religious group as a whole. As Cimet observes, 'Survivors never claimed martyrdom for themselves, but only for their dead' (2011: 138), and it was incumbent upon survivors and their community to bear witness to their martyrdom in a process which, according to Rachel Jablon's thought-provoking analysis of the interrelationship between Jewish mourning rituals and Holocaust memoir, mirrors the religious tradition of sitting[9] *shiva*, when, on each of the first seven days after burial, fellow Jews visit the bereaved family to offer comfort and prayers as 'acts of kindness' that 'contribute to healing' (2004: 308). As Jablon notes, group remembrance forms the cultural and religious cornerstone of Jewish mourning for the following reason:

> Although an individual mourns the loss of a loved one in a personal and distinct way, the community must be present in order to carry out certain mourning rituals. The community plays many roles during the mourning period, and each role has a special title, all of which include the Hebrew term for a 'group of people closely associated with some commonality': *khevrah* (plural: *khevrot*).
>
> (Jablon 2004: 309)

Indeed, some *yizkor* books describe survivors who meet to remember the dead as sitting *shiva* (Kugelmass and Boyarin 1983: 11).

Jablon extends the idea of the community of mourners from survivors to the readers of Holocaust memoir themselves (by implication, the broader Jewish community), who, she argues, come to constitute an essential audience for individual suffering – an audience with the capacity to listen to stories of traumatic loss, empathize with victims, soothe their pain and, ultimately, witness on behalf of the group as a whole (Jablon 2004: 308–309). What is especially striking about Jablon's focus on communal involvement in mourning is its relevance for understanding the problem of genocide remembrance in general, given that the crime of genocide is, by definition, a crime against a group, which, nonetheless, involves countless atrocities inflicted on countless individuals. And it is to the impact of genocide on individual memory that the discussion now moves as we shift our focus to Joseph's videotestimony.

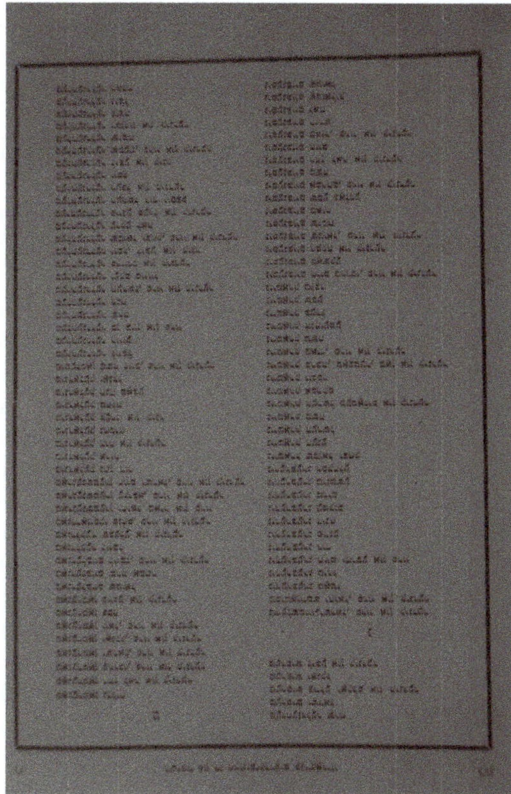

Figure 4.2 Black-bordered list of names of Kurow Jews who perished in the Holocaust. Source: M. Grosman (ed.) *Izkor book. In Memoriam of our Home-town Kurow*, Tel Aviv and New York: Residents of Kurow in Israel.

Joseph: ungovernable memory

Decades after his father's account of their survival was published, it was Joseph's turn to tell their story, this time through the medium of videotestimony as part of the Melbourne Jewish Holocaust Centre's videotestimony project. As he recalls his years of persecution, even at the age of seventy-one, it is clear that Joseph continues to be deeply scarred by the traumatic events he experienced. Although he frequently refers to his father's *yizkor* book chapter in the course of his interview, there is little evidence of the healing effect which, according to Jablon, exposure to Holocaust memoirs could provide. Joseph remains inconsolable. Most telling is his response to the interviewer when she asks how he 'kept himself going', after he provided a harrowing description of the brutalization of a group of 3,000 Jews, including the rape of old and young women, the murder of children and countless random shootings, all of which he had witnessed through the fence of his work camp. His reply, that he did not know how he 'kept going' at the time, except that 'you have to forget', underlines the personal cost he paid for what turned out to be the futile pursuit of erasing memory. In his next comment, Joseph confides that at home when, like the interviewer, his wife expresses concern about his emotional state and asks, 'What's the matter, what are you thinking about?', he says 'nothing', while in reality, it's 'everything coming into my head. Sometimes I can't sleep. I sleep to about two and three o'clock and it's finished. When I lie down I remember, everywhere, when. All the proceedings. What I had. Where I'm going. Who hit me. Just like animals you know' (Chanesman 1996).

Unlike Samuel, Joseph's memories are not based on any formal attempt to document his experiences at the time of their ordeal; indeed, in response to the interviewer's queries about his father's notetaking, Joseph reveals his father deliberately hid their contents from him until after the war. Joseph knew his father 'every day, doesn't matter where we went, he always got a piece of pencil with a piece of paper he written on what happens', even when hiding in the fields. Because Samuel 'described everybody, who was killed. And who, children', he was loath to 'upset' his son by revealing the wider picture to him (Chanesman 1996). Listening to Joseph's account and watching his agonized expression as he grasps for answers to the interviewer's questions, the viewer is left with the impression that he still struggles to make sense of what occurred, to construct a coherent picture of events. Certainly (as the transcribed excerpts from the videotestimony indicate), he has some problems with English, but his difficulties are far more profound. After giving a very confused response to a question about the Nazi bombing of the camp, he then jumps from these events to how he tried to protect his father, then to his mother's gassing, finishing with what can only be read as an existential statement relating to his experience as a whole, how he was (and one senses still is) overwhelmed by a visceral terror: 'I feel it in my body. Sometimes I'm so scared you know. Rain, rain I'm so cold. I haven't got anything. Only a sack'. He is consumed by the 'quivering reality' alluded to by Friedman. And then, maybe aware the interviewer is having trouble following his fractured narrative, Joseph asks if there is more she needs to know: 'Perhaps I can find something else to tell you? I don't know. It's coming around like a circle in my head' (Chanesman 1996).

Undoubtedly, what heightens the impact of Joseph's account is that it is being conveyed through the electronic medium of videotestimony. As the chapter's earlier discussion of Wieviorka (2006) suggests, characteristic of the audiovisual medium is its tendency to individualize experience and to direct the viewer's attention towards emotion. Importantly, videotestimonies held in the Jewish Holocaust Centre remain unedited, and, unlike the written word as it appears in *yizkor* books, they are not reordered after the event. The viewer is directly exposed to the unchecked expression of trauma. Aleida Assmann develops this idea further when she argues that by focusing specifically on the Holocaust, videotestimony comes to constitute a 'new genre' which is uniquely placed 'for registering and archiving individual incidents of the traumatic experience of the Holocaust' (Assmann 2006: 264). Contrasting written Holocaust memoir, constructed as conventional autobiography, to videotestimony, Assmann concludes:

> While the genre of autobiography creates meaning and relevance through the construction of narrative, the relevance of the video testimony solely lies in the impact of the historical trauma of the Holocaust. It registers events and experiences that are cruelly meaningless and thwart any attempt at meaningful coherence. It presents an incomprehensible event that defies all patterns of understanding, reflecting the naked terror of an alien agent and its unimpeded drive toward senseless destruction.
>
> (Assmann 2006: 264–265)[10]

It is as if Assmann wrote this passage explicitly with the contrast between Joseph's chaotic videotestimony and Samuel's highly structured narrative in mind, even taking into account that Samuel's *yizkor* book chapter is not strictly a formal autobiography. What enable the painful expression of traumatic memory are the 'technical' possibilities of the electronic medium of videotestimony. Unlike words circumscribed and fixed by the conventions of print, videotestimony 'leaves room for open-ended passages, such as pauses, periods of silence, uncompleted sentences, [and] innuendo' (Assmann 2006: 265). Verbal and visual cues appearing on the screen open up multiple interpretive possibilities for the viewer.

Holocaust videotestimony may amplify the voice of individual suffering, but this does not mean it is solicited in an institutional vacuum. Joseph's videotestimony is one of over a thousand conducted under the auspices of the Jewish Holocaust Centre in Melbourne, Australia. Worldwide, institutions including The Fortunoff Archive at Yale University, Stephen Spielberg's Shoah Foundation and, in Israel, the Holocaust Memorial Authority, Yad Vashem, to mention just a few, have collected over 80,000 videotestimonies (Krondorfer 2008: 199–200). Although interviews generally follow a similar structure, starting with questions about the subject's earliest memories, before moving to the direct experience of the Holocaust and then to its aftermath, each institution has developed its own interview protocols to reflect its particular mission. For example, because the pioneering Yale Fortunoff project, initiated by child survivor and psychotherapist Dori Laub, focused on the 'emotional sequelae' of the Holocaust for survivors and emphasized the therapeutic role testimony could play (Laub 2012: 72–73), its interviews tended to be open-ended and not constrained by a fixed time limit. With their emphasis on capturing factual data relating to the Holocaust as it occurred over a vast geographical expanse, Shoah Foundation interviews, by contrast, worked to a strict schedule, and, as far as possible, asked all interviewees the same questions.[11]

The Jewish Holocaust Centre's approach to videotestimony is influenced by another set of factors, the Centre's origins as a survivor-initiated organization. Established in 1984 to promote Holocaust education and provide mutual support for the substantial group of survivors who had settled in Melbourne, the Centre had started to collect the stories of its own community in videotestimonies by 1992 as a means not only of countering the dangers posed by Holocaust denial, but also of enabling survivors to share their experiences in a supportive environment (Maclean, Abramovich and Langfield 2008: 21). As Michele Langfield and I have noted previously (2009), this was not conceived of as a professional academic project, but as a communal one. Interviewers, including survivors, were volunteers drawn from the Jewish community. They received some training and were also provided with a question protocol that, as well as covering the Holocaust experience, sought to recover memories of pre-Holocaust Jewish life. Questions then turned to the Australian migrant experience. Although by no means as rigidly constrained by memorial conventions as contributions to the *yizkor* books, individual interviews were conducted within a collective framework of expectation of what would be told. Because so many survivors had come to Melbourne from Poland, especially from cities such as Lodz, where the Holocaust followed a 'straightforward' path of ghettoization, deportation, forced labour and/or extermination, questions were organized on the assumption that the interviewee's story would fit into this narrative of events. Even the most skilful of interviewers could find themselves at a loss, however, if the survivor's testimony deviated from this pattern and personal preoccupations, that could not be edited out of the raw recording, overrode the anticipated structure of the interview (Langfield and Maclean 2009). In Joseph's case, his competent and sensitive interviewer was hamstrung because the neglected historical topic of the 'Jew hunt' was not part of her interview protocol. Her attempts to impose order on his account by repeatedly asking him about his ghetto and work-camp experiences proved to be an exercise in futility. Joseph kept returning to his time in hiding.

Two recurring themes in his videotestimony, the reduction of his existence to that of an animal and the times he was forced to take responsibility for his father's welfare – reversing the 'normal' father–son relationship – suggest that for Joseph life on the run represented a total inversion of any 'normal' world order. Joseph rails against the dehumanization his Nazi-imposed relegation to the world of the animals represented. He recalls with distaste how, on the first day following their escape from the haystack, he and his father found refuge in a barn. Freezing and dressed only in underwear, Joseph assuages the cold by sleeping with the animals: 'When the animals is warm I just get to the animals and horse (you know) and keep me warm'. Worse still, during a later episode of hiding in haystacks, when local farmers refuse his pleas for water, he remembers, 'I use urine from the animals to have a drink'. Then, in his final period of hiding in an underground bunker, Joseph temporarily goes blind: 'I couldn't walk because I'm going my hand to my feet just like an animal' (Chanesman 1996). Far from losing his humanity in this period, however, Joseph assumes the uncomfortable role of his father's protector. Returning to the desperate period of survival in the winter of 1942/1943, Joseph recounts how he and his father were almost killed when they left their hiding places in search of food:

> I remember wintertime. I was so cold. And I said, 'Dad, are you alright?' And we went up to get some food. And so then the Germans caught us with the machine guns. This was the moon, you can see miles over the field ... And the Germans see us and start to shoot us with machine guns, and I fall down. And my father was lying down on the snow and I just wake up and I lift up my hand and my legs and I said, 'If I got my legs and my feet and you too dad, let's go. We can walk again'.
>
> (Chanesman 1996)

Lengthy silences and sighs punctuate Joseph's account, underscoring the depth of the responsibility he felt towards his father and his fear that he would let him down. When Joseph has finished recalling this episode, the interviewer asks, somewhat incongruously, his opinion of the '*Judenrat* in the ghetto'.

Certainly, Joseph's videotestimony is told from a very individualistic perspective and it resists fitting neatly into the narrative presuppositions of the Jewish Holocaust Centre community; nonetheless, he never loses sight of the fact that he was the target of genocidal intent because he was a Jew. Despite his awareness that Jews were the group targeted for destruction, in contrast to his father, Joseph positions himself as an individual observer of genocide, not as someone speaking on behalf of the group as a whole. He fondly remembers the thriving Jewish community as it existed in Kurow before the war, his attendance at Jewish schools and the local synagogue, and his father's support for Orthodox Zionists. Joseph's memories of Christian Poles prior to the German occupation are far less positive. He was aware of Polish anti-Semitism while he was still at school, and, despite his father's friendly business relationships with a number of non-Jews (who were later to prove critical in their survival), he is deeply suspicious of what he regards as their murderous anti-Semitism. Joseph's contempt for Poles intensified during his period in hiding, when so many rejected his pleas for help, believing such help was, 'not for Jewish people. Jewish people should die'. Polish anti-Semitism pales into insignificance, however, when compared with that of the Germans. Joseph witnessed and was subject to countless acts of brutality by German forces and was under no illusions as to their true intent. Commenting on the atrocious conditions of the Kurow work camp, where starving and powerless inmates lost all hope, Joseph observes: 'Very difficult life what the Jewish people have (you know) ... People sit in the camp every day expect they would die'. His conviction that Germans and Poles alike wanted Jews to die is encapsulated in the phrase Joseph uses throughout the testimony: Jews were meant to 'go to Abrahams' (Chanesman 1996).

Figure 4.3 Photograph of Samuel and Joseph Chanesman taken immediately after liberation.
Source: M. Grosman (ed.) *Izkor book. In Memoriam of our Home-town Kurow*, Tel Aviv and New York: Residents of Kurow in Israel.

Conclusion

Different memorial genres influence, but do not determine, how genocide is remembered. The two parallel accounts by Samuel and Joseph Chanesman – one embedded in the conventions of written *yizkor* books dedicated to the remembrance of specific communities destroyed in the Holocaust and the other recorded as part of the late-twentieth-century project to capture survivor testimony in audiovisual form – mobilize memory in contrasting ways. Samuel presents his personal story of survival in a well-structured narrative, which clearly fulfils its obligation to document the broader fate of other Kurow Jews. Joseph's testimony, reflecting electronic media's propensity to expose personal trauma, is chaotic and disorderly. Videotestimony, in particular, despite the best efforts of a community to homogenize and control the story being told, privileges the personal experience in a way that is not possible in written texts. Nonetheless, whether it is Samuel allowing private emotion to intrude on communal obligation or Joseph resisting attempts to contain his story in a preconceived narrative framework, memory of genocide cannot be harnessed in a predictable fashion. Regardless of how the 'Jew hunt' has been remembered here, the existence of such accounts ensures that knowledge of this lesser-known event is no longer lost to Holocaust history. Indeed, they more than confirm Browning's conclusion to the chapter titled 'The "Jew hunt"' in his groundbreaking study *Reserve Police Battalion 101 and the Final Solution in Poland* that the 'Jew hunt':

> was a tenacious, remorseless, ongoing campaign, in which the 'hunters' tracked down and killed their 'prey' in direct and personal confrontation. It was not a passing phase but an existential condition of constant readiness and intention to kill every last Jew who could be found.
>
> (Browning 1992: 135)[12]

Notes

The chapter is based on a paper originally presented in 2007 at the International Association of Genocide Scholars conference in Sarajevo. A Linkage grant from the Australian Research Council in association with the Jewish Holocaust Centre in Melbourne facilitated the research.

1 Browning (1996: 126) refers to grenades being thrown into bunkers.

2 Samuel's surname is transliterated from the Yiddish as Hanisman in translations of the *yizkor* book. To maintain consistency with the spelling of Joseph's name, I refer to both as Chanesman. Translations of Samuel's chapter are based on Tania Bruce's unpublished translation, together with Gloria Berkenstat Freund's translation on the JewishGen website: http://www.jewishgen.org/yizkor/kurow/kur235.html (accessed: 23 July 2013). The Kurow *yizkor* book is available online as part of the New York Public Library's excellent collection of 650 *yizkor* books: http://yizkor.nypl.org/index.php?id=2682 (accessed: 23 July 2013).

3 It is difficult to estimate how many *yizkor* books have been published that relate specifically to the Holocaust. A recent upper estimate suggests 1,000. *Yizkor* books started appearing already in the 1940s, with their numbers peaking in the 1950s and 1960s. Publication has continued into the 1980s and 1990s and beyond. Approximately three quarters of the books have now been published in Israel, and Hebrew has supplanted Yiddish as the predominant language of publication (Horowitz 2011: 1–2). *Yizkor* books were published prior to the Holocaust, documenting earlier Jewish catastrophes.

4 For a translation of the table of contents, see the JewishGen website: http://www.jewishgen.org/yizkor/kurow/kurow.html (accessed: 23 July 2013).

5 Feliks Tych notes survivors completed detailed questionnaires which formed the basis of their testimony (2008: 227–232).

6 Philip Friedman's (1980) collected essays, *Roads to Extinction*, remain a pivotal work for anyone interested in understanding the Jewish community's response to the Holocaust in Poland.

7 Particularly telling is Roskies's discussion of the failure of Leyb Rochman's successful Yiddish account of his Holocaust experiences to resonate in Israel once translated into Hebrew (2012: 83–84).

8 The *Torah* refers to Jewish scripture.

9 Traditionally, family members 'sit' on stools at a lower level than visitors, hence the phrase 'sitting *shiva*'.

10 Although quite applicable in this instance, Assmann's contention that Holocaust written memoirs are inherently coherent, whereas videotestimony is essentially disorganized and chaotic, is problematic. Having viewed many Holocaust video-testimonies and having interviewed many Holocaust survivors, I have encountered considerable variation in how survivors tell their stories. In Maclean (2006a), I examine non-standard narratives by Holocaust survivors whose videotestimonies give coherent accounts of their experiences by portraying them as adventures. Analysis of ethical dilemmas Jews faced during the Holocaust engages directly with traumatic memory (Maclean 2006b).

11 This was born of necessity, given that an estimated 52,000 interviews were conducted on behalf of the Shoah Foundation (Krondorfer 2008: 200).

12 Browning does not use Jewish survivor sources in his study.

Bibliography

Aleksiun, N. (2008) 'The Central Jewish Historical Commission in Poland, 1944–1947', in G.N. Finder, N. Aleksiun, A. Polonsky and J. Schwarz (eds) *Making Holocaust Memory, (Polin, Volume Twenty). Studies in Polish Jewry*, Oxford: The Littman Library of Jewish Civilization: 74–97.

Assmann, A. (2006) 'History, Memory and the Genre of Testimony', *Poetics Today*, 27.2: 261–273.

Browning, C.R. (1992) *Ordinary Men: Reserve Police Battalion 101 and the Final Solution in Poland*, New York: HarperPerennial.

——. (2006) '"Judenjagd". Die Schlussphase der "Endlösung" in Polen', in J. Matthäus and K.-M. Mallmann (eds) *Deutsche, Juden, Völkermord: Der Holocaust als Geschichte und Gegenwart*, Darmstadt: Wissenschaftliche Buchgesellschaft: 177–189.

Chanesman, J. (1996) 'Videotestimony No. 763', Melbourne: Jewish Holocaust Centre.

Cimet, A. (2011) '"To Hold our Own against Silence"', in R. Horowitz (ed.) *Memorial Books of Eastern European Jewry: Essays on the History and Meanings of Yizker Volumes*, Jefferson: McFarland: 122–142.

Friedman, P. (1980) *Roads to Extinction: Essays on the Holocaust*, New York: Jewish Publication Society of America.

Grosman, M. (1955) 'A Burial Place and a Memorial', in M. Grosman (ed.) *Izkor Book. In Memoriam of our Home-Town Kurow*, Tel Aviv and New York: Residents of Kurow in Israel.

Hanisman, S. (1955) 'Hurbn Koriv un di iberlebenishn fun Shmual Hanisman', in M. Grosman (ed.) *Izkor book. In Memoriam of our Home-Town Kurow*, Tel Aviv and New York: Residents of Kurow in Israel: 235–270.

Hesford, W.S. (2004) 'Documenting Violations: Rhetorical Witnessing and the Spectacle of Distant Suffering', *Biography*, 27.1: 104–144.

Horowitz, R. (2011) 'Introduction', in R. Horowitz (ed.) *Memorial Books of Eastern European Jewry: Essays on the History and Meanings of Yizker Volumes*, Jefferson: McFarland: 1–6.

Jablon, R.L. (2004) 'Witnessing as *Shivah*; Memoir as *Yizkor*. The Formulation of Holocaust Survivor Literature as *Gemilut Khasadim*', *The Journal of Popular Culture*, 38.2: 306–324.

Krondorfer, B. (2008) 'Whose Memory is it Anyway? Reflections on Remembering, Preserving and Forgetting', in P. Maclean, M. Langfield and D. Abramovich (eds)

Testifying to the Holocaust, Sydney: Australian Association of Jewish Studies: 199–222.

Kugelmass, J. and J. Boyarin. (1983) 'Introduction', in J. Kugelmass and J. Boyarin (eds) *From a Ruined Garden: The Memorial Books of Polish Jewry*, New York: Schocken Books: 1–50.

Langfield, M. and P. Maclean. (2009) 'Multiple Framings: Survivor and Non-Survivor Interviewers in Holocaust Videotestimony', in N. Adler, S. Leydesdorff, M. Chamberlain and L. Neyzi (eds) *Memories of Mass Repression: Narrating Life Stories in the Aftermath of Atrocity*, New Brunswick and London: Transaction Publishers: 199–218.

Laub, D. (2012) 'Testimony as Life Experience and Legacy', in N.R. Goodman and M.B. Meyers (eds) *The Power of Witnessing: Reflections, Reverberations, and Traces of the Holocaust*, New York: Routledge: 59–80.

Maclean, P. (2006a) 'Transforming the Holocaust into an Adventure in Videotestimony: An Unexpected Form of Discourse', *Quaderns de Filologia: Estudis Lingüistics, What is Critical Discourse Analysis?* XI: 125–143.

——. (2006b) '"You Leaving Me Alone?" The Persistence of Ethics during the Holocaust', *International Journal: Studies on the Audio-Visual Testimony of Victims of the Nazi Crimes and Genocides*, 12: 23–36.

Maclean, P., D. Abramovich and M. Langfield. (2008) 'Remembering Afresh? Videotestimonies Held in the Jewish Holocaust Museum and Research Centre (JHMRC) in Melbourne', in P. Maclean, M. Langfield and D. Abramovich (eds) *Testifying to the Holocaust*, Sydney: Australian Association of Jewish Studies: 3–28.

Roskies, D.G. (2012) 'Dividing the Ruins: Communal Memory in Yiddish and Hebrew', in D. Cesarani and E.J. Sundquist (eds) *After the Holocaust: Challenging the Myth of Silence*, London and New York: Routledge: 82–101.

Smith, M.L. (2012) 'No Silence in Yiddish: Popular and Scholarly Writing about the Holocaust in the Early Postwar Years', in D. Cesarani and E.J. Sundquist (eds) *After the Holocaust: Challenging the Myth of Silence*, London and New York: Routledge: 55–66.

Tych, F. (2008) 'The Emergence of Holocaust Research in Poland: The Jewish Historical Commission and the Jewish Historical Institute (ZIH), 1944–1989', in D. Bankier and D. Michman (eds) *Holocaust Historiography in Context: Emergence, Challenges, Polemics and Achievements*, Jerusalem: Yad Vashem: 227–244.

Waxman, Z.V. (2006) *Writing the Holocaust: Identity, Testimony, Representation*, Oxford: Oxford University Press.

Wieviorka, A. (2006) *The Era of the Witness*, Ithaca and London: Cornell University Press.

5 Set in stone?

The intergenerational and institutional transmission of Holocaust memory

Avril Alba

Introduction: Concepts and concrete

On 18 February 2013, the Sydney Jewish Museum (SJM) Board endorsed *An Obligation to Remember*, a master plan that outlined the SJM's major exhibition and education initiatives for the next ten years (Alba and X2 Design, 2013). On 3 March 2013, the Board reassembled for a workshop focused on a primary component of this plan, namely, the construction of a Holocaust and human rights centre to be housed at the SJM that would be the first centre of its kind in Australia. The decision to broaden the educational scope and reach of the SJM through establishing such a centre aligns with international trends, where explicit connections between Holocaust museums and associated ventures such as human rights and 'tolerance' museums are increasing in number (Moses 2012: 215–238).[1] Globally, these initiatives are more often than not partially or fully state funded, and hence the decision to broaden an institution's brief beyond the Holocaust is usually conceived as a way to make the historical information 'relevant' to the (mainly) non-Jewish public. Within the Australian context, however, such developments have been slow to eventuate and, where apparent, have not occurred as a result of significant changes in exhibition practices but rather, as has been the case with the SJM, through the creation of museum education programmes that have engaged comparative concepts to broaden the institution's educational scope (Alba 2007: 151–172).

From their inception, Australian Holocaust museums have always stood in contrast to their international counterparts as privately founded, privately funded and survivor-driven institutions (Berman 2001). However, with the passing of the survivor generation, the current SJM Board largely comprises sons and daughters of Holocaust survivors, the so-called 'second generation'. This generation has brought its own understandings of the utility of Holocaust history and memory to bear on institutional priorities and is currently harnessing these understandings to enact substantial change in line with international trends. This chapter charts significant junctures in the SJM's institutional development not only to assess the impact of these 'universalizing' international developments on a historically 'particularist' Australian context, but also to shed light on how intergenerational forces have generated and ultimately sanctioned such change. Utilizing and extending conceptual frameworks such as Marianne Hirsch's 'postmemory' (1997; 2001; 2008) as well as Gary Weissman's category of the 'non-witness' (2004) to illuminate the conceptual underpinnings of this very 'concrete' example, the chapter provides an alternate lens through which the dynamics of intergenerational transmission of the memory of genocide can be examined.

While Hirsch posits that the 'postmemory' of the second generation dominates intergenerational response to the Holocaust, Weissman challenges such a notion through delineating and exploring the category of the 'non-witness', a term which refers to those who have no first-hand, only received, knowledge of the Holocaust – *including* direct descendants. Weissman's category of the 'non-witness' extends the imperative to 'remember' the genocide of European Jewry beyond the children or grandchildren of survivors and, in so doing, enlarges our understanding of both the content and scope of the intergenerational transmission of Holocaust memory. By exploring where and how personal, familial and intra-communal memories (postmemory) intersect with more public expressions of Holocaust memory (non-witness memory), the following case study opens up a space in which these diverse and often contradictory memories can be examined. For while the memory of genocide is often superficially (mis)understood as a unifying force, an investigation of the effects of intergenerational forces on more public forms of Holocaust memory illustrates that such an outcome cannot be assumed. Indeed, in light of the multiplicity of meanings currently attributed to Holocaust memory, the chapter concludes by questioning the efficacy of the intergenerational transmission of this memory in the Australian public sphere and beyond.

Memory received or interpreted?

The influence of intergenerational change on the fields of Holocaust memory and representation is increasingly apparent. Indeed, one of the most salient features of the many imperatives to 'remember' the Holocaust is the call for intergenerational mechanisms to perpetuate the stories and legacy of the victims.[2] So strongly felt is this imperative within the now vast corpus of Holocaust 'memory forms' – forms that encompass, but are not limited to, cultural, religious, psychological, artistic and educational mediums – that intergenerational transmission has emerged as a dominant feature of both lay initiatives and scholarly debate.[3]

Within this corpus, Marianne Hirsch's theory of postmemory has dominated recent discussions concerning the dynamics of intergenerational transmission of Holocaust memory. Hirsch defines postmemory as 'the relationship of the second generation to powerful, often traumatic, experiences that preceded their births but that were nevertheless transmitted to them so deeply so as to seem memories in their own right' (Hirsch 2001: 103). Hirsch notes that her theory of postmemory contains an inherent contradiction or paradox. On the one hand, she asserts that members of the second generation feel the experience of their parents so deeply that they assume an immediate, affective knowledge of the events that have been transmitted. Yet, simultaneously, they are aware that they were not privy to these events and will remain forever unable to truly penetrate the stories transmitted to them:

> These terms reveal a number of controversial assumptions: that descendants of survivors (of victims as well as of perpetrators) of massive traumatic events connect so deeply to the previous generation's remembrances of the past that they need to call that connection *memory* and thus that, in certain extreme circumstances, memory *can* be transmitted to those who were not actually there to live an event. At the same time – so it is assumed – this received memory is *distinct* from the recall of contemporary witnesses and participants.
>
> (Hirsch 2001: 105–106, emphasis in the original)

Challenging Hirsch's self-confessed paradox, Gary Weissman acknowledges that children of Holocaust survivors will reach an understanding of 'what the Holocaust was' from a different subject position to those 'non-witnesses' with no familial connection to the Holocaust. However, this knowledge is not obtained because survivors' children *experience* the Holocaust and 'non-witnesses' do not. Rather, children of survivors *experience their parents' recollections, thoughts and feelings* about the Holocaust, their parents' 'memory'. Referencing novelist Melvin Jules Bukiet's introduction to an anthology of second-generation literature, Weissman concludes that, while the 'second generation will never know what their survivor parents knew in their bones, what the second generation knows better than anyone else is the first generation' (Weissman 2004: 18). Therefore, while the postmemory of children of survivors may be more visceral than that of others, it is still a *secondary* experience, what Weissman labels an experience of Holocaust 'representation' (2004: 20), *except* that the representation in question is familial and hence intensely personal and often enmeshed within the second generation's very sense of self.

However, Hirsch does not stop her exploration of the effects of postmemory at the familial level; she seeks to connect the intensely personal experience of postmemory with the concerns of Holocaust memory and remembrance more generally:

> At stake is not only a personal/familial/generational sense of ownership and protectiveness but also an evolving theoretical discussion about the workings of trauma, memory, and intergenerational acts of transfer, a discussion actively taking place in numerous important contexts outside of Holocaust studies. More urgently and passionately, those of us working on memory and transmission have argued over the ethics and

> the aesthetics of remembrance in the aftermath of catastrophe. How, in our present, do we regard and recall what Susan Sontag (2003) has so powerfully described as the 'pain of others'? What do we owe the victims? How can we best carry their stories forward without appropriating them, without unduly calling attention to ourselves, and without, in turn, having our own stories displaced by them? How are we implicated in the crimes? Can the memory of genocide be transformed into action and resistance?
>
> (Hirsch 2001: 104)

It is within these murky waters of 'appropriation' that debate concerning the nature and efficacy of intergenerational transmission is currently mired. Both Hirsch and Weissman's work illustrate that a primary concern of the second (and now third) generation of both children of survivors and 'non-witnesses' is to 'experience' rather than to 'learn about' the Holocaust. As Hirsch notes, 'postmemory's connection to the past is thus not actually mediated by recall but by imaginative investment, projection, and creation' (2001: 106–107).

I posit that such aspirations will remain vulnerable to the dangers of 'appropriation' unless the *interpretive* quality of these initiatives is made explicit and critically assessed. As Henry Greenspan has so persuasively argued, when providing testimony each survivor gives their unique perspective on the Holocaust, comprehensive only in the sense that it is the most accurate and detailed account they can provide of their experience (Greenspan 1998: 15). So too does the child of the survivor or non-witness have access to a *singular* experience, once removed. The assumption, therefore, that the children of survivors will ensure a more accurate recollection of and greater access to the past, or further provide some kind of collective representation of it, is unfounded. Indeed, if an accurate portrayal of the past is what intergenerational transmission seeks to achieve, those wishing to learn and pass on information about the Holocaust should turn instead to the numerous historical studies available, embarking upon the difficult task described by Holocaust historian Yehuda Bauer as anchoring 'the Holocaust in the historical consciousness of the generations that follow it' (Bauer 1978: 3).

However, the reception and transmission of historical information is clearly *not* what is at stake in either Hirsch's notion of postmemory or Weissman's exploration of the non-witness. And it is not the preoccupation of those members of the second and third generations – direct descendants and non-direct – who have undertaken the task of intergenerational transmission. For while a minority of this number will immerse themselves in the history of the Holocaust, the majority of those active in Holocaust commemoration will leave such ventures to professional historians, preferring to focus their energies on communal and institutional initiatives that might at best draw upon the fruit of the historian's labour.[4] Hence, when attempting to understand the workings of the intergenerational transmission of Holocaust memory, we must acknowledge that we are not dealing with an accurate transmission of events/history from one generation to another. Rather, we are faced with a complex and multilayered *interpretive* process, a process where the *meaning* or *utility* of the memory at hand is the key factor at stake.

From this perspective, one can argue that the process of intergenerational transmission both Hirsch and Weissman are seeking to describe might be better understood as a process of *interpretation*. More often associated with theological rather than historical enterprises, interpretation, or exegesis, is an intrinsically intergenerational and relational act. One interprets received texts in order to reaffirm their meaning and authority (in the case of Scripture) in the present. Textual interpretation in the Jewish tradition in particular also often contains an experiential element. The well-known adage of the Pesach *seder* (the Passover meal) provides a case in point. While celebrating the ritual meal, the participant is exhorted to remember the Exodus as if they too 'came out of Egypt'. Time momentarily 'collapses' as the 'historical' story is brought into the present through active identification with ancestors and 'events' long past. Further, the experiential is then often explicitly connected to the ethical, as is the case in the biblical injunction to 'not oppress the stranger for you were strangers in the land of Egypt' (Exodus 22:21).

Utilizing these concepts, the following examination of key junctures in the history of the SJM provides insight into the intergenerational and institutional transmission of Holocaust memory as an *interpretive* and *public* enterprise. As a community museum founded by survivors that is now dominated by the second generation, this site and the debates surrounding it provide an ideal case study for revealing the difficulties and potentialities involved in this process. What becomes evident is that the intergenerational transmission of memory at the SJM has been dominated by debates as to the meaning, and hence the utility, of the past in light of the concerns of the present. The 'future' of Holocaust memory from one generation to the next will by necessity, therefore, be a contested process, where the struggle to interpret and transmit this 'meaning' remains both a central and forever-changing element.

The first generation: building the Sydney Jewish Museum

The SJM is located in the Maccabean Hall, known colloquially as the 'Macc'. The building, opened formally on Armistice Day 1923 by the Jewish-Australian war hero Sir John Monash, also houses the New South Wales Jewish War Memorial. There was general agreement within the community at the time of building that a living communal centre would be the best way to commemorate those who served in the Great War. The walls of the forecourt are inscribed with names of nearly 3,000 Jewish-Australian service people, including 177 who died serving in the Australian forces in the First and Second World War.[5]

The centre quickly became a vital part of Jewish life in Sydney. As the original SJM catalogue recounts:

> The Macc instantly became a vibrant centre. There were meetings, dances, debates, revues, plays, movies, a library and a gymnasium. The hall housed High Holy Days services and a community Seder service at Passover. A singularly important flow-on effect was that countless marriages resulted from people meeting at The Macc.
>
> (Hammer 1992: 7)

In 1965, the building was remodelled as the 'NSW Jewish War Memorial Community Centre', with the focus changing from social events and activities to community administration. The arrival after the Second World War into Australia of the largest number of Holocaust survivors per capita to any nation except Israel profoundly changed the landscape of the Australian Jewish community. The survivors became involved in, and central to, all aspects of communal life and, in line with developments internationally, their need to recount and document their experiences became progressively more urgent as public consciousness concerning the Holocaust increased in the late 1970s and 1980s.[6] Subsequently, the Macc was again redesigned and refurbished, and, in 1992, the Sydney Jewish Museum was officially opened.

The choice to house the SJM in a pre-existing communal and memorial building stands in stark contrast to purpose-built Holocaust museums in the United States, Israel and Europe, and illustrates the intra-communal focus of the institution's founders. While a committee comprising a variety of survivor stakeholders originally initiated the project, Hungarian survivor and entrepreneur John Saunders commandeered it in 1989 and was, at its outset, the institution's sole benefactor.[7] Working hand in hand with the then Australian Association of Jewish Holocaust Survivors (AAJHS),[8] whose membership would provide the majority of guides and general volunteers for the SJM, Saunders's understanding of the task was clear; he wanted to build 'a *yiddishe* museum', a museum that would focus on the Jewish experience.[9] From the time of Saunders's leadership, therefore, Jewish survivors were dominant in developing and implementing the narrative and content of the museum space. As the original SJM catalogue proclaimed, this was to be a museum that would serve as 'a tribute to survivors, perpetuating the truth through their eyes and in their words' (Hammer 1992: 7).

From its inception, therefore, the 'telling' of the Holocaust at the SJM was presented from a survivor perspective that was at once equated with a singular 'true' or 'historical' rendering.[10] For example, when queried in a newspaper interview on the potential for a Holocaust exhibition to 'speak to' other historical events, the SJM's first curator, Sylvia Rosenblum emphatically stated, 'One cannot use the Holocaust to tell other stories'. Clearly, from Rosenblum's perspective, there was only one story to tell: a Holocaust museum should aim to 'tell the story of the Holocaust simply, truthfully and

Figure 5.1 The founder of the Sydney Jewish Museum, John Saunders, affixing a *mezzuzah* at the opening of the museum (with Alex Weinberger and Sol Schonberger). Reproduced with permission of the Sydney Jewish Museum, © Sydney Jewish Museum, 1992.

Figure 5.2 'The First Generation'. Marika and Alex Weinberger at the opening of the Sydney Jewish Museum. Reproduced with permission of the Sydney Jewish Museum, © Sydney Jewish Museum, 1992.

honestly so that it would never happen again' (Deutsch 1993: 10). She characterized such an approach as a 'survivor attitude to memorialization of the Holocaust', and defined this perspective as consisting of:

> The desire and/or need to fulfill the Jewish injunction to remember – *zachor* – and the desire or need to bear witness. These factors were paramount in the establishment of the Sydney Jewish Museum. Like its counterparts around the world, its memorialization of the Holocaust, therefore, is private, personal and Jewish, and has not been subjected to the problems of institutionalization and politicization of state-owned or state-subsidized museums.
>
> (Deutsch 1993: 10)

One might reasonably wonder why, if the central goal of memorialization at the SJM was 'private, personal and Jewish', that the task of building a *public* museum was undertaken in the first place.[11] Rosenblum's characterization of the complex undertaking of exhibition development and design as the curatorial equivalent of *wie es eigentlich gewesen*[12] belies the social, historical and political context within which the SJM emerged, the influence of key protagonists and the very process of exhibition practice – which is by definition one of selection and interpretation. An exhibition, like any other historical 'text', is influenced by a variety of factors; choice and availability of artefacts (sources), narrative shape, the perspective of those who create the exhibition and the space in which the display is ultimately placed all contribute to its final form. Rosenblum's characterization of the SJM's permanent exhibition as constituting a simple reflection of a pre-existing 'survivor attitude' masks several factors, key among these being what, exactly, such an attitude entails. Hence, what 'kind' of survivor built the SJM is left both assumed and unexplored. Given the centrality of survivors to the formation of the SJM, articulating the meaning(s) they attributed to their experience(s) is central to understanding how that meaning has been interpreted and changed by subsequent generations.

Ascertaining exactly what this meaning was, however, is no simple task. Even within the first generation of museum leadership, the meaning of the survivors' experiences was contested and therefore required interpretation. For, contrary to Rosenblum's assertion, prior to the transition of leadership and funding to John Saunders, it appears that no consensus existed as to what the museum's 'survivor perspective' might entail. In the initial planning, a 'personal, private and Jewish' museum was only one rationale among many given for the formation of the SJM. The diversity of reasoning behind the desire to build the museum is evident in a 1986 report compiled by the AAJHS. The AAJHS formed a working group for the express purpose of defining why such an institution should be built, which then embarked on a year-long process of deliberation. The working group met on ten occasions between March and September 1986 to discuss the desirability and feasibility of building a permanent Holocaust exhibition in Sydney and the proposed contents of such a museum.[13] Discussion centred on the following topics:

(i) Rationale and philosophy
(ii) The collection
(iii) Administration
(iv) Location

(Proposal 1986: 1).

The 'rationale and philosophy' discussion was primarily concerned with establishing the reasons for undertaking such a project, the 'need' for a Holocaust museum in Sydney, the 'role' such a museum would play, its intended audience and the overall philosophy or 'approach' of the proposed institution. Scholars have tended to point to the rise in Holocaust denial as the central motivating factor in the establishment of Australia's Holocaust museums (Berman 2001). The need to combat Holocaust denial is mentioned in the report (Proposal 1986: 2), but it remains only one point among many and cannot be understood to be the sole motivating factor.

Rather, the 'rationale and philosophy' discussion stressed the importance of the museum as a collecting institution. The availability of material culture pertaining to the Holocaust within the Sydney Jewish community is noted alongside the need to collect such memorabilia and make it 'available to the public' (Proposal 1986: 2). There is a sense of urgency in this mission: if the collecting process did not begin imminently, 'the memorabilia of survivors, many of whom are elderly, will be scattered, simply discarded or lost' (Proposal 1986: 3). Notably, throughout the report there is no mention of the idea of collecting outside of the Jewish community,[14] nor is there any discussion of a 'private/public' partnership that has characterized the building of many Holocaust museums internationally.[15] Rather, from the outset, the SJM was to be a private venture, initiated from within the Jewish community and reliant upon community funds, human resources and memorabilia.

Another significant factor cited for the emergence of an organized Holocaust commemorative body within the Sydney Jewish community was the shift to multiculturalism as official government policy in Australia in the 1970s, a political development that generated greater confidence and pride in ethnic identity (Rutland 1997: 369–371). Indeed, the *Proposal* states that 'in today's multicultural society, it is imperative that material evidence of one of Australia's significant ethnic minorities be housed in a permanent institution' (Proposal 1986: 2). This factor, combined with others, such as the increased international interest in Holocaust commemoration epitomized in the First International Gathering of Holocaust Survivors in Jerusalem in 1981 and the emergence of popular representation of the Holocaust (like the mini-series 'Holocaust' in the 1970s), all influenced the rise of public Australian commemorations. No doubt, all of these developments impacted the beginnings of organized Holocaust commemoration in Australia, but the *Proposal* does not stress a 'celebration' of this shift in Australia's political milieu, nor does it connect Holocaust memory to 'safeguarding' the rights of minorities in multicultural society.

Nonetheless, the *Proposal* does contain humanist elements that evince a desire to address Holocaust memory to non-Jewish Australians. A Holocaust museum, it says, stands as 'a warning against circumstances which give rise to the dehumanization of minorities, leading to genocide' (Proposal 1986: 2); it notes that, while 'attitudes towards the Holocaust will be set within the context of antisemitism generally,' the Holocaust will also be set 'within the context of persecution of minority groups' (Proposal 1986: 2, 6). Even so, these universal sentiments are not explicitly addressed. While universal issues may provide some context, the 1986 *Proposal* may not be as far removed from Rosenblum's later comments as first conceived. The *Proposal* indicates that the planned museum will address universal issues through inference rather than direct connection or the contextualization of the Holocaust into a pre-existing 'humanistic' framework. Instead, 'by highlighting the potential

Figure 5.3 'The First Generation'. SJM volunteers celebrate the International Year of the Volunteer. Reproduced with permission of the Sydney Jewish Museum, © Sydney Jewish Museum, 2001.

for evil in a totalitarian regime, it [Jewish Holocaust Museum] will promote commitment to democracy and freedom'. On this basis, the working group asserts that a 'project of such worth and lasting impact deserves the support of the Jewish and, indeed, the general communities' (Proposal 1986: 2). Hence, in its pre-formative and formative stages, even the most 'universal' statements would be premised on the desire to tell a 'particular' story, a supposedly unified and consistent first-generation 'survivor story', the *meaning* of which was initially debated and then, with the transition to Saunders's leadership, appears to be simply assumed.

The second generation: interpreting the memory

As is now well documented in a variety of studies, the meanings attached to Holocaust memory are constantly evolving. Further, as Edward Linenthal argues in his landmark study of the United States Holocaust Memorial Museum (USHMM), once a memory becomes a 'national trust', the shape of that memory is subject not only to the wishes of those who relay it, but also to the wishes of those who receive it (1995: 7). This need to understand the demands of a changing visitor base, a change in which intergenerational shifts play a significant role, is an important component of contemporary museum practice.

Increasingly, museum work is imagined as a relational act involving the active participation of both those who provide information and those who receive it. Museum displays and related education and public programmes are created with the 'active' museum visitor in mind. This visitor will 'choose' how much information they will delve into through immersion in a multilayered display that, through interactive media, provides a series of pathways and will then be encouraged to relate that information to contemporary life – the public programmes of the USHMM's Darfur campaign provide a case in point. The contemporary museum is no longer simply an elaborate 'cabinet of curiosities' but is more accurately imagined as an active researcher and educator. Indeed, the aforementioned master plan, *An Obligation to Remember*, explicitly states that the displays must now come to the forefront to replace the immediacy of the encounter with the survivor (Sydney Jewish Museum 2013: 14).

Given this shift in museum practice and visitor expectation, in its current incarnation the SJM can no longer retain an intra-communal focus if its leadership's explicit desire is to place the museum into the mainstream of Australian public life (Sydney Jewish Museum 2013: 12).[16] Rosenblum's vision of a 'personal, private and Jewish' museum will not enable the kind of expansion and shift that the current Board of Directors envisions for this growing institution. In a cultural landscape in which museums and memorials are increasingly understood as reflections of and contributors to issues of national import, it is little wonder that the particularistic emphasis of the SJM's founding survivors is being reassessed by their descendants in order to achieve the SJM's self-proclaimed mission of 'contemporary relevance' (Sydney Jewish Museum 2007). The question therefore arises: does the original particularistic focus of the SJM's founders sit in opposition to the institution's current mission 'to inspire mutual respect and cross-cultural understanding in our society' (Sydney Jewish Museum 2009), or can this emphasis be retained but recast to allow the universal resonance of Holocaust memory to be felt beyond the confines of the Sydney Jewish community? Debates concerning the museum's future hinge, therefore, upon this question of whether the invocation of Holocaust memory can serve to illuminate a variety of historical instances, political and social causes, and moral and ethical dilemmas *without* betraying its particular identity. Can the application of Holocaust memory at the SJM serve to highlight other instances of genocide and mass trauma to extend empathy and identification with victims of persecution? It is precisely these debates upon which the SJM's intergenerational battle lines are currently drawn.

An ever-evolving mission

Rosenblum's 'personal, private and Jewish' museum, if it ever really existed, exists no more. A new generation of 'memory guardians' are now charged with relating this memory to an ever-more diverse and demanding public – the majority of which no longer have any living memory of the Holocaust. Yet, within this generation, the meaning of the Holocaust is anything but self-evident. Rather, this meaning continues to be interpreted and changed, resulting in some instances in an almost complete reversal of the meaning(s) that the first generation attributed to their Holocaust experience.

One way this shift can be illustrated is through an examination of the change in focus evident in the institution's mission and vision. The SJM's first mission statement, written in the period dominated by the survivor generation, provides a clear example of the particularistic perspective evident in the early years of the museum's functioning:

> The Sydney Jewish Museum is a museum about a people. Created as a living memorial to the *Shoah*, it honors the six million who perished, the courage and the suffering of all those who were caught up and those who attempted to resist evil for the sake of what was right. We celebrate their lives, cherish the civilization that they built, their achievements and faith, their joys and hopes, together with the story of the Australian Jewish community and its culture.
>
> (Sydney Jewish Museum 2002)

Followed by a list of 'aims and objectives', the focus of the mission statement is overwhelmingly particularistic, although an implicit understanding of 'universal values' might be drawn from statements such as the resistance of 'evil for the sake of what was right' and the paying 'tribute to the individual rights and liberties we enjoy in democratic Australia'. The aims and objectives end with a sentence emphasizing the 'importance of religious and cultural tolerance so that these events will never be repeated'. Upon whom they might be repeated is left unspecified.

In contrast, the current version of the SJM mission statement, compiled by a Board that now comprises only three survivors, with the majority of members being second-generation descendants, *begins* with a universal statement and outlines the institution's vision thus:

> To inspire mutual respect and cross-cultural understanding within our society, with particular emphasis on the lessons of the Holocaust, in order that such a tragedy can never again happen to any people.
>
> (Sydney Jewish Museum 2009)

The mission statement continues from this premise to mention specifically 'the six million Jews murdered by the Nazis and their collaborators', and promises to 'honour the survivors and pay tribute to the Righteous Among the Nations'; it then contextualizes the Holocaust as a 'crime against humanity with contemporary and universal significance' (Sydney Jewish Museum 2009). A clear shift has occurred in which the particular memory of the Jewish survivor moves from being the *object* of the mission to its *conduit*, its channel to the larger concerns that emanate from a consideration of the Holocaust (Sydney Jewish Museum 2003).[17]

Similar changes are beginning to emerge in the built space of the SJM. The addition in 2005 to the permanent exhibition of *Serniki: Unearthing the Holocaust*,[18] a display that focuses upon the war crimes trials undertaken in Adelaide, South Australia in 1991–1993, provides a case in point. Culminating in a consideration of the 'global resonance' of these trials – as the forensic methods undertaken to present evidence to the South Australian court were then employed in similar such trials of the genocidal campaigns in the former Yugoslavia and Rwanda – the display is now utilized in a variety of educational programmes concerning issues of justice and human rights.[19] Increases in student visits for the museum's education programmes also bear witness to this change in the direction of Holocaust memory at the SJM. Student visitors comprise the only 'growing' segment of the museum's visitor base, and the number of students visiting the SJM has increased by over 100 per cent over a seven-year period (Sydney Jewish Museum 2010).[20] Despite the fact that there is no mandated study of the Holocaust in the New South Wales curriculum,[21] this increase was engendered through developing programmes that address both the historical 'facts' of the Holocaust and the ethical imperatives that stem from such a considered study (Alba 2005: 37–41).[22] In this manner, the Holocaust could be studied within history, but it could also address a far broader range of topic areas across the New South Wales syllabus. Education programmes do not have the same 'permanency' as exhibitions and, as a result, have traditionally been afforded more scope in the 'personal, private and Jewish' space of the SJM.

The success of the education programmes led to a desire to expand this section of the SJM's activities further with the 2008–2012 strategic plan, which identified a key goal for education as being the positioning of the SJM as 'the leading educator within Australia of anti-racism, social inclusion and genocide' through the establishment of a 'Centre for Anti-racism and Tolerance Education within five years' (Sydney Jewish Museum 2008). The proposed Centre became a focal point for debate on the SJM Board and was finally abandoned when the Board leadership changed in November 2010 due to a disagreement as to whether anti-racism was the logical extension of Holocaust memory at the SJM and, indeed, if it honoured the 'original intent' of its founders (Sydney Jewish Museum 2010). While some Board members (descendants) saw the Centre initiative as true to the survivors' original vision for the SJM, others held completely opposite opinions. Debate centred on who had 'interpreted correctly', who 'understood properly' the original intent of the survivor generation.

This 'interpretive' issue divided the SJM Board, and the matter was only finally resolved with the election of a new president (himself the son of survivors), who, while abandoning the idea of an anti-racism centre, did not yield on the need to expand the SJM's activities beyond a purely Holocaust-focused approach. The idea of an additional centre whose focus would be on

Figure 5.4 'The Second Generation'. SJM volunteer and non-witness Harry Taibel guides a school group. Reproduced with permission of the Sydney Jewish Museum, © Sydney Jewish Museum, 2007.

the universal issues that emanate from a study of the Holocaust was therefore not relinquished and, as noted in the introduction to this chapter, planning for a new 'Holocaust and human rights' centre is currently underway (Sydney Jewish Museum 2013: 23–25). While the content of the human rights centre is still evolving, the shift away from a 'personal, private and Jewish' museum is clearly evident as a new generation reinterprets, and hence reshapes, the Holocaust memory at hand.

As ownership of Holocaust memory at the SJM shifts from the first to the second generation, however, the shape of that memory continues to be a contested one that has become increasingly fractious both inside and outside the museum walls. An exchange on the Jewish internet news source 'J-Wire' between B'nai B'rith ADC[23] chairman Anton Block and AAJHS&D immediate past president George Foster and current president Anna Berger (both of whom also sat on the SJM Board at this time) provides a case in point. The debate centred on the appropriateness of evoking the memory of the Holocaust in relation to the tragic deaths of asylum seekers near Christmas Island (an Australian territory located close to Indonesia) on 15 December 2010 as they were attempting to reach shore. In the article, Block stated that 'the deaths of dozens of asylum seekers in treacherous seas near Christmas Island might have been prevented if Australia had better processing procedures in Indonesia and humanitarian resettlement of refugees' (Stone 2010). While Block admitted that his analogy was 'imperfect', he couched his critique and its legitimacy in the following statement:

> As Jewish Australians, many of us descended from those lucky survivors who did get refuge in Australia; we are tremendously pained to see asylum seekers a generation later drowning and suffering.
>
> (Stone 2010)

The response from Foster and Berger centred on just how 'imperfect' the analogy was. Berger began her reply by stating:

> The recent tragic death of asylum seekers is unquestionably worthy of heartfelt compassion and empathy by all decent people. The instincts of B'nai B'rith ADC in deploring this tragedy in their media release of 16 December 2010 are commendable, but their comparison of the asylum seekers' plight to that of Jews trying to escape certain murder by the Nazis and their allies is irresponsible.
>
> (Berger 2010)

Both Foster and Berger pointed out that the historical context of the current situation of asylum seekers and that of those Jews fleeing persecution under Nazism was radically different and objected to Block's statement on several counts, with Foster stating that 'current asylum seekers have not been marked out for, or subjected to, genocidal mass murder and have not actually been turned back by governments because of their religion or race, and do have choices. Many of them have been admitted into Australia after their claims have been processed'. In contrast to these cases, Foster ponders: 'During the *Shoah* where were the governments sympathetic to the Jewish plight? There was in the end nowhere for them to go and even the Australian representative at the fateful Evian Conference in 1938 said that "As we have no real racial problems, we are not desirous of importing one". It is outrageous to compare the current Australian government to that of 1938' (Foster 2010). Berger also contends that such analogies are unnecessary and that 'Jews do not need faux analogies to the Holocaust in order to make a strong moral statement on human rights issues. When we choose to make our voices heard we do so as proud, engaged Jewish Australian citizens with a strong ethos of *Tsedaka* and *Chesed* based on the ethical system which has been our people's unique gift to humankind' (Berger 2010).[24]

Both Foster and Berger are correct with regard to their historical qualifications as to the differences between the tragic events of Christmas Island and the events of the Holocaust sixty years earlier. However, both miss the point that Block's comparison was not made to make the case for absolute historical parity – the historical 'uniqueness' of *any* historical event ensures that this is never a real possibility. Rather, Block's invocation of Holocaust memory was rather an interpretation based on the perceived *utility* of Holocaust memory to highlight the moral indignities of one historical instance of tragedy through invocation of another.[25] Foster might rightly worry that such analogies 'trivialize' the events of the Holocaust, while Berger may well be correct that there are other ways for Jews to make such moral claims, but if Holocaust memory cannot and should not speak past its immediate context and community, then why place, indeed 'display', it in the public sphere? Can historical integrity be maintained ('the analogy is imperfect'), while contemporary empathy is also extended? As founding 'partners'[26] with the Sydney Jewish Museum, the AAJHS was instrumental in bringing Holocaust memory into the Australian public context. Now run by descendants (both Foster and Berger are children of survivors), this recent example of their misgivings as to whether Holocaust memory can and should be 'made relevant' to current and ongoing issues of racial intolerance and xenophobia that beset contemporary Australian life illustrates that the public utility of Holocaust memory at the SJM and beyond its walls remains a topic in flux to the next generation of Australian 'non-witnesses'.

Conclusion

As the Sydney Jewish Museum moves into its third decade, the continued influence of the second generation on institutional priorities ensures that their *interpretations of survivor memory* will remain the cornerstone in any discussion as to the 'shape' of that memory, at least for the foreseeable future. At the same time, it is increasingly evident that the second generation, much like the first, does not speak with one voice and is unlikely to ever do so. Indeed, the overview of both the formative stages of the institution's development and the current debates outlined in this chapter demonstrates, that there never was a singular meaning attributed to this memory, much as some would like to believe otherwise. Rather, what this historical consideration of the institutional and intergenerational process of the transmission of memory brings to light is that the intersection between Hirsch's largely private notion of 'postmemory' and Weissman's more public notion of 'non-witness' expressions of intergenerational response are deeply interlinked. The individual and private memories of the second generation will necessarily influence and shape the public expression of Holocaust memory at the SJM, but they cannot, and will not, dictate its final form or its public reception. Rather, the element of compromise that characterizes communal endeavours combined with the demands of public discourse will ultimately determine the shape of memory at the SJM.

And so, in conclusion, we return to Hirsch's poignant and pressing question: 'Can the memory of genocide be transformed into action and resistance?' (Hirsch 2008: 104). If the experience of the Sydney Jewish Museum is understood as a 'concrete' attempt to answer this question, then, based on a consideration of past and contemporary debates, our conclusions can only be tentative. What must be recognized is that the private memories that the generation 'postmemory', of 'non-witnesses', brings to their tasks are varied, often contradictory and always in debate. Their memories reflect their diverse interpretations of both a private and a communal history, producing interpretations that may, or may not, be deemed in harmony with a changing Australian public landscape. The challenge, therefore, facing the current museum leadership is to engage these intensely personal and diverse intergenerational memories while forging and maintaining a commitment to broader communal and institutional priorities. If the leadership of the SJM can maintain the centrality of the Australian community's distinct, yet diverse, experience of Holocaust history and memory while engaging with the broader concerns that emanate from these experiences – if it can hold the particular and the universal in tension while refusing to relinquish either – then the intergenerational and institutional transmission of Holocaust memory may indeed be realized.

Notes

1 The most recent example of such a venture is the Canadian Museum of Human Rights (see chapter 6 in this volume and Moses 2012).

2 One could argue that this demand actually begins within the period itself, for example, with initiatives such as Emanuel Ringelblum's *Oneg Shabbat* archive and Simon Dubnow's famous exhortation of '*Yidn, schreibt und farschreibt!* Jews, write and record!'

3 For an example of such studies within the Australian context, see the essays of Amelia Klein (2007) and Sharon Kangisser Cohen (2007). Klein also participated

in the making of a 2004 documentary *Who Owns the Memory?* by film-maker Marc Radomsky that followed the Australian March of the Living group throughout their travels in Poland in order to explore the topic of intergenerational transmission of memory.

4 Taking the New South Wales context as an example, neither the majority of SJM Board members, nor the members of the Yom HaShoah committees that organize annual commemorative events are professional researchers in Holocaust studies.

5 The per capita rate of Jewish participation in both the First and Second World War was higher than that of the general population.

6 For a summary of the rise of popular Holocaust consciousness in Australia, see Berman 2001.

7 John Saunders was the co-founder of the Westfield department store company with fellow Hungarian survivor Frank Lowy.

8 In 1994, the organization changed its name to include Descendants – an explicit recognition of the need for intergenerational transmission – to the Australian Association for Jewish Holocaust Survivors and Descendants (AAJHS&D).

9 Interview with Marika Weinberger, 11 October 2009.

10 This view was affirmed in an interview with Professor Konrad Kwiet on 2 December 2009. Professor Kwiet has served as the resident historian of the Sydney Jewish Museum since its inception.

11 Unlike the majority of Holocaust museums internationally, the SJM began as an entirely private venture and remains so today, with the majority of operating costs sourced from within the Jewish community. Government grants are applied for and obtained for distinct projects, but there is no ongoing source of government funding.

12 The definition of the historical enterprise attributed to the German historian Leopold von Ranke: 'to show what actually happened'.

13 While the SJM exhibition was finally placed in a pre-existing communal building, the Maccabean Hall, at this point there was no consensus as to where the display would be housed or whether a totally new building would need to be established.

14 The current collecting policy of the SJM prohibits the buying of Nazi paraphernalia for fear of participating in a black market of such items. However, it is asserted in Section B of the *Proposal*, 'Collections Policy', that 'objects for the permanent collection will be acquired by gift, bequest, purchase, exchange or any other transaction ... ' (Proposal 1986: 11).

15 Such a partnership is exemplified in the United States Holocaust Memorial Museum's structure.

16 This is perhaps the clearest statement of the SJM's current goal to engage in outreach as an institutional priority.

17 Interestingly, this shift occurs in the period of the 2003–2008 strategic plan, when it is acknowledged in the 'Stakeholder Analysis' that 'the external and general categories are the key and largest stakeholders and yet, most of the SJM's activities seem to be focussed on the needs of internal stakeholders/audiences'.

18 Serniki is a village in the Ukraine which was the site of a mass shooting of Jews in 1942.

19 Most recently, this exhibition and the research of chief historian of the Australian War Crimes trials, Professor Konrad Kwiet, have become the basis for an education programme commissioned by the Australian Institute for Police Management. The programme centres on the issues of ethical leadership and individual responsibility, and looks particularly at the role of police battalions in implementing the Final Solution.

20 At the end of 2002, the student visitor rate was 7,500 per annum. At the close of the 2011 school year, that rate had increased to 16,801 per annum.

21 The Holocaust will be included in Australia's new National Curriculum, which will begin implementation in 2014.
22 No doubt the structure and content of the education programmes will change yet again with the inclusion of the Holocaust in the history syllabus created for Australia's new national curriculum. However, it is becoming increasingly likely that the New South Wales Board of Studies will retain the subject as an elective only.
23 B'nai B'rith is the oldest Jewish service organization existent in the world today. Among its many activities is anti-defamation and advocacy against anti-Semitism and racism more generally. For the AAJHS&D, see note 8.
24 *Tsedaka* and *Chesed* are commonly translated as 'charity and lovingkindness', although the Hebrew root of the former is literally translated as 'justice'.
25 Interestingly, high-profile Australian publisher Louise Adler gave a similar interpretation of these events on the popular ABC (Australian Broadcasting Corporation) current affairs show *Q&A* on 25 June 2012 by evoking her parents' own journey to Australia as refugees from Nazism in 1939.
26 Marika Weinberger refers to this partnership as a 'handshake' between John Saunders and the AAJHS&D in which the former agreed to give the financial backing and the latter the 'manpower' to realize the project. At that point, the Association did not include '& Descendants' in its title. Interview with Marika Weinberger, 31 October 2006.

Bibliography

A Proposal for the Establishment of a Jewish Holocaust Museum in Sydney. (1986).

Alba, A. (2005) 'Teaching History and Teaching Ethics: New Perspectives on Holocaust Education', *Teaching History: Journal of the History Teachers Association of NSW*, 39.2: 37–41.

——. (2007) 'Displaying the Sacred: Australian Holocaust Memorials in Public Life', in T. Lawson and J. Jordan (eds) *The Memory of the Holocaust in Australia*, Portland and London: Vallentine Mitchell: 128–147.

Alba, A. and X2 Design. (2013) *An Obligation to Remember, Masterplan 2020*.

Bauer, Y. (1978) *The Holocaust in Historical Perspective*, Seattle: University of Washington Press.

Berger, A. (2010) 'Not the Holocaust', *J-Wire*, 27 December. Available at: http://www.jwire.com.au/news/not-the-holocaust/14161. Accessed: 2 January 2011.

Berman, J.E. (2001) *Holocaust Remembrance in Australian Jewish Communities, 1945–2000*, Crawley: University of Western Australia Press.

Deutsch, S. (1993) 'The Holocaust is Unique', *Australian Jewish News*, 23 July.

Foster, G. (2010) 'Response to Deborah Stone "Voyage of the Damned – Take Two"', *J-Wire*, 26 December. Available at: http://www.jwire.com.au/news/voyage-of-the-damned-take-two/13990.

Greenspan, H. (1998) *On Listening to Holocaust Survivors: Recounting and Life History*, Westport: Praeger.

Hammer, G. (1992) *Sydney Jewish Museum Catalogue*, Sydney: Sydney Jewish Museum.

Hirsch, M. (1997) *Family Frames: Photography, Narrative and Postmemory*, Cambridge: Harvard University Press.

——. (2001) 'Surviving Images: Holocaust Photographs and the Work of Postmemory', *The Yale Journal of Criticism* 14.1: 5–37.

——. (2008) 'The Generation of Postmemory', *Poetics Today*, 29.1: 103–128.

Kangisser Cohen, S. (2007) '"Remembering for Us": The Transgenerational Transmission of Holocaust Memory and Commemoration', in T. Lawson and

J. Jordan (eds) *The Memory of the Holocaust in Australia*, Portland and London: Vallentine Mitchell: 93–109.

Klein, A. (2007) 'Memory-Work: Video testimony, Holocaust Remembrance and the Third Generation', in T. Lawson and J. Jordan (eds) *The Memory of the Holocaust in Australia*, Portland and London: Vallentine Mitchell: 110–127.

Linenthal, E.T. (1995) *Preserving Memory: The Struggle to Create America's Holocaust Museum*, New York: Penguin Books.

Moses, A.D. (2012) 'The Canadian Museum for Human Rights: The "Uniqueness of the Holocaust" and the Question of Genocide,' *Journal of Genocide Research*, 14.2: 215–238.

Rosenblum, S. (1996) 'Are Museums the Best Place for the Memorialisation of the Holocaust?', *International Network on Holocaust and Genocide*, 11.4: 18.

Rutland, S.D. (1997) *Edge of the Diaspora: Two Centuries of Jewish Settlement in Australia*, Sydney: Brandl & Schlesinger.

SJM Mission Statement 2002. SJM Institutional Archive.

SJM Mission Statement 2007. SJM Institutional Archive.

SJM Mission Statement 2009. SJM Institutional Archive.

SJM Mission and Vision Statement 21 December 2009. SJM Institutional Archive.

SJM Strategic Plan 2003–2008. SJM Institutional Archive.

SJM Strategic Plan 2008–2012. SJM Institutional Archive.

SJM Board Minutes October 2010. SJM Institutional Archive.

SJM Education Department Report December 2010. SJM Institutional Archive.

Stone, D. (2010) 'Voyage of the Damned – Take Two', *J-Wire*, 16 December. Available at: http://www.jwire.com.au/news/voyage-of-the-damned-take-two/13990. Accessed: 2 January 2011.

Weissman, G. (2004) *Fantasies of Witnessing: Postwar Efforts to Experience the Holocaust*, Ithaca: Cornell University Press.

6 National memory and museums

Remembering settler colonial genocide of Indigenous peoples in Canada

Tricia Logan

Introduction

> We also have no history of colonialism. So we have all of the things that many people admire about the great powers but none of the things that threaten or bother them.
>
> Canadian Prime Minister, Stephen Harper, September 2009 (Ljunggren 2009)

During a 2009 speech to the G20 meeting in Pittsburgh, Pennsylvania, Canadian Prime Minister Stephen Harper made the now-famous statement that Canada has 'no history of colonialism'. In the days following the G20 meeting, Harper's representatives retracted his statement, claiming the use of 'colonialism' was taken out of context (Wherry 2009). The statement still infuriated Indigenous communities in Canada and illuminated a growing trend in Canada's national memory. The Prime Minister's remarks reminded Canadians that publicly or privately, national memories have blind spots when it comes to the real costs of building a nation. Ultimately, the First Nations, Métis and Inuit people in Canada[1] are still paying an enormous price. Settler colonial crimes committed in the pursuit of 'civilizing' the 'Canadian wilderness' and establishing a powerful, economically viable nation are often erased or ignored, and Indigenous peoples are often instructed to 'just get over it' (Mahoney 2013). This chapter argues that revisions to national memory in Canada are not only long overdue, but could potentially aid in altering colonial mindsets.

Misunderstood or misconceived definitions of settler colonial genocide in Canada and settler colonial genocide overall contribute to the lack of engagement by the non-Indigenous Canadian public. Settler colonial genocide is best known as a phenomenon that occurred in the United States or Australia (see Levene 2005: 69; Bloxham 2009: 283; Docker 2008: 94–96; Stannard 1993), and Canada is rarely mentioned. In Canada, Canadian historiography is critically flawed when it discusses genocide. Non-Indigenous Canadian historians regrettably use narrow definitions based on the 1948 United Nations Convention on the Prevention and Punishment of the Crime of Genocide (UNGC). Narrow definitions of genocide as a singular event (rather than as multiple events occurring over centuries) or based purely on 'killing' (rather than, for example, on the forcible removal of children) limit examination of Indigenous histories (McDonnell and Moses 2005).

Settler colonial genocide is not addressed in Canadian museums, and it is rarely addressed in Canadian mainstream historical narratives. Canada has created a mythology of nation-building and a national narrative that does not correspond to the realities of Indigenous peoples' experiences. The obtrusive omission of settler colonial genocide in Canadian museums speaks to the wider omissions of genocide in Canadian history. Public histories in Canada and institutions like museums have a considerable distance to bridge in order for an agreement between Indigenous peoples' accounts of history and public accounts of history to be reached.

In museums like the Canadian Museum for Human Rights (CMHR), due to open in Winnipeg in 2014, there exists a dominant narrative on genocide and human rights that features genocides perpetrated outside of Canada and the Americas. As the curator of Indigenous content at the CMHR, I was asked in July 2013 to remove the term genocide from the small exhibit on settler colonial genocide in Canada. While the museum itself relies heavily on a genocide narrative to build 'encounters with human rights', the dominant examples are the Holocaust and the Holodomor (the Ukrainian Famine 1932–1933). Atrocities against Indigenous peoples would remain in the museum, but I was no longer permitted to name them as genocide. Later in the chapter, I will draw on my own experience as the curator for Indigenous content at the CMHR to consider the way in which the experiences of Indigenous peoples are remembered in museums in Canada. I will first consider the question of settler colonial genocide.

Settler colonial genocide

There is a misconception that the idea of 'settler colonial genocide' is a recent innovation (McDonnell and Moses 2005). And yet, definitions of genocide conceived in the 1940s by Raphael Lemkin, the creator of the term 'genocide', included work on colonial genocides (see Docker 2010). Portions of what Lemkin found in the early part of the twentieth century are congruent with North American Indigenous peoples' conceptions of the same term, genocide. Lemkin's insistence that biological, physical and cultural techniques of genocide remain conceptually inseparable from each other is conceptually similar to how genocide is defined in Indigenous communities (McDonnell and Moses 2005). Dirk Moses examines the conceptual blockages that have created polarized comparisons of the Holocaust on the one hand and genocides in North America against Indigenous populations on the other (Moses 2002). According to Moses, the origin of these blockages lies in the differentiation between liberal and post-liberal theories on genocide (Moses 2002: 20–28). Moses argues that in their definitions of genocide, the post-liberal theorists 'contend that the first formulation of the concept included cultural genocide in its core; that is to say, genocide did not necessitate mass murder or even biological extirpation' (Moses 2002: 23). Churchill reinforces this point when he argues that physical life and death is inseparable from language, culture, land and spirituality according to Indigenous worldviews (Churchill 2004). In the same way, First Nations, Métis and Inuit of Canada do not distinguish between physical, biological and cultural death.

While there is little question from an Indigenous perspective of whether or not settler colonial genocide occurred in Canada, Canadian historians have failed to represent the processes and events of that genocide that took place over centuries (Woolford 2009). Shortcomings in both Canadian historiography and genocide scholarship have left a deficit in historical examination of genocide in Canada (Levene 2005; Bloxham 2009). Canadian histories rarely relate the long list of atrocities committed against Indigenous peoples in Canada as belonging to a larger process (or processes) of genocide. Often isolated as separate occurrences, the Indian residential school system,[2] massacres, disease and sexualized violence against Indigenous women are written about historically as a series of discrete colonial-driven events as a broad legacy of colonialism. As a result, genocide scholarship relies on incomplete Canadian histories in order to construct a narrative account of settler colonial genocide in Canada, with the result that it still remains largely unrecognized inside and outside of the country.

One of the challenges for remembrance is that the history of settler genocide can cover a period of centuries, as it does in the case of Canada. This is in contrast to the short periods of time in which other genocides occur. As a consequence, the tangible and intangible heritage associated with settler genocide available for museum exhibitions spans multiple epochs and events. Settler colonial eliminationist policies have been fragmented into isolated parts of a more complete process of genocide. Massacres, residential schools, forced relocations, slaughter of animals, dispossession, burning of homes and property and bureaucratic assaults against Indigenous peoples have, if they have been recognized at all, been entered as fragments into the Canadian institutional history. Recorded as discrete events and violations, these events appear in Canadian museums, but they rarely appear in the context of genocide. Settler genocide is, therefore, a profoundly complex story to tell in a museum, as it is not easily summarized into digestible museum exhibit portions.

The Government of Canada has officially recognized five legal cases of genocide with some guidance from the UNGC (1948): the Holocaust (1933–1945), the Holodomor (man-made famine in the Ukraine 1932–1933), Rwanda (1994), Srebrenica (1995) and Armenia (1915–1923).[3] The first Canadian public institution to include the five recognized genocides, as they relate to the UNGC and political recognition, will be the CMHR. By reaffirming a perception of genocides as short-lived anomalies, will the CMHR's treatment of these five recognized genocides further obscure the 'long-lived' quality of settler genocide in the Canadian context? Also, given the genocides that have been officially recognized, what kind of a role does political lobbying play in influencing Canadian memory and public institutions? What kind of advocacy 'promotes' a genocide into public memory and public institutions and to what extent does public or media attention highlight some advocacy over others? Are there determinants to inclusion or exclusion in public memory and public institutions? Moreover, to what extent do social, economic and political leverage or an assumed 'right to memory' influence the determinants of public memory?

The right to memory

In *Public Memory, Public Media and the Politics of Justice*, Philip Lee and Pradip Thomas (2012) expand the potential mandate for public memory and public media, and promote the role that these institutions could potentially play in providing a 'right to memory'. Not only should public institutions integrate a mandate to engage and influence national identity, there could be an additional role in promoting a 'right' for the victims of atrocity to be remembered, publicly. Lee and Thomas note that groups that are denied agency or representation in public or popular media may have been discouraged from remembering their histories or atrocities committed against them. Asserting a 'right to memory' creates space and agency for groups historically or politically marginalized by their nation-state; providing voice and agency to survivors thereby becomes part of post-atrocity repair.

Lee and Thomas cite the history of the residential schools in Canada when they describe the 'mental harm' (Article 2(b))[4] element of the UNGC of 1948 and the essential nature of memory in the interpretation of international human rights instruments. They identify the right to memory in the Declaration on the Rights of Indigenous Peoples (2007), Article 11 of which reads:

> Indigenous peoples have the right to practice and revitalize their cultural traditions and customs. This includes the right to maintain, protect and develop the past, present and future manifestations of their cultures such as archaeological and historical sites, artefacts, designs, ceremonies, technologies and visual performing arts.[5]

Lee and Thomas acknowledge that this 'human right to memory' is related to both justice and sociocultural rights. Moreover, and at least theoretically, public memory of atrocity or genocide could have an influence over the state of current or ongoing atrocities or genocides. Making space for the agency of civil society may allow under-represented groups to gain a level of control over how their lives and rights are represented in mainstream or public memory. The onus on the state to record events and histories into a national historic narrative remains. This is never a neutral role and is always influenced by both the public and policymakers (Lee and Thomas 2012: 15).

Indigenous peoples' public memories in Canada

The cultural property of Indigenous peoples has been appropriated or stolen for centuries (Battiste and Henderson 2000). In the past, objects, stories, artefacts and sacred items were simply taken from First Nations, Métis and Inuit, and used in the introverted function of the museum, for the museum's own collection (Dion 2009; Clapperton 2010: 7). In the past, the role for the museum was to preserve and remember a 'dying' race in which a salvage paradigm was applied to the colonial collections relating to Indigenous peoples worldwide. Fascination with the savage and the contrast to 'civilized' Europe meant that great value was placed on Indigenous pieces. That value was also amplified by a growing scarcity of Indigenous peoples in the colonies. Physical, spiritual, mental and emotional fragments/remnants of Indigenous peoples were appropriated by museums to preserve the last evidence of what was regarded by Europeans as a dying race. It can be argued that the 'salvage paradigm' promoted by museums was complicit in the neglect of Indigenous populations, as it supported the prevailing thought that 'they were just going to die anyway' (Clapperton 2010; Peyton and Hancock 2008).

Museum practice in Canada has changed considerably since the 1990s and has increasingly involved Indigenous communities in the creation of exhibits that involve Indigenous heritage. However, according to Clapperton (2010) the salvage paradigm is often still at play in Canada, where museums seem to still struggle with postmodern museums' representation of Indigenous peoples. Clapperton interviewed Museum of Anthropology at the University of British Columbia anthropologist James Clifford, who stated 'that works of culture or art are only considered authentic if they predate "tainting" by the "modern" world. Authenticity is lost once an object crosses a "modern" temporal and/or geographical line' (Clapperton 2010: 29). In other words, Indigenous artefacts can only be 'salvaged' from the past. This perceived or real inability for Canadian museums to regard Aboriginal Canadians as equals stands as a barrier to the integration of historical narratives about settler colonial genocide in Canada (Battiste and Henderson 2000). Canadian museum professionals acknowledge that significant concerns still need to be addressed and that revisions must be made to Indigenous heritage policies in public institutions in Canada (Clapperton 2010: 30).

Increasingly, public institutions in Canada are charged with taking a role in public advocacy and engage civil society in a way that museums have not done before (Trofanenko 2006). As critical spaces for public engagement, museums have extended their pedagogical role and are engaging visitors beyond stimulating their curiosity and desire to see their country's accomplishments and riches. Responding to visitor experience, there has been an increase in visitor-testing monitoring, which has changed the methodologies in museum practice (Grenier 2010; Falk 2009). No longer the 'cabinets of curiosity' holding static objects described with static didactic text panels, museums are increasingly interactive, text free, and experiential. Museums are asking more of their visitors, and in return, visitors are asking the same of the museums they visit.

The Federation of International Human Rights Museums (FIHRM)[6] constitutes a critical mass of professionals and academics marking these changes in museum practice. In an address at the fifth annual Stephen Weil Memorial Lecture in Shanghai in November 2010, David Fleming, president of the FIHRM, cited the impetus behind these changes as museums become more 'extroverted' than ever before (Fleming 2010). Fleming argued that museums needed to become more relevant and financially viable, and to carry social responsibility. In turn, they increasingly occupied the social mediator role and memorialized atrocity as well as national treasures. In other words, memory institutions are contributing to both national identity and social conscience, and new methodologies need to be developed to answer the extension of the international museum mandate. There is a role for museums to play as socially conscious institutions, namely, to build 'positive action' towards inclusion of marginalized voices or communities. Fleming stated that:

> Positive action means that the museum is joining the fight against social exclusion, joining with other socially responsible agencies to effect a difference at the personal, community and social levels. In other words, social responsibility means being socially inclusive, which leads ultimately to social value and the attainment of social justice: that's our primary aim, I would argue. Without social value, without achieving social justice, museums aren't worth having. This is our moral obligation.
>
> (Fleming 2010)

There is no doubt, therefore, that museum practice has changed, that it has moved towards experiential learning and that 'idea' museums or human rights-based museums have made space for genocides in national memory, where they did not appear before (Stone 2006). The role of institutions like Yad Vashem in Jerusalem; the United States Holocaust Memorial Museum (USHMM) in Washington DC; the Kigali Memorial Centre in Rwanda; or the Mémorial de la Shoah in Paris is to serve as an intermediary between the remembered and the public. The curatorial function of the museum has changed with expansion of genocide narratives into an already existing public history. However, the outcome of this process is open to question. As Stone (2006: 159) notes:

> Some argue that this turn to museums as repositories of memory is a reactionary 'compensation' for the ravages of time or an attempt by governments to 'help' people what to think; others that they are just another part of our consumer culture, in which a visit to a nicely packaged past is the heritage industry's equivalent of a day's shopping.

In Canada, what has emerged is this 'reactionary compensation', a government intervention into public memory, where the public is essentially being told what to think and what to remember. By emphasizing some stories or accounts of genocide and under-emphasizing others, are memories being effaced? By erasing stories or eliminating their mention from public institutions, are museums also helping the public turn away, as much as they are there to tell people what to think? Do these changes mean that settler colonial genocide in Canada is becoming part of public history and identity alongside other 'well-known' genocides, or is it hitting the curatorial 'cutting-room floor'? If Canada does begin to engage this history, will lessons from similar institutions be considered during their development?

Museums and Indigenous peoples in Canada

National museums in Canada have always dedicated exhibit space and a portion of their interpretive narrative to the First Peoples of Canada. Provincial and National museums in Canada, like the Canadian Museum of Civilization (Ottawa), the Glenbow Museum (Calgary), the Museum of Anthropology at the University of British Columbia (Vancouver), Pointe-à-Callière Museum (Montreal) and the emergent CMHR (Winnipeg), are a few large-scale museums in Canada that have built or are building a legacy of exhibit content that includes Indigenous peoples' narratives.

However, Aboriginal peoples in Canada have historically been relegated to the margins, as the Other in the museum, and have struggled to inject their histories into Canadian museums, let alone articulate a narrative of settler colonial genocide committed against them. The history of settler genocide exists in the Indigenous communities and oral histories of those who were violated through settlement plans by governments and churches in Canada. Although these stories appear in Canadian museums, the series of violations against Indigenous peoples are not framed as genocide in a single, explicit exhibit on genocide. Rather, they are portrayed as discrete, discontinuous episodes.

Internationally, museums have increasingly become institutions for memory of genocide and atrocity (see Williams 2007). Once a place of curiosity and collection, museums drew in visitors by capturing 'rare finds'. This was an objective of the traditional museum, to display the rare and the 'captured'. As institutions of colonial power, museums became repositories of the salvage paradigm, housing bodies and objects plundered from their colonies (Bickham 2005). As showpieces of European colonization and 'civilization', museums in Canada were and are places for 'socially and geographically broad audiences' (Bickham 2005) and fulfil a number of purposes, including entertainment and political statement.

And yet, Paul Born, President of Tamarack, an Ontario-based charity working on community empowerment, describes the important, emerging role museums are playing in Canadian community-building efforts:

> Often overlooked by community groups as dusty, unapproachable tourist destinations, museums can become important partners in campaigns

> for social change. They can bring important ideas, assets and resources to a table and act as catalysts for community conversation.
>
> (Born 2006)

Born suggests, therefore, that Canadians should rethink museums as a designated space for static or one-sided knowledge transfer. Museums, rather, are to be seen as 'catalysts' and as having a role in engaging the public; asking the public to consider their visit alongside a social conscience changes the entire relationship between museum and community. Museums are building what Born calls the 'conversation' between the museum and the visitor, rather than a model of a visitor simply entering gallery space, viewing exhibits and taking back an experience. Some museums are asking that visitors engage with what they've experienced beyond the walls of the museum and sign up for online newsletters, join advocacy groups or – in an ideal scenario for the museum – plan a return visit ('Curation as Social Activism' 2012).

In line with this trend, museums in Canada have changed from being a country's colonial trophy case to being centres of dialogue and visitor experience. Changes to operational policies for working with Indigenous communities at museums like the Museum of Anthropology at the University of British Columbia in Vancouver and the Glenbow Museum in Calgary have demonstrated to a significant extent how visitor experience, curation and direct input from Indigenous communities can improve institutional practices (Trofanenko 2006). In part, this is being done with what Susan Dion (2009) describes as '(re)tellings of testimony'. Transmission of stories and Indigenous knowledge comes to the museum with a type of intentionality that it had not had in the past as survivors enter their statements into public memory institutions as an act of social justice and social activism, and as a way to ensure that their experience is remembered (Reimer et al. 2010).

Pauline Wakeham (2008), however, warns that what ends up in the dominant narrative of the museum in a country with a colonial past like Canada can remain a state-orchestrated effort towards reconciliation. Reflecting on the opening of the National Museum of the American Indian (NMAI) in 2004 in Washington DC, Wakeham comments on the tension between the celebration of a valiant past of peaceful relations with Indigenous peoples and the brutal truths of eliminationist policies:

> … transformations in museum policy and practice are only one aspect of broader cultural, socioeconomic, and political changes crucial to reckoning with colonial violence in North America and working toward a future of social justice. As a result, the celebratory discourse of museological reconciliation lends itself to complicity with and co-optation by the state for the purposes of staging postcolonial rapprochement via the cultural milieu of museums while circumventing further restitution in the form of land claims, rights to natural resources, and compensation

> for the state's destruction of the environment on reservation territory, to cite only a few examples.
>
> (Wakeham 2008: 355)

Sending a precautionary warning to the builders of public, historic narratives, Wakeham is cognizant of the power that celebration has on gestures of reconciliation and remembrance. In Canada, there is a risk that the 'celebratory discourse' of museum-driven 'reconciliation' glosses over or sugar coats existing violations against Indigenous peoples. Often, the narratives of a state's own crimes do not appear in the museum even though those crimes often contribute to a nation-building narrative as much as the victories do. As a curator at the CMHR, I was consistently reminded that every mention of state-perpetrated atrocity against Indigenous peoples in Canada must be matched with a 'balanced' statement that indicates reconciliation, apology or compensation provided by the government. In cases where those issues are not reconciled or where accusations of abuse against the government continue to this day, the stories are reduced in scope or are removed from the museum. As curator, I have been ordered to limit coverage of stories of Aboriginal children in the child welfare system, missing and murdered women in Canada and climate change. These stories will still appear in the museum, but their treatment has been greatly reduced in each instance. As mentioned above, I was also instructed to remove the terms 'genocide' and 'settler colonial genocide' from all Indigenous exhibits. The atrocities committed against Indigenous peoples will be labelled in museum text and media productions as 'colonialism'.

In the case of the CMHR, both the museum's staff and board determine the relative weight and importance placed on objects, images or stories that the museum deems the 'primary' entry point for interpreting an exhibit. Interpretations of 'colonialism' need to be vetted through museum research and design, and reformulated into readable exhibit pieces. Edits to individual and collective accounts are made to build a visitor interface or experience. What is entered into public memory and what is essentially erased through the curatorial process and the 'cutting-room floor' has meaning. Omission from an exhibit can speak to visitors as much as the presence of a story. Especially in terms of atrocity or genocide, if the atrocity committed against you, your family or your community is not included, but another story is included, that exclusion will mean something to you, the visitor. In museums exhibiting human rights violations and atrocities, the unenviable task – of determining which stories make it 'in' to the museum and which ones will not enter public memory – in and of itself makes a statement to visitors.

Arguably, Canada has recently taken a step backwards in museum practice with an increase in government control and influence. Prior to the influence of the current Conservative government, museums had more autonomy in their messaging and narrative. In October 2012, the Canadian Department of Heritage announced that it would rename the Canadian Museum of Civilization

(CMC) as the 'Canadian Museum of History' (Butler 2012). The renaming or rebranding of the CMC has faced criticism for the level of control that the current Canadian government has gained over public history. Immediately after the CMC's name change, predictions started to surface about the effects this change would have on the already under-represented Aboriginal histories at the museum. Sincere fears are building about the new incarnation of the museum and how Aboriginal histories will be represented under what many believe to have been recreated and government mandated as a 'dominant culture's' history.

With increased government oversight of the narrative of museum content, the question remains about how a new, emerging museum will avoid glossing over and removing the mention of the history of colonial genocide. Museums in Canada may have changed their relationship with Indigenous peoples, but has it changed enough to face difficult histories and the challenge of representing settler colonial genocide in a national museum? The following section will consider the CMHR as an example of a public institution struggling with both the decolonization of Indigenous exhibits in the museum as well as the potential representation of settler colonial genocides.

Canadian Museum for Human Rights and the 'cutting-room floor'

One museum poised to approach new museum practice and revised historical narrative is the CMHR. The museum is scheduled to open in 2014 in Winnipeg, Manitoba, Canada. It is the second national museum built outside of the National Capital Region (Ottawa–Gatineau) and the first national museum to be built from the ground up since 1967. Envisioned as an 'ideas' museum, with a collection that will include stories, objects, images and art, the CMHR has been under debate since the early 2000s, when it was originally proposed as a private institution to be funded by the Asper Foundation.[7] The Foundation was started by Israel and Babs Asper in 1983 and has initiated a number of philanthropic projects based out of Winnipeg, including the 'Human Rights and Holocaust Studies Program' and 'The Friends of the Canadian Museum for Human Rights'.[8] The Asper Foundation drove the idea for a human rights museum based on a student programme that took student groups to Washington DC each year to visit the USHMM and a number of museums and memorials along the National Mall. At the time, CMHR founder and head of the Asper Foundation Israel 'Izzy' Asper had a desire to give Canadian students a similar museum experience in Canada. The first plans for the museum were to build a Holocaust or genocide museum. Over time, however, the museum vision was broadened, and it was to become a 'human rights' museum. After Izzy Asper's death in 2003, his daughter Gail headed the CMHR museum project, and the museum design firm Ralph Appelbaum Associates (RAA) was hired to design this new Canadian museum. RAA had also designed the USHMM and is considered to be an international-calibre museum design firm. In order to increase funding potential, the CMHR became a federal institution in 2008, and it has been on a long road to inaugural design and development since.

I was hired as the curator for all of the Indigenous content in May 2010. Before that, I had worked for around a decade with survivors of the Indian residential school system in Canada. When I started at the CMHR, the museum and gallery floor plans had already been drawn and construction on the building had started. There was little to be done about gallery size, location and structure. The CMHR gathered the initial group of Indigenous curators, elders and advisors in November 2009 and later retained two of the members to sit on a 'Human Rights Advisory Council'. One of the main recommendations from this group, which I received when I started at the museum, was to decolonize the way Indigenous peoples are consulted with and represented in the museum. Rather than relegate all Indigenous content into one 'corner' or gallery of the museum, advisors recommended that Indigenous stories be placed throughout the museum.

However, the conventional way in which the museum is organized is still laden with colonial presuppositions of Canadian heritage and westernized methods of memory and knowledge transfer. For example, I have often fought the museum professional's tendencies to want to categorize or label Indigenous stories, knowledge, art or objects. While there is a need, of course, for the museum to schedule, categorize, archive and digitally store each piece entered into the museum collection or exhibit, I have challenged the museum to reconsider its categories and labels. As an example, one piece of an Indigenous oral history or a piece of literature is categorized as 'art' by the CMHR. I have argued that the piece, while undoubtedly artistic, is also a beautiful story, passed down by generations, transmitted orally in keeping with Indigenous methodologies. A portion of the story describes violation of rights and atrocity, and the story can also be considered as an articulation of Indigenous law. Simply categorizing it as 'art' strips the piece of this greater significance. The way in which I have challenged such labelling is part of a wider problem, namely, my attempts to represent 'difficult knowledge' and histories of settler colonial genocide in the museum. I often faced challenges from the institution to interpret dark or traumatic history of Indigenous peoples, but the greater challenge is to transmit an Indigenous perspective on this history.

How Indigenous knowledge is translated through or with the structure and design of the CMHR relies on a constant questioning of the colonial nature of standard museums and museum practice. This occurs in both the physical construction of the CMHR and the exhibits and the ongoing operations of the museum. The mere presence of this opulent and masterfully built architectural wonder on top of the Forks of the Red and Assiniboine Rivers in Winnipeg, Manitoba, is also an intervention into and a dialogue with the transfer of 'difficult knowledge' in a sacred space. The site is a sacred space and has been an ancient meeting place for First Nations and

Métis for centuries. The location of the CMHR is therefore a curious place for dialogue on human rights. The museum's location was an early decision made by the Asper Foundation and the Friends of the Canadian Museum for Human Rights. Archaeological site mitigation digs were conducted from 2008 to 2012 and archaeologists involved in the first segment of the dig were concerned that First Nations communities were not being adequately consulted and that the conditions of the agreement to conduct the dig were not being met by the museum (Sanders and Martin 2011). As of April 2013, the museum had yet to officially meet with First Nations and Métis experts who have ancestral claims to the land on which the museum is built to discuss the archaeological dig yet a meeting was planned for later in 2013. As curator of Indigenous content I found that Indigenous communities are aware of this halted process and that, as a result, some have hesitated to work with the museum until matters are resolved. Based on my perspective as a curator at the museum and my experience working with First Nations and Métis communities in Canada, understanding how to engage with Indigenous communities is another area of museum operations that requires decolonization.

The majority of the debate and attention on the CMHR has been focused on the presence and representation of the Holocaust and other genocides at the museum (Moses 2012). Little or none of this attention has been paid to the possibility that the museum may also address settler colonial genocide within the borders of Canada. Design and development of exhibits has been accused of being motivated by public pressure and government influence (CBC 2012). A demand for more 'positive Canadian content' and promotion of a government-sanctioned history of Canada has increasingly relegated an already-marginalized Aboriginal history to a critically under-representative segment of the museum.

The creation of the CMHR has sparked a debate in Canada about the representation and remembrance of genocide. Lobbying efforts by members of Jewish-Canadian and Ukrainian-Canadian groups have kept a decade-long debate over representation of the Holocaust and Holodomor brewing in the museum and have undoubtedly impacted museum design and development (Moses 2012). A portion of the debate has resulted in a fight for museum floor space. The CMHR maintains that it will not support competitive suffering or become either a genocide museum or a memorial. Notwithstanding that promise, the dominant examples of genocide used to illustrate the connections between genocide and human rights discourse in Canada are the Holocaust and the Holodomor. Currently, there is a 4,500-square-foot gallery dedicated to the Holocaust and seven sections slated for inaugural exhibits on the Holodomor. Atrocities committed against Indigenous peoples in Canada and the Americas will collectively be named 'colonialism', and any mention of genocide will be removed.

In November 2012, the museum faced public criticism about the presence or absence of certain genocides. In the debate, focus was placed on the presence of the Holocaust, Holodomor and the Armenian Genocide. The criticism did not refer to the absence of settler colonial genocide in Canada (Winnipeg Free Press 2012). The CMHR administration answered the criticism by stating that they wanted to maintain balance in the museum and that they did not want a visit to the museum to be 'too dark'; they defended their choice to focus the exhibits on the five genocides that the Government of Canada officially recognizes: the Holocaust, the Holodomor, Armenia, Srebrenica and Rwanda (Kives 2012).

While Jewish-Canadian and Ukrainian-Canadian lobbyists have tirelessly encouraged the CMHR to reconsider the genocide and Holocaust galleries of the museum (Ukrainian Canadian Congress 2013), First Nations, Métis and Inuit communities and lobby groups have not engaged with the CMHR in the same way. Indigenous groups in Canada have focused their rights struggles 'on the ground'. In Canada, over one hundred First Nations communities do not have access to clean drinking water, over six hundred missing and murdered women's cases remain unsolved and environmental destruction seriously threatens Indigenous homes and lives across Canada. The efforts and energies of Indigenous rights lobbyists in Canada are focused on providing safe water, safe homes, food and better health conditions for Indigenous families. Whether they are lobbying for memory or rights, for many, a museum may not be the logical place to confront rights discourse in Canada for current and ongoing abuses.

In Canada, the successful and powerful Idle No More movement[9] has mobilized grassroots leaders and Indigenous peoples, and has manifested itself as a historic political power (CBC 2013a). The movement argues that only through the decolonization of government relations with First Nations, Métis and Inuit in Canada can a system that continues to violate rights be reformed. Campaigns by the Idle No More movement continue to focus on the passage of controversial bills through the Canadian House of Commons without adequate consultation with Aboriginal peoples; on land, water, resources and the oil sands of northern Alberta and Saskatchewan; on violence against Indigenous women and the growing number of missing and murdered women in Canada; the lack of access to clean running water in Aboriginal communities; inadequate education for Aboriginal children; calls for governance reform; and advocacy for children in the child welfare system (CBC 2013a). Having started in late 2012, Idle No More motivates both Indigenous and non-Indigenous Canadians to address the urgent need to provide access to clean drinking water and schools, to end systemic violence and racism, to secure the protection of environment and resources as well as to achieve ongoing political reform. As a national and international movement of Indigenous rights, human rights and land rights, Idle No More has motivated work on Canadian social justice and restorative justice issues in unprecedented ways. Lobbyists involved in the movement have invested countless hours, personal sacrifice and resources.

From my position as a curator at the CMHR, it was a lot to also ask communities in the process of advocating, protesting and hunger striking to lobby for floor space in a government-funded museum, especially for floor space that will exhibit the very stories and issues they are fighting so hard to be heard on. The violations and settler colonial genocide for Indigenous peoples is not only contemporary for the survivors and descendants of the victims of historic atrocities, but it is contemporary for those who are still affected by ongoing violence, environmental destruction and lack of basic human rights like access to clean water or adequate housing (Huseman and Short 2012). Indigenous communities are faced with some of the most severe economic, social and political impacts of poverty in Canada. Indigenous groups in Canada are unlikely to direct funding or time normally dedicated towards combatting ongoing issues of access to clean drinking water, missing and murdered women, housing crises and ecocide to give attention to a national museum on human rights. Indigenous groups have been engaged in the creation of the CMHR, but the highly contemporary nature of their stories makes their inclusion a special case.

A question may remain on how the exhibits on genocide or international human rights law are interpreted for all audiences. In an article about the inaugural vision for the National Museum of the American Indian (NMAI) in Washington DC, Paul Chaat Smith was influenced by the presence and approach of the USHMM. Smith states:

> The Holocaust Memorial Museum breaks every museum rule about how long text labels can be, or how educated visitors in Washington's museums are, and has defied expectations by creating a massive audience of people willing to spend half a day, even an entire day, reading labels that are more than seventy-five words long. The creators of the permanent exhibit at the Holocaust Museum gambled that the conventional wisdom was wrong and that millions of people craved deep knowledge about the Holocaust and not superficial treatment.
>
> (Smith 2008)

Smith believed that visitors to the NMAI would be held to a higher standard than 'prevailing museum practice' had dictated. The NMAI made a decision to strive for exhibit content on Indigenous peoples in America to reach an engaged, informed public and to expect more of a visitor than past museums had. Museum curators at the NMAI were well aware of the state of memory of Native American realities in American public historical narratives. Historical narrative can challenge or comply with public discourse and memory. It remains to be seen how the public will react towards more positive content at the CMHR and whether or not it will challenge any visitors in a way that they should be challenged when thinking about human rights in Canada. In contrast to the USHMM or the NMAI, the CMHR is currently hiding controversies and glossing over histories of gay rights, child welfare, climate change and corporate crimes against human rights. When other museums move to challenge visitors and provoke them to change, CMHR is accepting a model of complacency and promotion of the status quo.

Conclusion

Voices of First Nations, Métis and Inuit peoples in Canada are being heard in ways they have never been heard before. Social media, mainstream media and grassroots-led movements such as Idle No More have motivated all generations of the First Peoples of North America. These voices are clear with the message that settler colonial genocide continues and human rights violations are historic, traumatic and undoubtedly ongoing. Canada is still working to catch up with the inclusion of settler colonial genocide in public history institutions like museums. Moreover, the emergent museum, the CMHR, faces a great deal of pressure from stakeholders, government and community members to create a meaningful dialogue on human rights and the meanings of genocide and human rights. When the museum opens in 2014, a dominant narrative will emerge. It remains to be seen whether or not that dominant narrative will motivate visitors to act on social justice and human rights issues or whether or not it will, if at all, reflect realities of ongoing human rights violations in Canada. The museum should answer the questions about what the Holocaust and 'other' genocides mean for human rights discourse in Canada. In response, will the museum inform Canadians about settler genocide in Canada?

Notes

1 First Nations, Métis and Inuit are the three officially recognized groups of Aboriginal peoples in Canada. First Nations are people who have historically been referred to as 'Indians', status, non-status, treaty or non-treaty Indians. Métis are a unique group of Aboriginal people with origins in Canada and have a mix of European and First Nations parentage. Today, Métis have formed a distinct language, culture and identity separate from Euro-Canadians or First Nations. Inuit peoples were historically named the 'Eskimos' and reside in Canada's North.

2 The Indian residential school system was operated in partnership with the Government of Canada and both the Protestant and Catholic Churches for over one hundred years, commencing in the mid-1880s. The schools were a system of industrial, residential, day, boarding and mission schools designed to Christianize, civilize and assimilate First Nations, Métis and Inuit children in Canada. Schools were notorious for high rates of physical and sexual abuse, high student death rates, significant underfunding, low levels of education and enduring intergenerational impacts on students and their families.

3 The Government of Canada officially recognizes five genocides: the Holocaust, the Holodomor, Srebrenica, Rwanda and Armenia. See: Ukrainian Famine and Genocide ('Holodomor') Memorial Day Act, (S.C. 2008, c.19), Bill C459, 2008, available at: http://laws-lois.justice.gc.ca/eng/acts/U-0.4/page-1.html; Armenian Genocide, 19 April 2006, http://www.armenian-genocide.org/uploads/Affirmation/359.pdf; Srebrenica Remembrance Day Act, 2010, available at: http://www.parl.gc.ca/HousePublications/Publication.aspx?Mode=2&DocId=4610579&File=24&Language=E; Act to Establish Holocaust Memorial Day, 12 November 2003, available at: http://www.parl.gc.ca/LegisInfo/BillDetails.aspx?Language=E&Mode=1&billId=1095137; Motion to Recognize Genocide, Rwanda, 31 March 2004, available at: http://www.mobinajaffer.ca/senate-chamber/senate-speeches/senate-chamber-speeches-2004/march-31-2004-motion-to-recognize-genocide-in-rwanda-adopted.

4 Article 2(b) of the UNGC reads: 'In the present Convention, genocide means any of the following acts committed with intent to destroy, in whole or in part, a national, ethnical, racial or religious group, as such: (b) Causing serious bodily or mental harm to members of the group'.
5 UN General Assembly. (2007) 'United Nations Declaration on the Rights of Indigenous Peoples: resolution / adopted by the General Assembly'. 2 October. A/RES/61/295. Available at: http://www.unhcr.org/refworld/docid/471355a82.html. Accessed 15 November 2012.
6 http://www.fihrm.org/.
7 http://www.asperfoundation.com/site/index.html.
8 Friends of the Canadian Museum for Human Rights, www.friendsofcmhr.com.
9 http://idlenomore.ca/.

Bibliography

Aboriginal Peoples Television Network (APTN). (2012) *TRC Commissioner Changes Tune on Residential Schools as Genocide*, 27 February. Available at: http://aptn.ca/pages/news/2012/02/27/trc-commissioner-changes-tune-on-residential-schools-as-genocide/. Accessed: 8 March 2013.

Battiste, M. and J. Youngblood Henderson. (2000) *Protecting Indigenous Knowledge and Heritage: A Global Challenge*, Saskatoon: Purich Publishers.

Bickham, T.O. (2005) *Savages within the Empire: Representations of American Indians in Eighteenth-Century Britain*, Oxford: Oxford University Press.

Bloxham, D. (2009) *The Final Solution: A Genocide*, Oxford: Oxford University Press.

Born, P. (2006) 'Community Collaboration: A New Conversation', *Journal of Museum Education*, 31.1: 7–14.

Butler, D. (2012) 'Museum of Civilization Changes a Mistake, University Teachers Association Says', *Ottawa Citizen*, 17 October. Available at: http://www.ottawacitizen.com/travel/Museum+Civilization+changes+mistake+university+teachers/7405788/story.html. Accessed: 7 April 2013.

Canadian Broadcasting Corporation (CBC). (2012) 'Human Rights Museum Pushes "Positive" Stories', 3 December. Video. Available at: http://www.cbc.ca/player/Embedded-Only/News/Canada/Manitoba/ID/2312327648/. Accessed: 8 March 2013.

——. (2013a) *Idle No More Activists Gather on Parliament Hill*, 28 January. Available at: http://www.cbc.ca/news/politics/story/2013/01/28/parliament-hill-ottawa-setup.html. Accessed: 7 April 2013.

——. (2013b) *Ottawa Ordered to Provide all Residential School Documents*, 30 January. Available at: http://www.cbc.ca/news/canada/story/2013/01/30/pol-cp-truth-reconciliation-commission-documents.html. Accessed: 27 March 2013.

Canadian Press. (2013) 'Ukrainian Canadian Congress Unhappy with Winnipeg Human Rights Museum', 11 April. *Maclean's Magazine*. Available at: http://www2.macleans.ca/2013/04/11/ukrainian-canadian-congress-unhappy-with-winnipeg-human-rights-museum/. Accessed: 11 April 2013.

Cassie, A. (n.d.) 'Letter to Association of Manitoba Archaeologists', Canadian Museum for Human Rights. Available at: http://www.assocmanarch.com/resources/CMHR+response.pdf. Accessed: 7 April 2013.

Churchill, W. (2004) *Kill the Indian, Save the Man: The Genocidal Impact of American Indian Residential Schools*, San Francisco: City Lights Books.

Clapperton, J.A. (2010) 'Contested Spaces, Shared Places: The Museum of Anthropology at UBC, Aboriginal Peoples, and Postcolonial Criticism', *BC Studies: British Columbian Quarterly*, 165: 7–30.

'Curation as Social Activism'. (2012) *Searcher*, 20, 7, 36–37. Academic Search Premier. Web 12 May 2013.

Dion, S. (2009) *Braiding Histories: Learning from Aboriginal Peoples' Experiences and Perspectives*, Vancouver: University of British Columbia Press.

Docker, J. (2008) 'Are Settler-Colonies Inherently Genocidal? Re-reading Lemkin', in A.D. Moses (ed.) *Empire, Colony, Genocide: Conquest, Occupation, and Subaltern Resistance in World History*, New York: Berghahn Books: 81–101.

——. (2010) 'Raphaël Lemkin, Creator of the Concept of Genocide: A World History Perspective', *Humanities Research*, 16.2.

Falk, J.H. (2009) *Identity and the Museum Visitor Experience*, Walnut Creek: Left Coast Press.

Fleming, D. (2010) 'Museums Campaigning for Social Justice', 5th Stephen Weil Memorial Lecture, Shanghai, China.

Friends of the Canadian Museum for Human Rights. (2013) Available at: http://www.friendsofcmhr.com/. Accessed: 7 April 2013.

Grenier, R.S. (2010) 'All Work and No Play Makes for a Dull Museum Visitor', *New Directions for Adult and Continuing Education*, 127: 77–85.

Hinton, A. (2002) 'The Dark Side of Modernity: Toward an Anthropology of Genocide', in A. Hinton (ed.) *Annihilating Difference: The Anthropology of Genocide*, Berkeley: University of California Press: 1–40.

Huseman, J. and D. Short. (2012) '"A Slow Industrial Genocide": Tar Sands and the Indigenous Peoples of Northern Alberta', *The International Journal of Human Rights*, 16.1: 216–237.

Kives, B. (2012) 'Atrocities Gallery "too much"', *Winnipeg Free Press*. 30 November. Available at: http://www.winnipegfreepress.com/local/atrocities-gallery-too-much-181497341.html. Accessed: 28 March 2013.

Lee, P. and P.N. Thomas. (eds). (2012) *Public Memory, Public Media and the Politics of Justice*, New York: Palgrave Macmillan.

Levene, M. (2005) *The Rise of the West and the Coming of Genocide*, London: I.-B. Tauris.

Ljunggren, D. (2009) 'Every G20 Nation Wants To Be Canada, Insists PM', *Reuters*. 25 September. Available at: http://www.reuters.com/article/2009/09/26/columns-us-g20-canada-advantages-idUSTRE58P05Z20090926. Accessed: 2 April 2013.

McDonnell, M. and A.D. Moses. (2005) 'Raphael Lemkin as Historian of Genocide in the Americas', *Journal of Genocide Research*, 7.4: 501–529.

Mahoney, J. (2013) 'Canadians' Attitudes Hardening on Aboriginal Issues: New Poll', *The Globe and Mail*. 16 January. Available at: http://www.theglobeandmail.com/news/national/canadians-attitudes-hardening-on-aboriginal-issues-new-poll/article7408516/. Accessed: 14 March 2013.

Moses, A.D. (2002) 'Conceptual Blockages and Definitional Dilemmas in the "Racial Century": Genocides of Indigenous Peoples and the Holocaust', *Patterns of Prejudice*, 36.4: 7–36.

——. (2012) 'The Canadian Museum for Human Rights: The "Uniqueness of the Holocaust" and the Question of Genocide', *Journal of Genocide Research*, 14.2: 215–238.

Perkel, C. (2013) '"It was Obviously a Policy not to Report Them": New Research Finds at least 3,000 Confirmed Indian Residential School Deaths', *National Post*. 18 February. Available at: http://news.nationalpost.com/2013/02/18/it-was-obviously-a-policy-not-to-report-them-new-research-finds-at-least-3000-confirmed-indian-residential-school-deaths/. Accessed: 7 April 2013.

Peyton, J. and R.L.A. Hancock. (2008) 'Anthropology, State Formation and Hegemonic Representations of Indigenous Peoples in Canada, 1910–1939', *Native Studies Review*, 17.1: 45–69.

Powell, C. (2011) *Barbaric Civilization: A Critical Sociology of Genocide*, Montreal and Kingston: McGill-Queen's University Press.

Rawlinson, K., S. Wood, M. Osterman and C. Caro Sullivan. (2007) 'Thinking Critically about Social Issues through Visual Material', *The Journal of Museum Education*, 32.2: 155–174.

Reimer, G., A. Bombay, L. Ellsworth, S. Fryer and T. Logan. (2010) *The Indian Residential Schools Settlement Agreement's Common Experience Payment and Healing: A Qualitative Study Exploring Impacts on Recipients*, Ottawa: Aboriginal Healing Foundation.

Sanders, C. and N. Martin. (2011) 'Archeologists Dig for Information: "Buried" Findings at Forks Excavation Site', *Winnipeg Free Press*. 16 December. Available at: http://www.winnipegfreepress.com/local/archeologists-dig-for-information-135720188.html. Accessed: 8 April 2013.

Saul, J.R. (2009) 'Reconciliation: Four Barriers to Paradigm Shifting', in G. Younging, J. Dewar and M. DeGagné (eds) *Response, Responsibility and Renewal: Canada's Truth and Reconciliation Journey*, Ottawa: Aboriginal Healing Foundation: 309–320.

Smith, P.C. (2008) 'Critical Reflections on the Our Peoples Exhibit', in A. Lonetree and A.J. Cobb (eds) *The National Museum of the American Indian: Critical Conversations*, Lincoln: University of Nebraska Press: 131–143.

Stannard, D.E. (1993) *American Holocaust: The Conquest of the New World*. Oxford: Oxford University Press.

Stone, D. (2006) *History, Memory and Mass Atrocity: Essays on the Holocaust and Genocide*, London: Vallentine Mitchell.

Tatz, C. (1999) 'Genocide in Australia', *Journal of Genocide Research*, 1.3: 315–352.

Trofanenko, B. (2006) 'Interrupting the Gaze: On Reconsidering Authority in the Museum', *Journal of Curriculum Studies*, 38.1: 49–65.

Ukrainian Canadian Congress. (2013) Available at: http://www.ucc.ca/category/canadian-museum-for-human-rights/. Accessed: 11 April 2013.

Wakeham, P. (2008) 'Performing Reconciliation at the National Museum of the American Indian: Postcolonial Rapprochement and the Politics of Historical Closure', in A. Lonetree and A.J. Cobb (eds) *The National Museum of the American Indian: Critical Conversations*, Lincoln: University of Nebraska Press: 353–383.

Wherry, A. (2009) 'What he was talking about when he talked about colonialism', *McLean's Magazine*. 1 October. Available at: http://www2.macleans.ca/2009/10/01/what-he-was-talking-about-when-he-talked-about-colonialism/. Accessed: 28 March 2013.

Whitelaw, A. (2006) 'Placing Aboriginal Art at the National Gallery of Canada', *Canadian Journal of Communication*, 31.1. Available at: http://www.cjc-online.ca/index.php/journal/article/view/1775/1897. Accessed: 21 May 2013.

Williams, P.H. (2007) *Memorial Museums: The Global Rush to Commemorate Atrocities*, Oxford: Berg.

Winnipeg Free Press. (2012) 'Film on Holodomor for CMHR', *Winnipeg Free Press*. 21 December. Available at: http://www.winnipegfreepress.com/local/film-on-holodomor-for-cmhr-184386261.html. Accessed: 28 March 2013.

Woolford, A. (2009) 'Ontological Destruction: Genocide and Canadian Aboriginal Peoples', *Genocide Studies and Prevention*, 4.1: 81–97.

7 Memory at the site

Witnessing, education and the repurposing of Tuol Sleng and Choeung Ek in Cambodia

Elena Lesley-Rozen

Introduction

Both the former S-21 prison in Phnom Penh, where some 15,000 Cambodians were detained and tortured, and corresponding Choeung Ek 'Killing Fields', have become widely recognizable international symbols of the crimes of Democratic Kampuchea (DK), the communist regime that controlled the small Southeast Asian country from 1975 to 1979. While thousands of international visitors have travelled to these sites every year since they were preserved and curated by the Vietnamese-backed regime in the early 1980s to globally condemn the Khmer Rouge, until recently, many Cambodians had never visited S-21 (now the Tuol Sleng Museum of Genocide Crimes) or Choeung Ek. 'Study tours' that were first undertaken by civil society organizations in 2004 to bring groups of Cambodians to the two memorial sites and the United Nations-backed Khmer Rouge tribunal courthouse,[1] creating a narrative of violation and redemption, have now been largely co-opted and expanded by the Public Affairs section of the court itself. As the tribunal's second case unfolds, hundreds of Cambodians from around the country are bussed to the sites during proceedings in an effort to 'educate' them about their country's past and the cases underway at the court.

During a tour held in early September 2012, men, women and children from rural Takeo Province, located in the southern part of the country and bordering Vietnam, met at the local commune office at 4 a.m. to catch buses for the trip. Many said they had seen programmes about the tribunal and tours on TV that had motivated them to accept their village chief's offer to participate in the programme. 'I lost many relatives during the Pol Pot time. I want to know who was on top, who was responsible', one woman told me. 'I have watched on TV about the court, but I don't think *it is as clear as being here to see for myself*' (my emphasis). Itineraries of tours vary depending on time limitations and coordination with other groups. For example, one group may visit Tuol Sleng and/or Choeung Ek in the morning, while others start their day at the tribunal itself. Before relatively rushed and unmediated afternoon tours of Tuol Sleng and Choeung Ek, the Takeo group began the day at the Extraordinary Chambers in the Courts of Cambodia (ECCC) building with a briefing from a press officer about the history of the tribunal and the proceedings that had taken place to date. In a somewhat politically truncated narration of the court's creation – which will be explained in greater depth later on in this chapter – the press officer said that the ECCC had come into being through the efforts of Prime Minister Hun Sen, who had requested the United Nations create a court to 'discover who was really responsible for crimes committed by the Khmer Rouge'. Several older members of the audience interjected to express their support for this effort, saying that they had also 'worked hard in the fields' and never had enough to eat during the DK period. Another man in attendance, however, more nervously inquired as to who, exactly, was being investigated. 'I was the head of a collective during that time', he said, 'and I never knew of any killings or any orders to execute people'. To reassure him, the press officer explained the mission of the court is to try 'senior leaders and those most responsible' for the atrocities committed during the DK period. 'The court is not interested in small people', he said, 'only the people who made policy. You do not need to worry'.

The exchanges that took place at this press briefing illustrate some of the tensions inherent in the current judicial and educational efforts underway in Cambodia. For reasons both political and social, the ECCC and its corresponding study tours aim to create a historical narrative of the DK period that emphasizes the culpability of a few top leaders and fail to address

Figure 7.1 ECCC Study Tour participants outside the courthouse. © Elena Lesley-Rozen.

crimes committed throughout the DK power structure. While responsibility for crimes was actually much more widespread, the narrative promoted by the government grants de facto amnesty to lower-level perpetrators, shielding former Khmer Rouge in the current regime (including Hun Sen) from greater scrutiny and, officials argue, facilitating social reconciliation. As part of this effort, memorial sites that were originally created primarily to justify Vietnamese occupation of the country to an international audience have now been repurposed to serve as explanatory devices for the work of the ECCC to Cambodians. Yet ECCC-coordinated tours often provide little in the way of interpretation or historical context, relying on the physicality of evidence at Tuol Sleng, Choeung Ek and even the court itself to convey this state-sanctioned version of history. In many ways, the lack of clarity serves the government's purpose – too much explanation and discussion could lead to questions that subvert the authority of the official narrative being formed. Yet codification of a generally agreed-upon history of DK is still very much evolving, and Cambodians bring their own experiences, ideas and biases to these study-tour encounters, affecting the extent to which the government's message is accepted, rejected or incorporated to varying extents into pre-existing narratives.

Numerous scholars have written about the politically charged process of memory formation in Cambodia after the fall of DK, wherein the Vietnamese-backed People's Republic of Kampuchea (PRK) regime sought to legitimize itself both domestically and abroad by highlighting Khmer Rouge atrocities. While sociologist Serge Thion argues that the PRK's efforts 'obliterated' (Thion 1993: 183) the ability of Cambodians living under the regime to form their own narratives of the period and Michael Vickery (1984) contends that the version of history promoted by the government did not correspond to the majority of Cambodians' experiences under DK, Judy Ledgerwood writes that the PRK narrative served as the starting point for Cambodians to construct an understanding of DK (Ledgerwood 1997: 93). Of course, this would have only been true for those Cambodians living in PRK-controlled areas of the country throughout the 1980s, not those who continued to fight with a repackaged Khmer Rouge coalition force from near the Thai border. While Cambodians were urged by the state to move beyond the past in the 1990s in the interest of reconciliation, the establishment of the ECCC in 2003 has launched a new era of outreach, education and memorial efforts. Many of these have involved work by civil society organizations[2] informed by international discourses related to human rights, democracy and transitional justice.

This chapter focuses on one such effort – the tribunal study tours – which began largely as a civil society initiative, but which has now been co-opted to a great extent by the ECCC itself. By exploring the reactions of Cambodians who participate in such tours, the chapter makes two major claims: (1) that although there is always variation in individual experience, the ways in which Cambodians respond to the government-backed narrative put forth at the

ECCC and memorial sites appear to be highly dependent on whether participants lived in a PRK-controlled area or a Khmer Rouge stronghold after the fall of DK in 1979, and; (2) that, while many Cambodians say they joined the tours in order to learn more about the DK period, they often leave with numerous unanswered questions due to the lack of clarity and explanation. Concerning the latter claim, Cambodians are frequently able to derive satisfaction from the experiential and performative aspects of their visits as acts of bearing witness to atrocity. Their reactions are similar to those that Rachel Hughes found among foreign tourists to Tuol Sleng (Hughes 2008: 326).

My findings are drawn from ethnographic work conducted in Cambodia from late August to early November of 2012, a period in which I interviewed 52 people (some multiple times) and also engaged in participant observation with select individuals who worked at the two memorial sites I was researching. My informants consisted predominantly of Cambodians who participated in study tours, hailing from both former PRK-controlled areas as well as Khmer Rouge strongholds. They were drawn primarily from two major areas – the previously mentioned Takeo Province and Pailin Province, a notorious former Khmer Rouge stronghold in the northwest of Cambodia near the Thai border. Several of the current defendants at the ECCC had been living freely in Pailin before they were arrested in 2007. My informants also included staff at Tuol Sleng and Choeung Ek as well as Cambodians from other organizations who worked with the memorial sites in some capacity. This study builds upon the two-and-a-half years I had previously lived in the country, a period I spent working as a journalist and frequently interviewing Cambodians about the disastrous period of 'three years, eight months and 20 days'.[3]

Nationalism, memorialization and mass death

In the process of forming 'national biographies', Benedict Anderson describes how historical tragedies must be both remembered and forgotten; in other words, they must be remembered in particular ways as part of a people's *shared* national story (Anderson 2006: 206). For example, Americans are encouraged to view 'the hostilities of 1861–1865 as a great "civil war" between brothers rather than between – as they briefly were – two sovereign nation-states' (Anderson 2006: 201). Ledgerwood references Anderson when examining the narratives formed through S-21, which was transformed into the Tuol Sleng Museum of Genocide Crimes after the Vietnamese invaded Cambodia in 1979: 'Unlike individuals, nations cannot write their biographies as a string of natural "begettings". Rather than births, the fashioning of narrative is marked by deaths' (Ledgerwood 1997: 82). The nation co-opts and shapes the remembering and forgetting of 'suicides, martyrdoms, assassinations, executions, wars and holocausts to serve the national purpose' (Ledgerwood 1997: 82). This process is particularly fraught, however, in countries like Cambodia that have experienced massive internal violence that cannot easily be understood and interpreted as serving a greater, nation-building purpose (Williams 2007: 20). To this day, Cambodians often lament the 'senseless' nature of killing under DK and are particularly upset and bewildered by the concept of 'Khmer killing Khmer'.

In his work on the emergence and proliferation of the memorial museum, 'a specific kind of museum dedicated to a historic event commemorating mass suffering of some kind' (Williams 2007: 8), Paul Williams describes how war monuments traditionally served to forge narratives of unity in the wake of mass death. Soldiers who died in battle can be seen as having given their lives for the nation, their deaths interpreted as sacrifice for the homeland. Yet it is difficult for the victims of genocide and other forms of atrocity to inhabit this commemorative model. Scholars such as Hughes have drawn connections between Cambodians killed during DK rule and Giorgio Agamben's discussion of *homo sacer*, 'a figure from Roman times whose existence fell outside the scope of the law, and who could thus be killed but not sacrificed' (Hughes 2006: 18). The initiative to create a shared national biography was further complicated by continued fighting between the PRK and a repackaged Khmer Rouge coalition force, which propagated a far different narrative of the DK period and of the Vietnamese invasion of Cambodia. It is partly due to the fact that this fighting continued into the 1990s that the project of forging a national biography of 'reassuring fratricide', as described by Anderson, remains very much in flux in Cambodia.

Demonizing Democratic Kampuchea

After repeated incursions by the DK into Vietnamese territory, a combined force of Khmer Rouge defectors and Vietnamese military forces invaded Cambodia in late December 1978, taking control of Phnom Penh in January 1979. Although Vietnam ended the brutal DK period, during which an estimated 1.7 million people had died through overwork, starvation and execution, its invasion of the country was condemned by the United States, China and other nations allied against the Eastern Bloc within the Cold War context. Thus, the new Vietnamese-backed PRK immediately set about justifying its actions through broadcasting evidence of Khmer Rouge crimes to the international community. This proved somewhat complicated considering that Vietnam needed to vilify a fellow communist country. Historian David Chandler writes that, in order to distance Vietnam and the PRK regime from the crimes committed by the Khmer Rouge, the country's new leaders created a narrative that cast DK as:

> A 'fascist' regime, like Nazi Germany, rather than a Communist one, recognized as such by many Communist countries. Finally, it was important for the Vietnamese to argue that what had happened in Cambodia under Democratic Kampuchea, and particularly at S-21, was genocide, resembling the Holocaust in World War II, rather than the assassinations

> of political enemies that at different times had marked the history of the Soviet Union, Communist China and Vietnam.
>
> (Chandler 2001: 29)

Labelling DK a 'genocidal' regime and ascribing blame for its crimes to the 'Pol Pot–Ieng Sary Clique' served as a symbolically resonant and tactical move, even though the majority of the killing that took place from 1975 to 1979 does not fit with the legal definition of genocide. According to the 1948 UN Convention on the Prevention and Punishment of the Crime of Genocide, the crime must be committed against a 'national, ethnical, racial or religious group'. Minorities protected under the convention, such as the Cham Muslims or Vietnamese living in Cambodia, were indeed targeted during the DK period, but the vast majority of killing was Khmer on Khmer, and thus not in keeping with the legal definition. Nonetheless, the events that occurred during this period are widely referred to as genocide. In addition, scholarly communities often adopt a broader definition of the term, allowing for the possibility of collectivities such as political and social groups as potential targets of genocidal crimes. Today, Cambodians use a number of different terms to describe the period of DK. They may use '*bralay pouchsah*' (to kill one's own race or family line), 'the Pol Pot time', the 'period of three years, eight months and 20 days' or the '*kosang*' (establishment) period.

Casting DK as a fascist and genocidal regime enabled the PRK to draw on international genocide/Holocaust discourses and also to vindicate those 'innocent' Khmer Rouge, including members of the new PRK government, who had become victims of a deviant communist system. Such messages featured prominently in the curation of S-21. The mass graves at Choeung Ek, where the majority of S-21 prisoners were taken to be killed, were exhumed around a year after the Vietnamese invaded Cambodia. At that time, the human remains were treated with chemicals and placed in a wooden memorial pavilion. Further curation of the site was not proposed until the mid-1980s, and the now-famous glass memorial *stupa* filled with bones was not constructed until 1988 (Hughes 2006: 97).

Around two months after the fall of DK, even before Tuol Sleng opened to the public, private tours were arranged for foreigners from sympathetic socialist parties. According to Brigitte Sion, the museum was used primarily to show international guests the cruelty of the DK regime, and Cambodians were only allowed to visit on Sundays, generally to find information about missing relatives (2011: 5). My own interviews with those who worked at the site in its early years support this version of events. Foreign delegations, particularly from Eastern Bloc countries, were frequent visitors to the museum, where they would often be given guided tours by some of S-21's few survivors. This partially explains the lack of extensive explanatory signage at the site. Tuol Sleng was initially created to be interpreted by those who had experienced its horrors, who functioned as artefacts of authenticity in ways not unlike the iron shackles that bound prisoners and various torture devices used to extract confessions. Tours to Tuol Sleng were in fact compulsory for early visitors to the PRK, a condition of visa approval; international visitors were expected to act as witnesses of genocide, bringing stories of their experiences back to their home countries and even the global community (Hughes 2008: 326). Despite the aggressive efforts of the PRK to establish its legitimacy on the mass graves of the DK regime, countries such as the United States and China continued to recognize the repackaged Khmer Rouge coalition fighting from the Thai border as the official government of Cambodia until the fall of the Soviet Union.

While the PRK disseminated a narrative internationally of Pol Pot's genocidal regime, the state also devoted considerable effort to crafting a history of DK for those Cambodians living under its authority. Starting in 1983, directives were put forth for the creation of village-level memorial *stupa* to commemorate those who died under the Khmer Rouge (Hughes 2006: 30); these served as focal points for the 20 May Day of Anger that was inaugurated in the same year. Hughes concludes that:

> Overall, authorities constructed memorial narratives that emphasized collective suffering under the 'Pol Potists'. Memory was rhetorically linked to the affirmations of the political accord the PRK enjoyed with

Figure 7.2 Exterior of the S-21 prison in Phnom Penh. © Elena Lesley-Rozen.

> its socialist allies, and to Cambodians' loyalty and vigilance in bringing an end to the civil war that still divided the country.
>
> (2006: 33)

Although some groups of Cambodians were brought to visit Tuol Sleng and Choeung Ek during the PRK period, these were drawn mostly from people living in the Phnom Penh area. Travel from remote areas was too costly and dangerous on a large scale. Still, Cambodians who lived under the PRK learned about the sites through other means. They heard about them through radio broadcasts, including a popular song about Tuol Sleng. Several people I talked to recalled reading about Tuol Sleng in school; indeed one fourth-grade writing text from the Ministry of Education included two essays about the prison (Hinton 2008: 71).

With the end of the Cold War and massive UN intervention in Cambodia from 1992 to 1993, the government began to downplay some of its anti-DK rhetoric as the UN attempted to involve Khmer Rouge fighters in the political process. Still, officials maintained an ambivalent relationship with the history of DK, and Hun Sen appeared to highlight Khmer Rouge atrocities when he found it politically expedient to do so. He did indeed write to the UN in 1997, requesting the creation of an international court, but he changed his position soon afterwards; many believe this was because the initial request was a tactic to intimidate remaining Khmer Rouge military forces into surrendering and reintegrating into society. Yet, international pressure for a tribunal continued, and Hun Sen's government entered into protracted negotiations with the UN. Hearings in the first trial, against former S-21 chief 'Comrade Duch', did not begin until 2009, and since its inception, the tribunal has been plagued by allegations of corruption and political interference. In particular, critics of Hun Sen charge that he has refused to allow the court to pursue prosecutions beyond five 'scapegoat' defendants because casting a wider net could implicate members of the current political establishment (Giry 2012).

Representatives from civil society organizations report that they launched the first study tours to Tuol Sleng, Choeung Ek and the tribunal for Cambodians in 2004 to put pressure on the government to begin trials at the ECCC. Since the curation of Cambodia's most prominent memorial sites after the fall of the Khmer Rouge, international tourists had continued to make up the bulk of visitors. The chilling photographs taken of seemingly dazed, frightened and sometimes even resigned S-21 prisoners have become some of the most powerful representations internationally of Khmer Rouge atrocities. Although some improvements and upgrades were made to the sites over the years, however, they still lacked comprehensive explanatory signage and could be difficult for visitors to interpret. While Hughes's interviews with foreigners at Tuol Sleng revealed that many had come to the site in order to gain a greater understanding of what had happened during the DK period, 'tourists generally exit the museum in a state of confusion' (2008: 325). Quite frequently:

> While many arrive at the museum with the expectation of a better understanding of the Pol Pot period, they leave with the hope that their 'being there' was at least significant. In other words, the experience is no longer *epistemological* but *testimonial*, not 'I now know more' but 'I visited'.
> (2008: 326)

Similar reactions are not uncommon among Cambodians who visit the sites as part of the ECCC study tours, depending on how the tours are conducted. However, as will be discussed shortly, the stakes are somewhat different for tourists hoping to fulfil a moral and humanitarian obligation in a foreign land, and for Cambodians struggling to understand and narrate the history of their own country.

The initial local study tours conducted by organizations such as the Documentation Center of Cambodia (DC-Cam) and the Center for Social Development (CSD) often selected respected members of local communities and involved multi-stage processes of outreach, discussion and visitation. Peter Manning followed a 2008 outreach effort conducted by CSD wherein Cambodians from a former Khmer Rouge stronghold were taken on tours of the sites in Phnom Penh and later participated in a large public forum on 'Justice and Reconciliation' in the town of Pailin (at which I was also present). Commenting on the way history is being portrayed through such efforts, he writes that 'ECCC prosecutions are reflective of the way blame for DK is represented at Tuol Sleng and Choeung Ek and, as such, they are deployed to help persuade groups that participate in the ECCC outreach about the truth of the DK period and the need of the ECCC as a response to it' (Manning 2011: 178). Participants from Pailin were disturbed by, and sometimes unreceptive to, the information presented to them through the outreach process and through tours of the memorial sites. Partly, this is due to the fact that 'members of communities such as Pailin largely experienced KR rule in a setting of agrarian cooperativism, receiving more favorable treatment, rather than in incarceration and torture facilities in an urban setting' (Manning 2011: 170). A number of participants questioned the mandate of the court and could not understand why culpability had been limited to crimes committed between 1975 and 1979. If the ECCC is to try former leaders of DK, those responsible for the American bombing in Cambodia before 1975 and for crimes committed by PRK and Khmer Rouge forces after 1979 should also be held to account, they argued. Extracting DK from its historical context, many felt, did not tell the 'whole story' (Manning 2011: 177).

As hearings for the first trial began in 2009, outreach efforts expanded and intensified, as both international and domestic visitation to somewhat updated memorial sites increased. Tuol Sleng and Choeung Ek now feature informational displays about the five defendants on trial at the tribunal. Tourists at

Tuol Sleng can even interact with the prison's two remaining survivors. They sit across from each other on the site's main pathway, each presiding over a desk filled with materials for sale related to their experiences and Khmer Rouge history. Both are happy to sign books and pose for photos with visitors. Meanwhile, at Choeung Ek, which since 2005 has been jointly managed by the Cambodian government and the private JC Royal Company, new signboards and a small museum-style building have been erected. Within the last year, a multilingual audio tour has been created by an Australian company, although most of the Cambodians I interviewed who had participated in study tours had not had access to the audio guide.

When actual trial hearings began in the case of Comrade Duch, the atmosphere at the ECCC was completely transformed. Until that time, proceedings had been sparsely attended, the five-hundred-seat courtroom occupied by a smattering of international observers and participants from the occasional civil society outreach tour. But with the start of the trial and appointment of a new head of Public Affairs, hundreds of Cambodians began to be bussed to the court each day as part of large-scale study tour efforts undertaken by the ECCC. Every seat in the expansive courtroom was now filled; overflow participants watched proceedings from outdoor simulcasts, and weary tour members (often children and the elderly) rested outside in the open-air canteen area. In an interview for publication, the late head of Public Affairs

Figure 7.3 Visitors inspect the *stupa* filled with glass skulls at Choeung Ek. © Elena Lesley-Rozen.

Reach Sambath told me that he had advertised trips to the court on radio, TV and through the grassroots political network of the ruling Cambodian People's Party (CPP). He said response was overwhelming, with constant calls from village leaders to arrange tours and groups from some areas requesting to come multiple times. While civil society organizations continued to do outreach – and some still organize smaller-scale study tours to this day – they were eclipsed in number by the ECCC programme, and today the vast majority of study tours are coordinated by the tribunal.

Reactions to the study tour narrative

The narrative of culpability disseminated by organizers of the tours that bring Cambodians to Tuol Sleng, Choeung Ek and the ECCC remains one of limited responsibility assigned to the top echelons of the DK power structure. In an essay about other sites of atrocity throughout the country that have gone without official recognition, Alvarez, Colucci and Tyner note that:

> The overemphasis on these two sites serves to spatially and temporally frame the Cambodian genocide, thereby contributing to the political uses of memory evinced by the government. The genocide is rendered spatially to the Tuol Sleng–Choeung Ek nexus, suggesting that the violence was confined geographically. Likewise, the genocide is temporally circumscribed, restricted to those events that transpired at those locations. (2012: 9–10)

They conclude that this same framing can be seen in the work of the ECCC. In other words, both sites, along with the court, work to limit the framing of atrocities in Cambodia according to a government narrative that restricts geography, time and accountability. In my research, I found that Cambodians interacted with this rendering of history in a number of different ways, particularly depending on whether they had lived in PRK- or Khmer Rouge-controlled areas after 1979.

Of tour participants who lived in PRK-controlled areas, I will distinguish further between those old enough to have some memories of the DK period and those who are not. Talking with those of the older generation, I found that while they may not necessarily narrate their experiences chronologically, they tend to focus on events that took place after the massive forced relocations of 1975. As Aafke Sanders (2006) discovered during her research among Khmer Rouge survivors, they often narrate their stories of DK thematically, focusing on food/starvation, hard labour, family members lost, executions and appropriate behaviour in keeping with a revolutionary consciousness. I also found this to be the case. In addition, people tended to focus on seemingly fragmented personal experiences without connecting them to a larger political or historical narrative. Sanders writes that survivor stories were remarkably consistent and that starvation had generally left the strongest impression on people; there was an overemphasis on food and underemphasis on perpetrators. She ascribes this partly to the formation of 'catastrophe tales', collective myths or standardized stories created in communities to blunt the pain of individual memory (Sanders 2006: 11–12).

While this is quite possible, there may also be a political element at play. Those who lived through DK have received shifting messages throughout the years about how to remember the history of the highly secretive regime – the leadership of which was known to many simply as *angkar* ('the organization') – and whom to blame for its disastrous legacy. Under the PRK, they were told to harness their *chheu chap* (rage born of grief and betrayal) to prevent the return of the 'Pol Pot–Ieng Sary Clique', which aimed to *bralay pouchsah*, commit genocide against or exterminate the Khmer race, line or species (Ledgerwood 1997: 91–93). Then in the 1990s, the government instructed Cambodians to forget the past in order to move forward and achieve reconciliation. Nonetheless, with the start of the ECCC, international and civil society actors launched new educational and outreach campaigns, encouraging Cambodians to address the past, often assuming they had remained frozen in a changeless state of dysfunction since the end of DK (see Hinton 2013). Given these conflicting messages, perhaps Cambodians have found it safer to draw upon their limited experience when discussing DK, unsure of whether the historical/political narrative they would construct is accurate or endorsed by current and future authorities.

This tendency for survivors to focus on personal narratives also emerged in conversations with tour participants too young to have memories of DK, who often said their parents had emphasized stories of hard labour and starvation under DK, but never narrated a more comprehensive history for them of the period. 'For many years, I thought the Khmer Rouge was just something that happened to my family. I didn't realize it was everywhere in the country', explained Srey Oun,[4] 28, from Takeo. Younger people frequently told me that they had indeed started to learn more about the DK period through the outreach activities related to the ECCC, particularly through what was featured on TV. Yet even after participating in the study tours, they often said they still did not understand why killing had taken place during the DK years and who should be held accountable. In a recent survey, researchers from Impunity Watch found that in the absence of clear display materials and tour guides at Tuol Sleng, young Cambodians may resort to 'mythological' explanations for what they see at the museum, generally that it is a Vietnamese hoax (Impunity Watch 2012). (While I did not encounter this response among the younger people I interviewed in former PRK-controlled areas, it did emerge during my conversations in the Khmer Rouge stronghold of Pailin.) Nonetheless, members of the younger generation in Takeo and their parents were mostly supportive of prosecutions underway at the ECCC. Moreover, those who lived through DK often confided that they had been aware of killing that took place in their local areas and that they thought more people should be brought to justice.

Figure 7.4 Women from a Cham Muslim village receive outreach materials from the ECCC Public Affairs office. The Cham were targeted by the DK regime. © Elena Lesley-Rozen.

Those study tour participants from former Khmer Rouge strongholds had far more conflicted feelings about the narrative put forth by the study tours and the existence of any prosecutions at the ECCC. Because most of those I interviewed had lived through the DK period, I do not feel comfortable dividing responses into those from older and younger generations, as I did in Takeo. In contrast to the older tour participants I spoke with in Takeo, Pailin residents tended to begin their narrations of DK *before* 1975, generally with stories of the US bombing of Cambodia, Khmer Rouge recruiters coming to rally men in their villages to fight against 'American imperialism', and their claim that they joined the movement partly because it was supported by the late King Norodom Sihanouk. Some said they were aware that people 'disappeared' and were killed during DK, but most claimed they were unaware of this. When the Vietnamese invaded the country, they reported that they ran for their lives to the Thai border, convinced they would be slaughtered by the advancing troops. Until the mid-1990s, many said they lived 'like a frog in a well' (a common symbol of isolation), convinced they were fighting to liberate the country from the Vietnamese and largely unreceptive to stories of execution and even genocide under DK.

Some study tour participants were receptive to the information that they had been presented, but they still questioned whether the former DK leaders were truly responsible and whether they knew about the killing. Those who said they had begun to acknowledge that 'mistakes' were made during DK, however, still seemed uncertain about who was to blame and whether anyone – leaders, lower-level perpetrators or larger international actors like the United States and China – should be punished. Like many former Khmer Rouge soldiers I interviewed in Pailin, Sokha, 57, told me that 'the Khmer Rouge had the best policies and sacrificed everything for the people'. He said he thought the leaders may not have known about the extent of the killings, but that it might be fair to hold them accountable: 'it is like in a family. If a child does something wrong, then the parents are responsible'. Rith, 46, also a former Khmer Rouge soldier, said he thought lower-level cadre must have misinterpreted the orders of their superiors. He said he had lived in Pailin with the former leaders and their families:

> [They] were just normal people. I met the wife of Khieu Samphan on Pchum Ben day. She chatted with me and asked about the DK time. She said people had told her they had no rice to eat. I told her my family just had a big pot of water – you couldn't even find the rice inside. She said she had no idea at that time that people were starving.

Like other former Khmer Rouge soldiers, he assigned potential blame to a number of outside sources, including the Cold War, the United States and even karma. Some older people think that Cambodia was destined to go through a period of mass internal violence 'no matter who the leaders were', he explained. Vuthy, 49, thought the policies themselves may have been responsible for the brutality that occurred during DK:

> We were following good policies and principles. But it became stricter and stricter and people became crazy. Leaders at the grassroots level are the ones who made the mistakes. The top leaders never said anything about killing or execution; they just talked about building the country and building solidarity.

Some visitors from Pailin rejected outright the work of the court and what they had been shown on the study tours. Ratana, 56, a former Khmer Rouge nurse, said the leaders 'wanted us to have a good and happy life' and that only a small amount of killing had taken place near the end of DK because 'Vietnamese spies were trying to undermine the regime'. She recalled how helicopters had come to Pailin to arrest Nuon Chea, considered chief ideologue for the Khmer Rouge, and said she pitied the elderly former leaders, who she thought should be released. She went on to say that she only participated in the study tour because the village chief had asked her to – he felt they needed a woman representative, in accordance with CPP policy to promote female involvement in the programme – and that she did not believe the DK leaders were responsible for the crimes showcased at S-21 and Choeung Ek:

> Many people died during the fighting between the Khmer Rouge and Lon Nol and there were many bodies. We don't know whose bodies

> those are. And the clothes at Choeung Ek don't look like the same material of the Khmer Rouge clothes. I have no interest in going back to that place.

Several other Pailin residents I interviewed questioned the origin of the bones displayed at Choeung Ek, seemingly contradicting the justifications often invoked for exhibiting remains of victims of mass slaughter: that it is incontrovertible 'evidence'. As Sara Guyer has written, 'any body can make bones' (2009: 156).

The human remains and artefacts displayed at the sites were a flashpoint for tour participants from both former PRK-controlled areas and former Khmer Rouge strongholds. In the absence of clear explanatory displays or even tour guides for many of the groups, visitors left with a number of unanswered questions about DK, yet stressed in our conversations the impact the physical objects had left on them. Sina, 56, a villager from Takeo who has participated in three study tours told me, 'I don't understand how Cambodia fell into this. That's why I have gone many times. I keep going, but still no answers'. Nonetheless, he went on to describe the powerful impression the torture devices had left on him, and how he continued to visualize them at times when he closed his eyes. I heard similar statements from a number of those I interviewed and found that their narrations of their experiences tended to focus on the artefacts they had encountered – shackles, skulls, paintings depicting the ways in which people were tortured – rather than on a description of the functioning of DK, how the regime had come to power and why its reign had been so deadly. Chenda, 28, a farmer

Figure 7.5 An ammunition box and chain inside a cell at S-21. © Elena Lesley-Rozen.

from Takeo, offered a narrative typical for study tour participants who had lived in former PRK-controlled areas. She said that she had only heard stories from her family of labour and starvation under DK and that she 'was shocked and frightened to see the torture materials and chains at Tuol Sleng. I did not expect it to be so cruel. I still do not really understand why the Khmer Rouge happened and why people were killed'. While Ratana and other participants from former Khmer Rouge strongholds may have doubted the authenticity of artefacts at the sites, they were in the minority among those I interviewed. As will be discussed in the final section of this chapter, given the general inability of the tours to convey new context or information to participants, many Cambodians draw upon international discourses of witnessing atrocity in order to reconceptualize their visits in a meaningful way.

Local witnesses to global atrocity

In my conversations with Vuthy, a former Khmer Rouge soldier, I noted that a particular moment of his visit to Tuol Sleng had left a profound impression on him: 'I was looking at all the photos of the prisoners and then I saw three foreigners standing there and crying. They were looking at the pictures of some children who had been killed. It made me so upset. I still think often about those foreigners crying'. Throughout our talk, even as he narrated stories of his experiences before 1975, during DK and as a soldier fighting the PRK, he paused several times to remark again about the foreigners crying at Tuol Sleng and how that had engendered a feeling he could not quite describe – sorrow, disappointment, anger, perhaps shame. For some reason, watching foreigners take pity on his country affected him in a way that seeing fellow Cambodians grieve for their own history had not. Perhaps the foreigners were a striking reminder to him of a truth he was still struggling to understand – that the movement he had followed for decades is now considered a murderous, genocidal regime by most of the outside world. But even beyond that, Vuthy's experience raises questions about the ways in which Cambodians are interacting with international discourses related to the humanitarian obligation to bear witness to atrocity, a project that becomes particularly fraught when witnessing an internationalized site designed to disseminate the history of your own country.

Because foreigners comprised the majority of visitors to Tuol Sleng and Choeung Ek throughout the 1980s and 1990s, it is hardly surprising that most scholarly accounts of visitation to the sites focus on the non-Cambodian experience. Nonetheless, these works can still shed light on some ways in which Cambodians consume and engage with the sites, especially in an era when messages about their international significance as evidence of atrocity have in many cases trickled down to the village level. As previously noted, Hughes has described how foreign visitors often feel confused by the material presented at Tuol Sleng and, unable to use their visits to fill gaps in their understanding of Cambodian history, 'respond to this situation by reconceptualising their visit to Tuol Sleng in terms of a symbolic gesture. In this sense, tourism is considered as a form of second-order humanitarian work' (Hughes 2008: 327).[5] For Williams, 'the primary feature of Tuol Sleng and Choeung Ek is their untouched appearance' (Williams 2004: 242), and although the process of transforming a killing centre into a memorial museum demands manipulation of the sites – especially in terms of what to include and exclude, what to downplay and what to highlight – they are nevertheless presented to visitors as *authentic*. Because those who died there can no longer bear witness to their suffering, through contact with the location and preserved artefacts, visitors in some way perceive themselves as appropriating this role.

Patrizia Violi contends that places such as Tuol Sleng, which she designates as 'trauma sites', and memorial museums located where actual traumatic events occurred *testify* to the past (Violi 2012: 39). She builds on Primo Levi's assertion that because the dead can no longer speak for themselves, only the traces of their existence can testify for them. Thus, at sites such as Tuol Sleng and Choeung Ek, bones, clothing, shackles, and other artefacts seemingly serve as conduits for testimony – and visitors as those who can receive and bear witness to their messages. Tuol Sleng, in Violi's argument, is 'a museum to be felt rather than to be known or understood' (Violi 2012: 48). Those who visit the site:

> are invited to participate, at least for the duration of their visit, in a fully embodied immersive experience that can be seen as a form of re-enactment of the traumatic experience itself; in doing so they change roles: they are no longer merely visitors looking around and gathering information, they become, at least to some extent, a part of the historical narrative itself. They become, in a sense, witnesses themselves.
>
> (Violi 2012: 51)

It is this process that enables tourists to reconceptualize their experience of Tuol Sleng and Choeung Ek. While they may not feel they have attained a deeper understanding of Cambodian politics, history or the DK period, they can justify their encounter through global discourses that stress the importance of bearing witness to atrocity – or at least fragments of the instruments of atrocity – in the wake of the Holocaust. Visitation becomes an act of humanitarian recognition.

Cambodians are not immune to these discourses of bearing witness and humanitarian exposure. Particularly since the launch of numerous outreach initiatives in 2003, many have come to understand Tuol Sleng and Choeung Ek as sites of international importance that, if given the chance, one has an obligation to visit. I was frequently told by those I interviewed that they had developed an interest in joining the ECCC study tours after they saw others participating in such efforts on TV. Despite widespread poverty in Cambodia, 90 per cent of the population has some access to TV, and this has proven to be one of the most effective mediums for communicating information about the internationalized court and its various related activities (Brady 2009). Thus, before even travelling to Phnom Penh, they had some sense that the tours and the locations they would be visiting – Tuol Sleng, Choeung Ek and the ECCC – were of international significance. This does not mean everyone, or even most participants, necessarily entered the process with the intention of bearing witness to global atrocity sites. Rather, most of those I interviewed said they joined the study tours because they wanted to learn more about the Khmer Rouge and why they had killed people. However, like the foreign tourists in Hughes's study, when this objective began to seem less and less attainable, they also sought to recast their visits as symbolically resonant acts of 'being there'.

While the ECCC's efforts have brought tens of thousands of Cambodians to Tuol Sleng, Choeung Ek and the court itself, they have received criticism for privileging 'head count' over actual education and rushing participants through the sites with little explanation. Experiences varied for the different participants I interviewed, although they frequently told me that they had 'run out of time', so they had not been able to visit all the sites expected or that their experience at sites had been cut short. Many reported that they had only thirty minutes to visit Tuol Sleng or Choeung Ek, and that they were offered no official guides to help them interpret the sites. Although participants often told me that they agreed to join the tours because they were hoping to gain a better understanding of the Khmer Rouge period, they left feeling confused by many of the displays and artefacts. In particular, they had difficulty distinguishing between Tuol Sleng staff and those who had been purged in the photo displays: 'I saw a girl from my village in the photos, but I don't know if she was a prisoner', Ratana from Pailin told me, 'maybe she was just a cook'. There were also misunderstandings about what kinds of torture methods were used, with tour participants often believing that a device used to position the heads of prisoners while their photographs were taken was actually a torture machine that drilled into the skulls of its victims.

Nonetheless, with the exception of those who rejected the authenticity of the sites or those who found them spiritually disturbing,[6] most participants said they were glad they had joined the tours. They reported deriving a sense of satisfaction from having *seen* Tuol Sleng and Choeung Ek for themselves. This was in spite of the fact that I was often told that they had not felt particularly compelled to journey on their own to the sites during the 1980s and 1990s, or before being given an organized opportunity by ECCC outreach. As Sina told me, 'we had a place like that near here where people were killed and we go to make offerings. Before, I did not see a reason to travel all the way to Phnom Penh to see such sites'. Interestingly, the act of witnessing also extended to the proceedings at the ECCC. The work of the tribunal is highly legalistic and difficult to follow, especially if one only comes in to watch a few hours of proceedings, as is the case for study tour participants.

However, those I interviewed explained that while they may not have understood the intricacies of the proceedings, they relished the opportunity to see the defendants in person, as well as the courthouse with all the domestic and international lawyers and judges. While at Tuol Sleng and Choeung Ek, Cambodians could bear witness to atrocity as filtered through a post-Holocaust lens intended for a foreign audience; at the ECCC, they could witness international conceptions of *justice being done*.

Conclusion

Given the lack of explanation provided by the study tours, the highly sensory nature of Tuol Sleng and Choeung Ek, and the widely disseminated discourses about the international significance of the sites as evidence of atrocity, it is not surprising that many Cambodians appear to re-imagine their visitation as acts of bearing witness. In a country where assignment of blame and creation of a generally agreed-upon narrative of internal violence is still contentious, this process may indeed serve the government's agenda to a certain extent. Providing more nuanced information, or an experience more complicated than exposing study participants to piles of bones and artefacts of Khmer Rouge torture methods, could lead to uncomfortable and divisive conversations that might subvert the authority of the state. Yet, the ECCC study tours are not uniform – some appear more comprehensive than others – and civil society organizations are also continuing to bring Cambodians to the sites on a limited basis, often with more extensive orientation and discussion sessions. Thus, this research project is but a starting point, a call for further study related to how Cambodians are interacting with these sites that were largely created for international consumption. While they are beginning to understand the global significance of Tuol Sleng and Choeung Ek – as illustrated by the experience of Vuthy, who was deeply moved to see foreigners crying in front of photos at Tuol Sleng – the impact of exposing Cambodians to representations of their history crafted for foreigners is unclear. Of particular significance is that it remains to be seen whether Cambodians interpret their visitation to these sites as acts of bearing witness to *internationalized* spaces located on Cambodian soil, or as engagement with national symbols of collective memory and suffering.

Notes

1 The Khmer Rouge tribunal is officially known as the Extraordinary Chambers in the Courts of Cambodia (ECCC). An agreement to create the hybrid court was reached by the United Nations and Cambodian government in 2003. Its mandate is to try senior leaders and those most responsible for the crimes committed during the Democratic Kampuchea (DK) period.

2 A few examples of such organizations include the Documentation Center of Cambodia, Khmer Institute of Democracy and Center for Social Development.

3 This is a term Cambodians often use to refer to the DK period.

4 The names of my informants have been changed in order to protect their confidentiality.
5 Of course, as Hughes explains, this is not necessarily the case for all those who engage in what has been described as 'dark tourism'. For example, some may conceptualize their visit as adventure tourism, of Cambodia as a destination to be 'survived'.
6 In Cambodia, there is particular concern that those who die bad, or 'unnatural' deaths may linger on earth and cause misfortune for the living. Hughes (2006) has written in 'Fielding Genocide: Post-1979 Cambodia and the Geopolitics of Memory,' that for this reason Choeung Ek in particular is considered a dangerous place and that many Cambodians refuse to visit the site. Yet, as I describe in 'Death on Display: Bones and Bodies in Cambodia and Rwanda' (forthcoming chapter, F. Ferrandiz and A.C.G.M. Robben (eds) *Down to Earth: Exhumations in the Modern World*, Philadelphia: University of Pennsylvania Press), I received mixed responses from Cambodians regarding this issue.

Bibliography

Alvarez, G.B., A. Colucci and J. Tyner. (2012) 'Memory and the Everyday Landscape of Violence in Post-Genocide Cambodia', *Social and Cultural Geography*, 13.8: 853–871.

Anderson, B. (2006) *Imagined Communities*, New York: Verso.

Brady, B. (2009) 'Lights, Camera, Genocide!', *Global Post*. 20 November. Available at: http://www.globalpost.com/dispatch/asia/091116/cambodia-genocide-tribunal-television. Accessed: 10 January 2013.

Chandler, D. (2001) 'Tuol Sleng and S-21,' *Searching for the Truth*, 18: 29.

Giry, S. (2012) 'Necessary Scapegoats? The Making of the Khmer Rouge Tribunal', *The New York Review of Books*. Available at: http://www.nybooks.com/blogs/nyrblog/2012/jul/23/necessary-scapegoats-khmer-rouge-tribunal/. Accessed: 12 January 2013.

Guyer, S. (2009) 'Rwanda's Bones', *Boundary 2: An International Journal of Literature and Culture*, 36.2: 155–175.

Hinton, A. (2008) 'Truth Representation and the Politics of Memory after Genocide,' in A. Kent and D. Chandler (eds) *People of Virtue: Reconfiguring Religion, Power and Moral Order in Cambodia Today*, Copenhagen: Nordic Institute of Asian Studies Press: 62–81.

——. (2013) 'Transitional Justice Time: Uncle San, Aunty Yan, and Outreach at the Khmer Rouge Tribunal', in D. Mayersen and A. Pohlman (eds) *Genocide and Mass Atrocities in Asia: Legacies and Prevention*, London: Routledge: 86–98.

Hughes, R. (2006) *Fielding Genocide: Post-1979 Cambodia and the Geopolitics of Memory*, Dissertation, The University of Melbourne.

——. (2008). 'Dutiful Tourism: Encountering the Cambodian Genocide', *Asia Pacific Viewpoint*, 49.3: 318–330.

Impunity Watch. (2012) 'Breaking the Silence: International Memory Initiatives Exchange Forum', Perspective Series Conference Report, Phnom Penh. 25–29 September.

Ledgerwood, J. (1997) 'The Cambodian Tuol Sleng Museum of Genocidal Crimes: National Narrative', *Museum Anthropology*, 21.1: 82–98.

Manning, P. (2011) 'Governing Memory: Justice, Reconciliation, and Outreach at the Extraordinary Chambers in the Courts of Cambodia', *Memory Studies*, 5.2: 165–181.

Sanders, A. (2006) *The Evil Within: Genocide, Memory and Mythmaking in Cambodia*, Thesis, Radboud University Nijmegen.

Sion, B. (2011) 'Conflicting Sites of Memory in Post-Genocide Cambodia', *Humanity: An International Journal of Human Rights, Humanitarianism and Development*, 2.1: 1–21.

Thion, S. (1993) *Watching Cambodia*, Bangkok: White Lotus.

Vickery, M. (1984) *Cambodia 1975–1982*, Boston: South End Press.

Violi, P. (2012) 'Trauma Site Museums and Politics of Memory: Tuol Sleng, Villa Grimaldi and the Bologna Ustica Museum', *Theory, Culture and Society* 29.1: 36–75.

Williams, P. (2004) 'Witnessing Genocide: Vigilance and Remembrance at Tuol Sleng and Choeung Ek', *Holocaust and Genocide Studies*, 18.2: 234–255.

——. (2007) *Memorial Museums: The Global Rush to Commemorate Atrocities*, New York: Berg.

8 Contested notions of genocide and commemoration

The case of the Herero in Namibia

Henning Melber

> Remembrance of the colonial era is a controversial issue everywhere, and it enters into many debates that are concerned with the present day as well as with the past.
>
> (Conrad 2012: 200)

In 1884, the German Empire had declared large parts of the territory which is known today as the Republic of Namibia as its first colonial prey, and named it 'German South West Africa'.[1] The process of colonization that took place in the following two decades took the form of settler colonial physical penetration and occupation in the central, southern and eastern parts of the country. This confrontation also provoked violent anti-colonial resistance by local communities, mainly among different groups of the Nama (derogatorily called 'Hottentots') and the Herero. These isolated acts of resistance were met in return by military oppression. Since the beginning of the twentieth century, an escalation of the invasions by German traders and settlers resulted in a major concerted occupation of the territory originally under the control of the local cattle herders. The confiscation of land, forced removal and displacement resulted in organized rebellion. Herero communities under the leadership of Chief Samuel Maherero rose up against German colonial rule with planned attacks on German settlers in January 1904. These attacks caught the colonial authorities by surprise, but were soon countered by the full force of the military, with the mobilization by the Empire of massive detachments of troops and weapons.

Within nine months, the Herero resistance was decisively broken and the commander of the German troops, General von Trotha, issued the now notorious 'extermination order' (for a debate of its significance, see Lundtofte 2003: 39ff.). The text, issued on 2 October 1904 and rescinded in December of the same year by the Kaiser under pressure from public protests within the German Empire, declared the following (among other things):

> I, the Great General of the German Soldiers, address this letter to the Herero people. The Herero are no longer considered German subjects. They have murdered, stolen, cut off ears, noses and other parts from

> wounded soldiers, and now refuse to fight on out of cowardice … The Herero people will have to leave the country. Otherwise, I shall force them to do so by means of guns. Within the German boundaries, every Herero, whether found armed or unarmed, with or without cattle, will be shot. I shall not accept any more women and children. I shall drive them back to their people – otherwise, I shall order shots to be fired at them.
>
> (Quoted in Drechsler 1980: 156f.)

Witnessing the uncompromising repression, Nama communities under Chief Hendrik Witbooi followed the Herero example, taking up arms against the Germans from October 1904 onwards. Engaged in a form of flexible guerrilla warfare, which dragged on until 1908, they were also ruthlessly defeated. The surviving Herero and Nama were detained as prisoners of war in concentration camps and used for forced labour. Some of the Nama were deported to the German colonies in West Africa. Many of the local people who survived the conflict tragically did not survive the subsequent ordeal. While figures remain contested and a matter of (at times) highly speculative and dubious arithmetic, it is widely believed nonetheless, that substantive parts of these communities – more than half, if not two-thirds, of the Herero originally estimated at some 80,000 and one-third to a half of the Nama originally estimated at 30,000 to 40,000 – were eliminated. The intent to destroy was the decisive element of the warfare applied. More than a century later, these colonial wars, and in particular the extinction strategy applied by the German troops – including the destructive effects on the communities through the establishment of a system denying them the continued reproduction of their original forms of living – remain a contested subject of intense public and academic debate.

This chapter focuses mainly on the remembrance of genocide. Initiatives to remember were to a large extent originally taken by Herero descendants, since they had been given voice and agency within an independent Namibian state.[2] This chapter also summarizes the parallel efforts in parts of the German academic community to provide more insights into the historical processes of this genocide and thereby contribute to a memory culture in Germany in recognition of this period. This is contrasted with the reluctant, if not evasive, position adopted by various German governments when confronted with the issue following Namibia's Independence in 1990. While the Herero and descendants of the other victims, in particular among the Nama but also the Damara (another ethnically distinct local group living often partly among the Herero and Nama communities), continued to demand justice through an apology and compensation as part of reconciliation between the German and Namibian peoples, the German responses were at best lukewarm and short of an apology. This coincided with the Namibian government at first adopting a similarly evasive position by refusing to take sides and instead stressing the need for good bilateral relations. Only twenty years after Independence, the political leadership of the former liberation movement, now the Government of the Republic of Namibia, seems to have readjusted its position and sided with demands to give adequate recognition to the historical injustices and crimes committed against specific sections of the Namibian population.

Building on their long-standing engagement in earlier campaigns for remembrance and compensation, the Herero played a central role in the memorial discourse and commemorative events a century after the Genocide. They also actively and visibly articulated demands for historical justice and compensation. The focus on Herero initiatives for remembering genocide, however, does not suggest that more credit and credibility should be given to Herero claims over and above the legitimate demands of other groups. Other groups significantly affected by the direct physical violence of the German colonial regime's practices – most notably the Nama, but also the San (Bushmen) as well as the Damara – have no less important or legitimate claims for remembrance and consolation because they exercise less visible agency in the current policy debates. Rather, this chapter reflects critically on the selectivity of remembrance by various actors. This chapter presents evidence based on the Namibian case. It reminds us of the widely popularized words of William Faulkner in his play 'Requiem for a Nun' (1950), which ring as true today as ever: 'The past is never dead. It's not even past' (Act I, Scene III).

In the preface to his recent (locally published and undated) literary narrative that recalls memories of the anti-colonial struggles of his forefathers, Rukee Tjingaete (n.d.: ii) places the remembrance of the atrocities committed against them into the Namibian context of the early twenty-first century:

> We cannot free ourselves from the past until both the victims and villains are atoned with Germany's imperial past in Namibia. The past is like the shade of a thorn tree that covers a pile of thorns for those stepping on it ... It is like a weeping grave of an angry ancestor.

The genocide debate and its implications

Already during the late 1960s, historians from the two German republics – Horst Drechsler from the German Democratic Republic (1966; 1980) and Helmut Bley from the Federal Republic of Germany (1968; 1971) – provided different yet complementary and convincing evidence for, and competent analysis of, the totalitarian practices and subsequent methods of mass destruction applied by colonial forces in German South West Africa. The pioneering, seminal contributions of these two historians to Namibian historiography were further strengthened by the more theoretically based work of Peter Schmitt-Egner (1975). His approach was reinforced decades later in various nuanced treatments and empirically substantiated by Gewald (1999),

Krüger (1999), Zimmerer (2001) and Bühler (2003). It is noteworthy that all these explorations dating from the late 1960s to the turn of the century were originally dissertations. They have since then been complemented by more popular works – most prominently those of Olusoga and Erichsen (2009) and Sarkin (2011), but also those in Zimmerer and Zeller (2003, 2008), Förster et al. (2004), as well as Melber (2005a) – on the occasion of the centenary of the outbreak of what is at times dubbed the 'German–Namibian War'.

These studies agree that German warfare conducted at the beginning of the twentieth century in so-called German South West Africa can be described as tantamount to genocide. The Whitaker Report, commissioned by the United Nations and published in 1985, concluded that the events in German South West Africa that took place between 1904 and 1908 constituted the first genocide of the twentieth century. The Whitaker Report is so far the most explicit document produced within a United Nations body and therefore represents a kind of official international frame of reference. It was drafted by the special rapporteur Ben Whitaker upon a request from the UN Sub-Commission on Prevention of Discrimination and Protection of Minorities/Commission on Rights of the UN Economic and Social Council.[3] In addition, most, if not all, internationally published reference works on genocide include the German colonial war against the Herero and Nama between 1904 and 1908 as an example of genocide.[4] Disappointingly, the otherwise well-informed overview by Conrad (2008, 2012) avoids confronting the issue of genocide. By contrast, Wallace's historical overview (Wallace 2011: 155–182) presents a concise, in-depth review of the German–Namibian War and concludes that genocide was, in her view, committed 'beyond reasonable doubt' (2011: 177).

Nevertheless, many involved in the current debate on the German side (both in Germany and among the German-speaking community in Namibia, estimated currently at about 15,000 to 20,000 members) continue to contest the notion of genocide. The most striking phenomenon in dealing with the historical events more than a century later is that analyses and conclusions still differ fundamentally in public perception as well as scholarly and political discourse – insofar as the Genocide, its understanding and its classification are considered or cared about at all.[5]

More generally, for the wider German public, this colonial episode – despite these (at times) strongly divided opinions – has been largely ignored or forgotten (if, in fact, awareness of these events had existed at all – at least in the German states after the Second World War) in the larger collective memory. In contrast to this widespread amnesia or indifference in Germany, the trauma lives on among substantial parts of the Namibian population, most notably the Herero and the Nama who bore the brunt of the colonial onslaught. Moreover, the strong collective memory has resulted in growing demands by sections of Namibian society for recognition of, and compensation for, the war crimes committed in the former colony, as well as for forcing the descendants of German colonial settlers, who as farmers still own a disproportionately large portion of commercial lands, to deal with the historical record (or in many cases to deny it). The colonial legacy and how it is treated remains a battlefield on which there are often uncompromising exchanges on how to come to terms with the past in the present.

As maintained elsewhere,[6] in the early twentieth century the Namibian Genocide contributed significantly to the establishment of a new extermination perspective. The inherent racism of settler colonialism worked to lower the tolerance threshold to mass killings, with similar examples to be found in the Americas, Australia and southern Africa. In the Namibian case, this also links up with a more distinctively German trajectory, where we can observe continuities with accounts and novels read by a mass readership; with military practice; with the activities of specific persons, as well as with military doctrines and routines that linked strategic ideas of 'decisive battles' to the concept of a 'final solution' and the extinction of the enemy that evidently culminated in the Holocaust of the 1940s.

The following discussion focuses on the different ways in which memory has been cultivated (if at all) in the two countries from a Herero-centred perspective. This chapter thereby seeks to counteract the German-centred focus and tendency in the wide range of literature on the subject in German

Figure 8.1 German monument. © Henning Melber.

(as documented in the bibliography). While most recent writing reflects some degree of concern among German scholars, new approaches carry risks, which this contribution also cannot avoid. According to the sensitive observation by Wallace (2011: 181), 'the genocide debate can also be a hindrance to inquiry, and above all, to situating the Namibian War as an event in *Namibian*, rather than German history' (her emphasis).

As the following section will show, the perseverance by groups of the Herero (who are by no means homogenous and who often engaged in inter-Herero rivalries and sectional in-fighting) more recently affected commemoration and the genocide discourse in several ways. Firstly, raising the issue of genocide since Independence in 1990 gave voice to agencies who were denied taking a floor internationally during the times under South African foreign rule. Secondly, the Herero-initiated campaigns resulted by the end of the twentieth century in a much wider awareness of German colonial warfare and its devastating effects both inside Namibia and also, to some extent, in Germany, as the marked increase of scholarly engagement (documented above) indicates. Thirdly, Herero agitation managed to put the issue on the agenda of bilateral Namibian–German relations, albeit originally only soliciting a reluctant response. Fourthly, a German civil society component (as tiny as it might be) was able to utilize the centenary of German warfare in its colony to draw attention to the genocide in then South West Africa and thereby impacted to some extent upon the inner-German political discussion by political parties in parliament as to how best to respond. Fifthly, other directly affected groups among the Nama and Damara started to mobilize with more determination and visibility to advocate their own similar demands for recognition of, and compensation for, historical injustice committed against them. Sixthly, the Namibian government finally responded, having been partly provoked by a German refusal to engage more openly, which in its forms of refusal bordered on paternalism and patronization and which thereby offended the highest Namibian political office-bearers.

Thus, the notion of genocide and commemoration, including forms of adequate recognition and compensation, has emerged recently more than ever as a topical policy issue foremost in Namibia, with the government more responsive to the demands of the local agencies seeking adequate recognition. The new relevance of this issue has also been reflected in the first restitution of skulls from collections in German institutions. These were transferred in late 2011 to Namibia and have contributed to a growing awareness that the past is 'not even past'.

Forms of Namibian genocide remembrance

More than twenty years after Independence, ultimately achieved on 21 March 1990, the specific blend between physical remnants of the colonial past and the

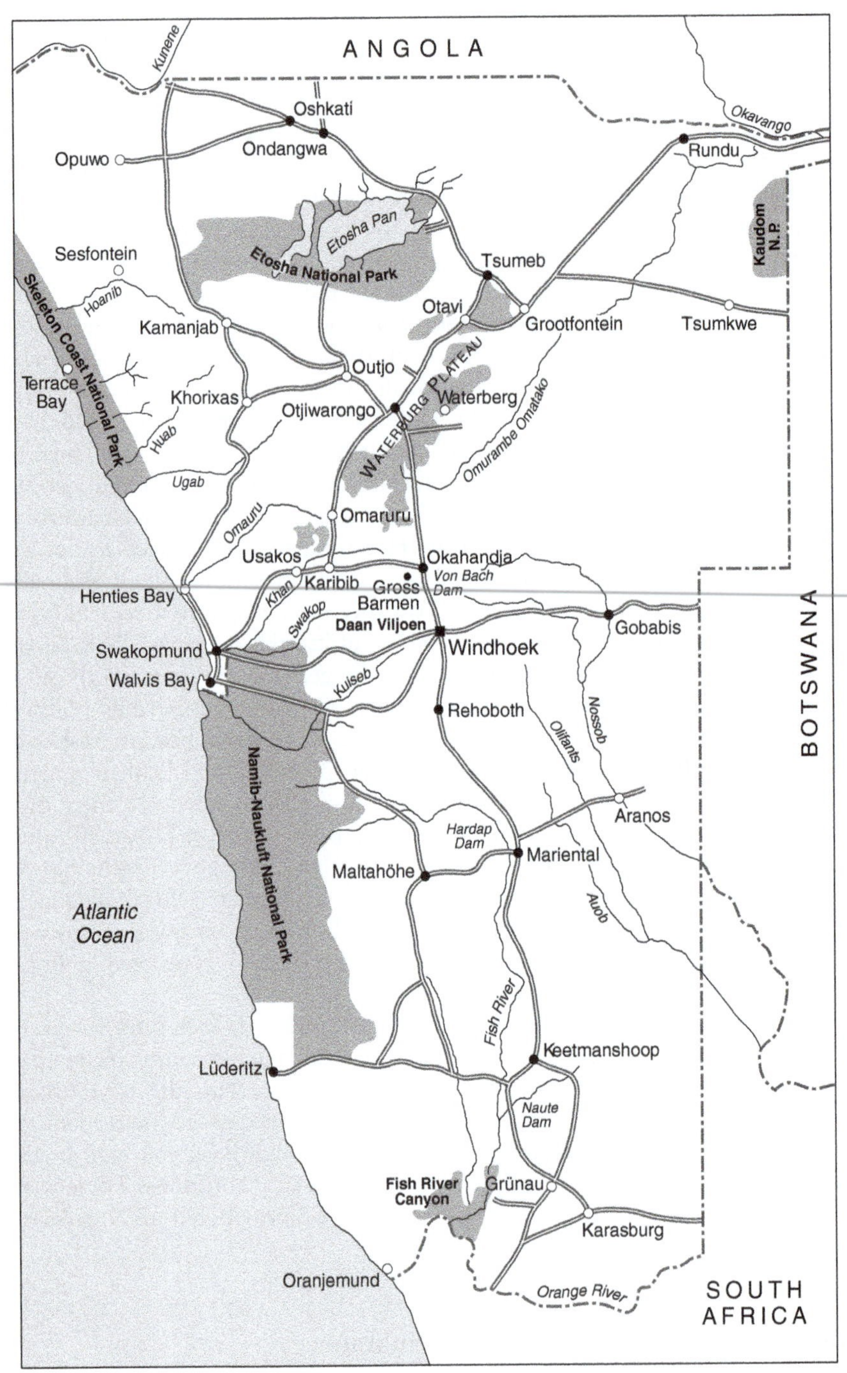

Map 8.1 Namibian locations of warfare and genocide. Adapted by Henning Melber.

newly emerging symbols of the anti-colonial struggle which are celebrated in the dominant postcolonial nation-building process create a rather peculiar public sphere and memory 'landscape' in Namibia's physical environment (Kössler 2003). This tension plays out in an ongoing transition from the architectural and monumental remnants of the colonial past towards an increasingly growing space for new symbols of a postcolonial patriotic history. This manifests itself in forms such as the Heroes Acre and the Independence Museum (both of North Korean design) in Windhoek, but also newly created sites of 'struggle commemoration' in northern Namibia and a military museum in Okahandja. These and similar insignia of the new power executed by the former liberation movement SWAPO (South West Africa People's Organization),[7] now the dominant party in political control over the state, emphasize the 'heroic narrative' of the anti-colonial struggle as it emerged since the 1950s (Melber 2003; 2005c). In contrast, it initially offered little recognition and public space for the period of primary resistance to German colonial rule. This exclusivist post-independence discourse reversed earlier acknowledgements of the different relevant stages of the country's liberation history that were not all directly connected to SWAPO and preceded the formation of the organization. As the liberation movement's official history summarized almost a decade prior to Independence:

> Out of the country's pre-colonial population, only the Ovambo escaped the full rigour of German rule … the Germans, preoccupied with their subjugation of the Herero and Nama and deterred by Ovambo numbers and military power, left them alone. Even when, after the genocidal suppression of the 1904–1907 national uprising, the colonial economy became heavily dependent on Ovambo migrant labour for its mines and railways, the colonial regime limited its contacts with the Ovambo kings strictly to 'protection' treaties and diplomatic 'persuasion'.
>
> (Department of Information and Publicity/SWAPO of Namibia 1981: 14f.)

Interesting is the acknowledgement that Oshivambo-speaking communities originally living in the parts of the colonial territory called Ovamboland situated north of the Police Zone (a dividing line introduced by the German colonial administration, which left the northern parts of the colony mainly under indirect rule) and nowadays representing more than half of Namibia's population as the decisive support base for the party in power remained, to a large extent, outside of the active anti-colonial resistance against the Germans. As interesting is the surprising and contrary reference to this anti-colonial resistance as a 'national uprising'. Such an appropriation and generalization ironically echoes the equally dubious tendency towards monopolization of primary resistance history, which at times was claimed by some among the traditional leaders of the Herero communities.

Figure 8.2 Waterberg. © Adelheid Esslinger.

Already during the 1920s, the 'Herero Day' in Okahandja became an annual celebration. The Paramount Chief Samuel Maherero, who had been in command over the Herero attacking the Germans in 1904 and who had fled to Bechuanaland after the battles at the Waterberg in August 1904, was buried after his death in Bechuanaland in 1923 at a separate small cemetery in Okahandja where other Herero chiefs were also laid to rest. Every last weekend of August since then, the different Herero communities gather there to remember their ancestors. This remains the most significant singular symbolic remembrance commemorating the forefathers who fought the Germans. The Herero Day is a forum not only to claim the Herero identities and traditions, but also to cultivate the memory of the war against the Germans (Kössler 2011: 242ff.). At the 'Herero Day' in 2002, Herero Paramount Chief Kuaima Riruako made an effort to justify the private claims for reparations from the German government and a few German companies, which upon his instructions had been presented to a United States court in late 2001 (Sarkin 2009). Riruako was so carried away that he declared the question of land redistribution in Namibia – a much-contested notion since Independence – to be solely a Herero issue (Heise 2002).[8] Even if this were in line with the admission made in the SWAPO publication quoted on p. 159, that the communities north of the Police Zone – introduced during German colonial rule as a demarcation line separating the direct territorial administration from the regions with forms of indirect rule – had not been directly affected, it represents a blatant denial of the sacrifices made by other communities also living inside the Police Zone, especially the Nama, as well as the Damara and the San.

The sort of logic that allowed the paramount Herero leadership to claim the sole and authentic status of victimhood in relation to the Genocide largely dominated subsequent events during the centenary commemorations in 2004. This monopoly of victimhood was, moreover, not limited to the Herero's own arrangements and commemorative events, but was also evident during the two large conferences organized in August 2004 at the University of Namibia in Windhoek and in November 2004 in Bremen, where, in contrast to other conferences on related subjects, the Herero presence was almost exclusively visible. Apart from the dominant perceptions by foreign and local White presenters, on both occasions other Namibian views were mainly confined to Herero positions, which often claimed to represent the only valid perspective.

The Namibian government, by contrast, kept a demonstratively low profile. No government-sponsored public events or other initiatives were organized in order to commemorate the occasion (and by doing so flag the commitment to honour the primary resistance as part of early nation-building). Instead, such constructive engagement was left to private initiatives mainly taken by groups among the Herero (and to a lesser extent Nama) communities. It should be noted that mainly through the initiative of the Evangelical-Lutheran churches, convened as the so-called 'Bishops' Committee', a few members of the local German-speaking community also showed a willingness to respond and take the initiative to participate in such activities. When the then Minister of Information and Broadcasting, Nangolo Mbumba, announced on behalf of Cabinet the decision to honour the centenary of the Genocide by issuing a special commemorative stamp, he was adamant that this would not single out particular groups such as Germans (as perpetrators) or Herero (as victims). The stamp initiative should instead be seen as an effort to contribute to a wider and general reconciliation as a declared guiding principle for postcolonial Namibian society. Namibia's government, as he explained further, did not subscribe to the initiative by a group of Herero to seek reparations from Germany (Hofmann 2003). In complementing the claim for an inclusive national significance for the war, but from a slightly different perspective, the Minister of Higher Education, Nahas Angula (Namibia's prime minister between March 2005 and December 2012), expressed the opinion during a panel debate that the commemoration of the Genocide should involve all Namibians and also be seen as a part of the wider Namibian struggle for liberation (Schreiber 2003).

As a result of this intervention, one would have expected the government to play a more active role during the subsequent centenary commemorations. Instead, the Namibian president and other senior government officials did not accept an invitation by the Herero leadership to attend the ceremonies in Okahandja, which marked the one hundredth anniversary of the beginning of the Herero war against German colonial occupation in January 2004 (Kuteeue 2004a). Significantly, President Sam Nujoma's designated successor as Head of State, Hifikepunye Pohamba, did attend the ceremony commemorating the military encounters around the Waterberg, held at Ohamakari near Okakarara in August 2004. The main reason for this significant gesture might, however, have been the presence of the German Minister for Economic Cooperation, especially since government representatives were absent again when the Herero gathered for their annual Otjiserandu commemoration activities (the 'Herero Day') during the last weekend of August in Okahandja. Instead, government officials gathered at a new monument in the north, which was erected in memory of the beginning of the armed struggle between SWAPO and the South African regime in 1966. The government thereby only recognized the Waterberg event when a German minister was in attendance, but it showed a cold shoulder to any other Herero-initiated commemorative event during the centenary. This suggests that bilateral relations with Germany set the agenda, rather than the commemorative activities by local groups.

The year 2004 was, however, not the end, but the beginning for increased efforts by the Herero – and ultimately also representatives of various groups among the Nama and Damara – to keep the past alive and to further pursue claims for recognition of their sacrifices and the injustices committed against them. Since then, Herero and Nama have cultivated commemorative events even more consciously and created a vibrant memory culture focusing on the war against the German colonial occupation as a mobilizing factor for renewed pressure to give adequate recognition to the demands of the descendants (Kössler 2010b, 2011).

Figure 8.3 Centenary commemoration. © Larissa Förster.

German governmental evasiveness

Throughout the centenary, the Namibian government seemed to be in almost silent agreement with the majority of the German-speaking minority in Namibia as well as those representing the official position of the German government, preferring to keep a lid on the issue of genocide and possible forms of compensation for the injustices and crimes that were committed. At the 11 January 2004 commemoration ceremony in Okahandja, the German ambassador to Namibia reiterated his government's position on the reparation issue raised by the Herero by stating: 'It would not be justified to compensate one specific ethnic group for their suffering during the colonial times, as this could reinforce ethnic tensions and thus undermine the policy of national reconciliation which we fully support' (quoted in Kuteeue 2004b). In contrast to official German inaction, there were a sizeable number of initiatives and commemoration activities, mainly by NGOs, that took place in Germany. Joachim Zeller (2005) has compiled an impressive overview of relevant activities he was able to identify until mid-2005. They include six distinct exhibitions in German towns and over twenty different seminars, panel debates, public lecture series and conferences from mid-2003 until mid-2005 in Germany – far more than in Namibia. In addition, several public acts of commemoration were initiated in different locations. It is noteworthy, however, that none of these had an official character in the sense of being initiated (or attended) by German state authorities. The proliferation of activities suggested a new awareness among parts of a younger generation which combined their anti-racist convictions in their fight against xenophobic tendencies with a critical retrospective on the legacy of the German colonial era.

Consecutive German governments, regardless of their political hue, had consistently downplayed the colonial record as a marginal episode in German history and evaded making a formal apology for any injustices committed under the banner of German civilization. The government declined making an apology to the Herero on the grounds that it might constitute an argument for the descendants of the survivors to seek legal redress and compensation for damages past and present. Shamefully, German state visits to independent Namibia reinforced cordial relationships with German-speaking Namibians while stonewalling calls for a response to the consequences of colonial genocide. As late as 2003, German Foreign Minister Josef ('Joschka') Fischer (from the 'progressive' Green party!) formulated the official political position that no apology would be offered insofar as it could be associated with a call for compensation. In January 2004, the Social Democratic German Chancellor, Gerhard Schröder, during his first series of official visits to African countries, meticulously avoided Namibia, a move which allowed him to simply skip the historical debate around German–Namibian relations with regard to the Genocide.

Nonetheless, during the August 2004 commemoration of the military encounters around the Waterberg at Ohamakari near Okakarara, the actions of German Minister for Economic Cooperation and Development Heidemarie Wieczorek-Zeul seemed to suggest a marked deviation from the previous official denial by the German government. In an emotional speech, the minister expressed what could only be interpreted as an admission of guilt, as well as heartfelt remorse. She suggested that, as seen from a twenty-first-century perspective, the German conduct during the war against Herero and Nama communities constituted war crimes and genocide. Asked for an apology (the word did not appear in the text she read out), she confirmed that her whole speech was supposed to be an apology. This took the audience by surprise and wholly changed the dynamic of the event; it gave it a far more conciliatory tone.

However, there were subsequently no visible results to indicate a change of policy towards related issues of compensation. In May 2005, Minister Wieczorek-Zeul announced the intention to establish a Namibian–German Panel on Reconciliation as a long-term initiative to financially assist the groups that had mainly been affected by the Genocide. According to the minister, twenty million euros were earmarked for its implementation during a period of ten years (two million euros annually). At the same time, the minister announced an increase in bilateral development aid for Namibia. Germany prides itself on being the most important donor country to Namibia because of the historical legacy, with Namibia being the recipient of by far the highest per capita aid expenditure in Germany's development aid programme for African countries, reinforcing that, since Namibia's Independence, Germany had been willing to accept a 'special historical responsibility' for the former colony, a phrase that has been frequently and repeatedly stressed ever since it was first adopted in a parliamentary resolution, carried on the occasion of Namibia's Independence in 1990. It has become an evasive euphemism for the ongoing denial of Germany's responsibility for genocide with regard to any of the local communities.

Identities and commemoration

For those considered to represent the descendants of the perpetrators – the so-called '*Suedwester*' ('Southwesters'), who by means of origin and tradition were socialized within a culture of settler-colonial European domination and imperialism – re-entering the belly of the beast might be a particular challenge. Descendants are confronted with the possibly very painful task of decolonizing their own mindsets by means of critical introspection into the fatal consequences for those at the receiving end of the dominant colonial paradigm of the civilizing mission. A similar challenge remains for those in Germany who remain either ignorant, or in denial of, the dark side of the so-called 'good old days', which culminated in the intention to exterminate people considered to be barbarians or brutes because they resisted foreign domination (Kössler 2010a; Kössler and Melber 2012a, 2012b; Melber 2013a, 2013b).

A challenge also remains for those claiming the legacy of the 'wretched of the earth' to the extent that this occurs at the expense of others. The logic of claiming the sole and authentic status as victims of the German genocide was actively cultivated within interventions dominated by Herero groups on various occasions of the commemoration as a dubious exclusivity (Schaller 2011). A spokesperson for the 'Coordinating Committee for the First Official Commemoration of the Ovaherero Genocide' stated as late as August 2004 that the term 'genocide' would, in Namibia, only apply to what happened to the Herero.[9]

Claims to genuine Herero identity have been, from Independence until recently, increasingly and inseparably linked to sole victim status under the colonial genocide. It created or reinforced an aura of exclusivity and consequently an 'us-and-them divide' against the rest of the world:

> Historically, Herero speakers were divided amongst themselves. Not all sections of Herero society were equally affected by the genocide, let alone in the Apartheid years. Yet discourse on the genocide allows people to paper over these distinctions. It is thus the first truly shared experience of all Herero speakers in the present.
>
> (Gewald 2003: 303)

Members of the group had the tendency to brush aside the concern expressed over such monopolization of victim status. They abused their 'biological authenticity' as successors to the victims in a way that excluded any serious debate about dissenting views. Instead, accusations of racism and eurocentrism were handy tools that readily allowed for an off-hand dismissal of any discourse on how best to advocate on the issue in order that it might serve the interests of more than just one group. A prominent leading intellectual of the Herero community, for example, strongly resisted the argument that the Herero were not the only victims of colonial genocide by warning that it is 'important to call attention to the insensitive intellectualization about Namibia and the genocide debate' (Kandetu 2005: 66). According to him:

> The context of historical analysis by some academics of euro-centric orientation is infested with insensitivity and masqueraded in arrogance. For they prefer to use historical events selectively ... This parochial perception is reinforced by the belief on the part of these experts that they as descendants of European cultures have everything to teach others and nothing to learn from them.
>
> (Kandetu 2005: 65)

This polemical rebuttal of what is shrugged off as unwanted interference denied others the right to a dissenting view and prevented any meaningful dialogue or debate. In the then frequently expressed view among Herero activists seeking recognition as victims who qualify for compensation, the Herero were the sole group entitled to claim this status. The motives of those, who in such a reductive way were seeking the recognition so far denied to them, might have been perfectly understandable. They wanted to pursue and achieve, in their own view, historical justice. But this happened in an exclusivist way at the expense of others who remained outside of the arena defined by public interest and who were therefore denied their recognition as victims. Those seeking to advocate an approach which gave recognition to all groups directly affected by the genocide were – as in the statement by Kandetu quoted on p. 165 – accused of lecturing the Herero and seeking to undermine their claims. This phenomenon of a 'competition among the victims', resulting in claims for monopoly of victim status, is a tendency certainly not confined to the Namibian case, but it was illustrated yet again under these particular centenary-related circumstances in a rather obvious way.

When introducing a motion in the Namibian Parliament on 19 September 2006 demanding adequate commemoration of and reparations for the Genocide, Kuaima Riruako as MP and paramount chief of the Ovaherero justified the exceptional sacrifices of his one ethnic group by stating: 'The Ovaherero was the only group singled out to be exterminated by an official legal order' (quoted in Schaller 2011: 274). Such a claim by segments of the Herero people for being exclusive genocide victims under German colonial rule was only one of the many selective ways of revisiting the past. The Namibian government's longstanding tendency to deny the descendants of the main victim groups of the time their rightful acknowledgement and specific entitlement to compensation was another (which for obvious reasons suited the German government's reluctant remorse). What had been concluded with regard to the Holocaust and its organized memory politics was until not so long ago applicable to the different parties and their interests in the case of Namibia's colonial genocide too:

> An integral component of representation is simplification. Practices of memory are not only about inclusion, but also exclusion. Some facts just don't fit with the co-creation of memory groups, national myths, propaganda agendas, or sell photos. As a consequence some groups are marginalized, histories unwritten and complexities reduced.
>
> (Fleming 2005: 122)

Recently, however, this has changed. The final part of this chapter summarizes recent tendencies which seem to suggest the formation of a more unified Namibian position towards the German government in finally demanding the outstanding recognition of the historical guilt and its obligations to deal with it more adequately.

When history is not past: the recurrent debate

While the Namibian Parliament adopted in late 2006 the motion by Chief Riruako, which in principle recognized the demands for the compensation of and reparations to those groups affected by the Genocide, the government did not follow up on this politically within the bilateral relationship with Germany. The situation only changed after the first transfer of skulls in October 2011 created a new focal point for restitution and commemoration among the most affected Namibian communities. The continued evasiveness of the German government finally led to the Namibian government becoming more motivated than it ever had been before to take sides and challenge the German position: its highest-ranking political representatives expressed their irritation towards the attitude displayed by the German government.[10]

As part of the genocidal practices evident during the 1904–1908 war, Herero and Nama skulls were shipped from the colony to German universities for human anthropological research, which was at that time obsessed with the physical measurement of people to substantiate the claims for racial superiority. Some of the skulls were positively identified in the basements of institutions, such as Greifswald, Freiburg and the Charité in Berlin. The Charité in particular was a centre that promoted the dangerous Aryan ideology of the Nazi regime. A first batch of the skulls identified there was, after several years of negotiations, finally returned in September/October 2011 to an official delegation of mainly Herero and Nama representatives headed by the Minister of Youth, National Service, Sport and Culture, Kazenambo Kazenambo, himself a descendant of the directly affected groups.[11]

However, what was supposed to be a solemn and spiritual act of restitution, turned into an embarrassing affront and ended in a disaster. The delegation was offended and humiliated by the lack of sensitivity displayed by the German government and its officials. For these domestic policy priorities (by claiming that the delegation was hijacked and manipulated by the 'wrong' political interests in Germany) counted more than coming to terms with a colonial past and its Namibian descendants. The German government did not offer the delegation and its head any appropriate courtesy according to protocol, as no meeting on a ministerial level was arranged. To add insult to injury, the state secretary in the German foreign ministry, representing the government during the commemorative act – irritated by some heckling from the floor by members of local anti-racist groups – abruptly departed from the ceremony after delivering her short statement and before the Namibian minister spoke.

Upon return to Windhoek, the delegation was questioned in particular by a White Namibian journalist about a variety of aspects of the visit (not least the size of the delegation and the costs for Namibian taxpayers). In response to the criticism of having incurred a great deal of expenses to fund a large delegation, published in a local newspaper on 11 November 2011, Minister Kazenambo called a press conference on 16 November, where, enraged over the issue, he lambasted the newspaper that had carried the report, called the journalist a 'bloody *boer*', and stated that Black Namibians' patience with the colonial mentality that surfaced in such criticism was running out. With reference to the continued disproportionately high ownership of land by

White commercial farmers, he suggested that the constitution could be set aside if the Whites were to 'scratch too far'. His reaction, as undiplomatic as it was, simply testified to the deep-seated sentiments and hurt feelings provoked by the arrogance that was on display during the visit to Germany.

Egon Kochanke, Germany's ambassador to Namibia, added fuel to the flames. At the signing of a new cooperation agreement worth over N$660 million on 16 November 2011, he complained that the Namibian delegation had visited Germany with a hidden agenda and had created a negative impression of bilateral relations between the two countries. Far from improving the situation, such pronouncements contributed to a further deterioration in relations. During a courtesy visit in the State House – the office and residence of Namibia's president – in late January 2012, German ambassador Kochanke suggested to Namibia's President Hifikepunye Pohamba that the demands of the Namibians and their views on German colonialism were initiated by a radical minority in Germany. A reportedly enraged president, offended by what he felt was a patronizing attitude, showed him the door. The prime minister at the time, Nahas Angula, commented on the incident:

> As a diplomat you have to understand the mood in the country where you are. The atrocities committed [by Germans] are a concern not only to the communities directly affected, but to the entire [sic] Namibia. These were tragic events and as an ambassador one should have that sense.
>
> (Quoted in Sibeene 2012)

Shortly afterwards, the one hundredth anniversary celebrations of the equestrian monument, erected by the German colonial administration in 1912 in memory of the German soldiers who died during the war against the local population, took place at the end of January 2012 in the presence of colonial-apologetic delegates from Germany. The Namibian minister of information, speaking for his government, criticized this as insensitive provocation. The event, which took place from 1 to 3 February 2012 coincided with the official visit of Walter Lindner, Director General of African Affairs in the German Foreign Office, for high-level meetings. He confirmed the reactivation of the suspended special initiative originally announced in 2004, which had earmarked €20 million for projects to benefit historically affected communities. Although Germany had allocated some €700 million in bilateral aid since Independence, the atmosphere remained frosty and the Namibians displayed little gratitude for the financial offer. Lindner visited Namibia again on 14 May 2012, without matters being resolved. It is therefore somewhat ironic that Ambassador Kochanke replaced Lindner as head of the Africa department in the foreign ministry in Berlin in August of that same year.

Kochanke's replacement did not, however, bring the finger-wagging posture to an end. In early February 2013, the new German ambassador, Onno Hückmann, clashed with Prime Minister Hage Geingob. During a courtesy visit, Hückmann called on the Namibian government not to use the good bilateral relations for what he termed 'endless discussions about reparations'. In marked contrast to the earlier low profile of the government on this issue, Geingob dismissed this advice. He asserted that the Namibian People would not stop talking about reparations, given how many people had died at the hands of the German imperial forces, asserting that Namibians had the right to express themselves. Under the title 'Rude, crude and undesirable', the editorial in the weekly *Windhoek Observer* posted on 8 February 2013 gave voice to Namibian frustrations:

> The fact that Germany keeps sending us such arrogant, crude and tactless ambassadors is clearly their way of telling us what they think of us.
>
> Who the hell is Hückmann to tell Namibians what they can, and cannot, talk about?
>
> Imagine how German chancellor Angela Merkel would react if the Namibian ambassador walked into her office and started telling her the German people must stop talking about this or that.

In the end, official German foreign policy, as represented by its diplomats in Namibia, most likely achieved more effectively than any earlier initiatives by members of the most affected local communities, government identification with their cause, which now sided with their demands.

Another visit by the former minister Wieczorek-Zeul was much better received. As an MP for the opposition Social Democratic Party, she had displayed strong empathy when attending the ceremonial handover of the skulls. In late January 2013, she was in Namibia to bring back to life the special initiative she had introduced as a minister after her visit in 2004. Her host was the Namibian–German Parliamentary Friendship Group, whose members visited Germany in March 2013. Underlying all public statements on both occasions was an eagerly stressed willingness to find adequate ways to deal with a common past. But an amicable solution does not seem (yet?) to be in sight. Those among the Herero and Nama who are close to the initiatives demanding compensation continue to express scepticism. For them, such exchanges have the taste of yet another effort to duck and dive, and to thereby avoid dealing with the real issue, namely, that of reparations (Matundu-Tjiparuro 2013a; 2013b).

Conclusion

More than a century after the Genocide took place in what was then labelled 'German South West Africa', commemoration of the events is closely related to the still – albeit less – contested notion of genocide and the adequate forms of dealing with this past. Only Namibian Independence in 1990 allowed the descendants of the directly affected local population groups, most prominently representatives of various Herero communities, to bring their case to a wider, international, audience. They did this originally in a rather exclusivist fashion, claiming almost sole victim status, while other directly affected groups such as the Nama and Damara did not enjoy similar levels of visibility and representation due to a lack of agency and an absence of similarly concerted efforts.

Parallel to the emerging claims by the Herero is the discussion over the warfare by German colonial troops being tantamount to the classification as genocide. This discussion gained a hitherto unknown dynamic in Germany and the German-speaking community in Namibia at the beginning of this century and in anticipation of the centenary of the decisive battles that defeated the Herero during the military encounters that started in mid-1904. Both the German and the Namibian governments largely abstained from this discourse and avoided entering any commitments as to the unresolved issues of recognition and compensation.

More recently, debates over current policy have had a direct impact on Namibian–German bilateral relations. Contributing factors extended beyond the well-publicized Herero case. From 2004, representatives of the Nama and Damara adopted a more visible role, reinforcing wider demands to come to terms with the past. Similarly, taking 2004 as their point of departure, members of German civil society groups engaged in a visible campaign of international solidarity that dealt in particular with the German colonial past – a campaign that managed to occupy at least some limited public space in Germany. Both Namibian and German governments subsequently became engaged to some greater extent with these issues, if only by the mere force of circumstance, with other parties setting the agenda.

This might have also been a supporting factor for the initiatives to seek clarification with regard to the whereabouts of skulls brought to Germany for anthropological research during the war against the Herero and Nama. A first transfer of such skulls identified beyond any doubt subsequently took place in late 2011. The Namibian government played a more official role than it had ever played before and, significantly, the Namibian delegation was composed of members of nearly all affected groups. The German government's response and approach to handling the matter then created frustration among the Namibian officials. Further insensitivities by German diplomats subsequently resulted in a new alliance, contributing to a closer common understanding between groups of the Herero, Nama and Damara on the one hand, and the Namibian government on the other hand vis-à-vis the official German position that evaded responsibility by dismissing claims and blaming victims for 'unreasonable' behaviour. As a result of this realignment, the demands for an adequate treatment of the historical record have become more prominent and pressing than ever before.

Notes

1 At the beginning of the First World War, South African troops fighting as part of the allied forces invaded under the command of General Smuts the territory and

forced the Germans to surrender after several military encounters. As part of the Treaty of Versailles, the former German colonies were transferred under the mandate of other colonial powers of the time. South West Africa was declared a C-mandate under the trusteeship of the League of Nations, and the Union of South Africa was tasked with executing the mandate on behalf of the British Crown. Despite being a founding member of the United Nations, South Africa refuted the organization's claim to supervise the mandate through its Trusteeship Council. In the 1950s and 1960s, the issue became a contested notion in international law. The conflict escalated with the founding of the anti-colonial movement SWAPO (South West African People's Organization). A UN Council for Namibia was established in the early 1970s, and negotiations over a decolonization haven been taking place since the mid-1970s. A UN-supervised transition to Independence was finally implemented in 1989–1990. Only since then have the Herero and other local groups as citizens of the sovereign Namibian state had the formal right and access to seek recognition and compensation through international legal bodies for injustices and crimes committed against them earlier on.

2 Parts of this chapter are based on an earlier publication (Melber 2011).

3 The document was adopted as 'Revised and Updated Report on the Question of the Prevention and Punishment of the Crime of Genocide' (Document E/CN.4/Sub.2/1985/6, 2 July 1985).

4 For a discussion of the relevance of colonial atrocities for the development of the genocide convention and the definition of genocide, see Melber (2008).

5 For a summary of the opposing positions and an overview of their protagonists, see Böhlke-Itzen (2004). Many among them refer to Lau (1989, 1995) as a central source. Dedering (1993) and Hillebrecht (2007) presented major contributions dismissing Lau's position.

6 See Melber (2005b); Kössler (2005); Zimmerer (2008). Critics of these views tend to construct a notion of linearity, determinism or monocausality between the subsequent events, which none of us would formulate (cf. Kundrus 2005). Interestingly enough, she presents a range of challenging research topics, much in line with the suggested explorations by those she had just criticized.

7 The South West Africa People's Organization (SWAPO) – later renamed SWAPO of Namibia and since Independence renamed Swapo Party – has since its establishment in 1960 become the decisive local movement to fight for self-determination. It has held absolute political power ever since Independence.

8 The particular Herero perspective of the Genocide and its consequences informs the work of Jan-Bart Gewald (summarized in Gewald 2003).

9 Quoted in 'Whose Genocide? Why are Only the Herero Taking the Bull by the Horns?', *Insight*, September 2004: 20.

10 The following summary of events is based on a variety of newspaper reports and other articles not cited in detail. For related summaries, see, inter alia, various articles in *afrika süd*, esp. 5 (2011) and 2 (2012), Melber (2013a, 2013b) and the various reports in *Pambazuka News. A Weekly Electronic Forum for Social Justice in Africa*, 577, Special Issue: Germany and Genocide in Namibia. 20 March 2012, as well as the continued postings on the following websites: http://www.berlin-postkolonial.de/cms/, http://www.freiburg-postkolonial.de/ and http://www.africavenir.org/project-cooperations/german-genocide-in-namibia.html.

11 Kazenambo Kazenambo was born in Botswana. He was the son of a Herero family that had sought refuge from German colonial extermination by fleeing through the Kalahari into neighbouring Bechuanaland. He joined the anti-colonial liberation struggle conducted by SWAPO in exile and returned to the land of his ancestors after Independence. An outspoken and unorthodox minister, he was replaced in a cabinet shuffle in December 2012. He always felt strongly about German colonial history. In September 2010, he was in transit at Munich Airport

(returning from a UN conference in Mexico), suspected of carrying a forged passport and subsequently interrogated. He missed his connecting flight, and the incident resulted in a brawl during which he exchanged heated words with members of the German border police. On 14 September 2010, the state-owned Namibian local daily *New Era* quoted him as accusing German officials of an attitude like that exhibited when they 'massacred and committed genocide here' and of behaving 'like neo-Nazis and neo-Hitlers [sic]'.

Bibliography

Bley, H. (1968 and 1971) *Kolonialherrschaft und Sozialstruktur in Deutsch-Südwestafrika 1894–1914*, Hamburg: Leibniz. English edition: *South West Africa under German Rule, 1884–1915*, London: Heinemann.

Böhlke-Itzen, J. (2004) *Kolonialschuld und Entschädigung. Der deutsche Völkermord an den Herero 1904–1907*, Frankfurt am Main: Brandes & Apsel.

Bühler, A.H. (2003) *Der Namaaufstand gegen die deutsche Kolonialherrschaft in Namibia von 1904–1913*, Frankfurt am Main: IKO.

Conrad, S. (2008 and 2012) *Deutsche Kolonialgeschichte*, München: Beck. English edition: *German Colonialism: A Short History*, Cambridge and New York: Cambridge University Press.

Dedering, T. (1993) 'The German–Herero War of 1904: Revisionism of Genocide or Imaginary Historiography?', *Journal of Southern African Studies*, 19.1: 80–88.

Department of Information and Publicity/SWAPO of Namibia. (1981) *To Be Born a Nation: The Liberation Struggle for Namibia*, London: Zed Books.

Drechsler, H. (1966 and 1980) *Südwestafrika unter deutscher Kolonialherrschaft. Der Kampf der Herero und Nama gegen den deutschen Imperialismus (1884–1915)*, Berlin: Akademie Verlag. English edition: *'Let Us Die Fighting' – The Struggle of the Herero and Nama against German Imperialism (1884–1915)*, London: Zed Books.

Fleming, M. (2005) 'Holocaust and Memory', *Ethnopolitics*, 4.1: 115–123.

Förster, L. (2010) *Postkoloniale Erinnerungslandschaften: Wie Deutsche und Herero in Namibia des Kriegs von 1904 gedenken*, Frankfurt am Main: Campus Verlag.

Förster, L., D. Henrichsen and M. Bollig (eds). (2004) *Namibia – Deutschland. Eine geteilte Geschichte.Widerstand – Gewalt –* Erinnerung, Köln and Wolfratshausen: Edition Minerva.

Gewald, J.-B. (1999) *Herero Heroes: A Socio-Political History of the Herero of Namibia 1890–1923*, Oxford: James Currey, Cape Town: David Philip and Athens: Ohio University Press.

——. (2003) 'Herero Genocide in the Twentieth Century: Politics and Memory', in J. Abbink, M. de Bruijn and K. van Walraven (eds) *Rethinking Resistance: Revolt and Violence in African History*, Leiden and Boston: Brill: 279–304.

Heise, S. (2002) 'Herero-Häuptling greift Deutschland an', *Allgemeine Zeitung*. 27 August. Also available at: http://www.az.com.na/politik/herero-huptling-greift-deutschland-an.3564.php.

Hillebrecht, W. (2007) '"Certain Uncertainties" or Venturing Progressively into Colonial Apologetics?' *Journal of Namibian Studies*, 1: 73–95.

Hobuss, S. and U. Lölke (eds). (2007) *Erinnern verhandeln: Kolonialismus im kollektiven Gedächtnis Afrikas und Europas*, Münster: Westfälisches Dampfboot.

Hofmann, E. (2003) 'Briefmarke zur Versöhnung', *Allgemeine Zeitung*. 27 November. Also available at: http://az.com.na/lokales/briefmarke-zur-vershnung.6475.php.

Kandetu, V. (2005) 'Namibia: Cold Discourse upon Chronic Pain', *New African*, 436: 64–66.

Kössler, R. (2003) 'Public Memory, Reconciliation and the Aftermath of War: A Preliminary Framework with Special Reference to Namibia', in H. Melber (ed.) *Re-examining Liberation in Namibia: Political Culture since Independence*, Uppsala: Nordic Africa Institute: 99–112.

——. (2005) 'From Genocide to Holocaust? Structural Parallels and Discursive Continuities', *Afrika Spectrum*, 40.2: 309–317.

——. (2010a) 'Genocide and Reparations: Dilemmas and Exigencies in Namibian–German Relations', in A. du Pisani, R. Kössler and W.A. Lindeke (eds) *The Long Aftermath of War: Reconciliation and Transition in Namibia*, Freiburg: Arnold Bergstraesser Institut: 215–241.

——. (2010b) 'Political Intervention and the Image of History: Communal Memory Events in Central and Southern Namibia', in A. du Pisani, R. Kössler and W.A. Lindeke (eds) *The Long Aftermath of War: Reconciliation and Transition in Namibia*, Freiburg: Arnold Bergstraesser Institut: 371–402.

——. (2011) 'Communal Memory Events and the Heritage of the Victims: The Persistence of the Theme of Genocide in Namibia', in M. Perraudin and J. Zimmerer with K. Heady (eds) *German Colonialism and National Identity*, New York and London: Routledge: 235–250.

Kössler, R. and H. Melber. (2012a) 'The Genocide in Namibia (1904–1908) and its Consequences: Toward a Culture of Memory for a Memory Culture Today – A German Perspective', *Pambazuka News. A Weekly Electronic Forum for Social Justice in Africa*, 577. Special Issue: Germany and Genocide in Namibia, 20 March.

——. (2012b) 'German–Namibian Denialism. How (not) to Come to Terms with the Past', *Pambazuka News. A Weekly Electronic Forum for Social Justice in Africa*, 577. Special Issue: Germany and Genocide in Namibia. 20 March.

Krüger, G. (1999) *Kriegsbewältigung und Geschichtsbewusstsein: Realität, Deutung und Verarbeitung des deutschen Kolonialkrieges in Namibia 1904–1907*, Göttingen: Vandenhoeck & Ruprecht.

Kundrus, B. (2005) 'From the Herero to the Holocaust? The Current Debate', *Afrika Spectrum*, 40.2: 299–308.

Kuteeue, P. (2004a) 'Nujoma to Miss 1904 Genocide Service', *The Namibian*. 9 January. Also available at: http://allafrica.com/stories/200401090214.html.

——. (2004b) 'No Apology, No Payout for Herero', *The Namibian*. 12 January. Also available at: http://www.namibian.com.na/indexx.php?archive_id=5107&page_type=archive_story_detail&page=5705.

Lau, B. (1989 and 1995) 'Uncertain Certainties: The Herero–German War of 1904', *Mibagus*, 2: 4–8. Reprinted in *History and Historiography. 4 Essays in Reprint*, Windhoek: National Archives of Namibia: 39–52.

Lundtofte, H. (2003) '"I believe that the nation as such must be annihilated ... " – the Radicalization of the German Suppression of the Herero Rising in 1904', in S.L.B. Jensen (ed.) *Genocide: Cases, Comparisons and Contemporary Debates*, Copenhagen: Danish Centre for Holocaust and Genocide Studies: 15–53.

Matundu-Tjiparuro, K. (2013a) 'Namibia: Special Initiative a Trojan Horse against Reparations Cause?', *New Era*. 25 January. Also available at: http://allafrica.com/stories/201301250546.html.

——. (2013b) 'Whither the Special Initiative?', *New Era*. 1 March. Also available at: http://allafrica.com/stories/201303011140.html.

Melber, H. (2003), '"Namibia, Land of the Brave": Selective Memories on War and Violence within Nation Building', in J. Abbink, M. de Bruijn and K. van Walraven (eds) *Rethinking Resistance: Revolt and Violence in African History*, Leiden and Boston: Brill: 305–327.

——. (ed.). (2005a) *Genozid und Gedenken: Namibisch-deutsche Geschichte und Gegenwart*, Frankfurt am Main: Brandes & Apsel.

——. (2005b) 'How to Come to Terms with the Past: Re-visiting the German Colonial Genocide in Namibia', *Afrika Spectrum*, 40.1: 139–148.

——. (2005c) 'Namibia's Past in the Present: Colonial Genocide and Liberation Struggle in Commemorative Narratives', *South African Historical Journal*, 54: 91–111.

——. (ed.). (2008) *Revisiting the Heart of Darkness: Explorations into Genocide and Other Forms of Mass Violence*, Uppsala: Dag Hammarskjöld Foundation.

——. (2011) 'The Genocide in "German South West Africa" and the Politics of Commemoration: How (Not) to Come to Terms with the Past', in M. Perraudin and J. Zimmerer with K. Heady (eds) *German Colonialism and National Identity*, New York and London: Routledge: 251–264.

——. (2013a) 'Dealing with the Past: Colonial Shadows', *Development and Cooperation (D+C)*, 40.2: 76–77.

——. (2013b) 'German–Namibian Relations Remain Fragile', *The Namibian*. 15 February. Also available at: http://allafrica.com/stories/201302160327.html.

Olusoga, D. and C. Erichsen. (2009) The Kaiser's Holocaust: Germany's Forgotten Genocide and the Colonial Roots of Nazism, London: Faber & Faber.

Sarkin, J. (2009) *Colonial Genocide and Reparations Claims in the 21st Century: The Socio-Legal Context of Claims under International Law by the Herero against Germany for Genocide in Namibia, 1904–1908*, Westport and London: Praeger.

——. (2011) *Germany's Genocide of the Herero: Kaiser Wilhelm II, His General, His Settlers, His Soldiers*, Cape Town: UCT Press and London: James Currey.

Schaller, D.J. (2011) 'The Struggle for Genocidal Exclusivity: The Perception of the Murder of the Namibian Herero (1904–1908) in the Age of a New International Morality', in M. Perraudin and J. Zimmerer with K. Heady (eds), *German Colonialism and National Identity*, New York and London: Routledge: 265–277.

Schmitt-Egner, P. (1975) *Kolonialismus und Faschismus: Eine Studie zur historischen und begrifflichen Genesis faschistischer Bewusstseinsformen am deutschen Beispiel*, Giessen and Lollar: Achenbach.

Schreiber, I. (2003) 'Debatte um Gedenken. 1904 – nationale oder ethnische Gedenkfeier?', *Allgemeine Zeitung*. 1 December. Also available at: http://az.com.na/lokales/debatte-um-gedenken.6503.php.

Sibeene, P. (2012) 'German Ambassador Peeves Pohamba', *Windhoek Observer*. 27 January–2 February.

Tjingaete, R. (n.d.) *The Weeping Graves of our Ancestors*, Windhoek: Capital Press.

von Trotha, T. (2003) 'Genozidaler Pazifizierungskrieg: Soziologische Anmerkungen zum Konzept des Genozids am Beispiel des Kolonialkriegs in Deutsch-Südwestafrika, 1904–1907', *Zeitschrift für Genozidforschung*, 4.2: 31–58.

Wallace, M. with J. Kinahan. (2011) *A History of Namibia: From the Beginning to 1990*, London: Hurst.

Zeller, J. (2005) 'Genozid und Gedenken: ein dokumentarischer Überblick', in H. Melber (ed.) *Genozid und Gedenken: Namibisch-deutsche Geschichte und Gegenwart*, Frankfurt am Main: Brandes & Apsel: 163–188.

Zimmerer, J. (2001) *Deutsche Herrschaft über Afrikaner: Staatlicher Machtanspruch und Wirklichkeit im kolonialen Namibia*, Münster: LIT.

——. (2008) *Von Windhuk nach Auschwitz? Beiträge zum Verhältnis von Kolonialismus und Holocaust*, Münster: LIT.

Zimmerer, J. and J. Zeller (eds). (2003 and 2008) *Völkermord in Deutsch-Südwestafrika: Der Kolonialkrieg (1904–1908) in Namibia und seine Folgen*, Berlin: Ch. Links. English edition: *Genocide in German South-West Africa: The Colonial War of 1904–1908 and its Aftermath*, London: Merlin Press.

9 Burying genocide

Official remembrance and reconciliation in Australia

Damien Short

Introduction: Reconciliation, settler colonialism and genocide

Within the now well-established fields of transitional justice, reconciliation and memory studies, academic analysis of 'post-conflict' responses usually focuses on the associated institutional 'innovations' (Lederach 1999) such as 'truth telling' commissions, victim hearings, perpetrator amnesty provisions and various forms of collective memory production. When 'reconciliation' processes attempt to accommodate the key concerns such as truth, justice, vengeance and forgiveness, they often utilize a combination of symbolic measures – such as official apologies, commemoration memorials and the like – and more practical measures – such as truth commissions and reparations tribunals – in an attempt to repair societies torn apart by gross human rights violations and/or war.

The complexion of reconciliation initiatives will of course vary depending on the context. For example, Rwanda and the former Yugoslavia, which suffered acute ruptures over relatively short time frames, exhibited considerable differences in their approach to post-conflict peace-building and reconciliation, but perhaps more significant differences exist between such contexts and the less-spectacular, but more pervasive, long-term colonial 'conflicts' between Indigenous peoples and settler states in countries like Australia, Canada, New Zealand and the United States. In the latter contexts, any notion of 'reconciliation' that seeks to build a common identity is deeply problematic, given that the Indigenous peoples therein have strongly defended their alterity in the face of hundreds of years of colonization. The 're' in reconciliation seems inappropriate in these contexts, as the two sides were never 'together' as such (Short 2005).

Australia's attempt at 'reconciliation' is interesting due to the nature of 'settlement', the origins of the reconciliation process itself and the official, albeit belated, 2008 apology from the prime minister for the child removal practices which were deemed genocidal by the landmark Human Rights and Equal Opportunity Commission's report – *Bringing Them Home: National Inquiry into the Separation of Aboriginal and Torres Strait Islander Children from Their Families* (HREOC 1997), generally known as *Bringing Them Home*

(BTH), a report which consequently caused much controversy. The question of genocide in the Australian past, with very few notable exceptions (Barta 1985; Tatz 1999), was only seriously interrogated after the landmark BTH report had been released in the latter half of the ten-year reconciliation process which began with the Council for Aboriginal Reconciliation Act (CARA) 1991.[1] The subsequent scholarly works that consider the question of genocide in Australia focused on the 'dispersal' extermination campaigns of the 1800s and/or the issue of the 'Stolen Generations' (the term commonly used to refer to Indigenous children removed from their communities) (Moses 2004: 16). Much discussion in these studies concerned the ubiquitous problem of genocide scholarship – the search for positive and provable genocidal intent – which is commonly interpreted as a specific intent to destroy a social group *because of who they are*. Such a focus in the Australian case is perhaps understandable, since in the early years after invasion many Indigenous fatalities were not the direct consequence of an intended policy of extermination. Unknown illnesses such as smallpox accounted for the greatest number, while alcohol, malnutrition, demoralization and despair played their fatal part. Furthermore, it could be argued that the colonizer's intent was to take over a land, not to eradicate an ethnic or religious group. In this sense, we could say that territoriality is settler colonialism's specific, irreducible element (Wolfe 2006: 388). Yet, the British desire to plant colonies in Australia meant *supplanting* the property of Indigenous populations (Barta 2008a: 115), and as Patrick Wolfe (2006: 387) observes, 'land is life – or, at least, land is necessary for life (and) thus contests for land can be – indeed, often are – contests for life'. The land grab that followed involved significant amounts of violence and population 'transfers' of Indigenous groups, such that when considered alongside the effects of illness and malnutrition, it seemed 'inevitable' that the Indigenous peoples of Australia would die out and disappear (Barta 2008a). Tony Barta, in a now seminal essay that originally appeared in 1987 and which avoided an overly intentionalist take on the question of genocide in Australian history, argued that 'it is not too simplistic to see in this dominant opinion (that Indigenous groups would simply "die out and disappear") the most comfortable ideological reflection of a relationship which could only be recognised in good conscience for what it was – a relationship of genocide' (Barta 2000: 248).

While writers like Barta, Wolfe, and more recently myself (Short 2010), imply that genocidal structuring dynamics are still at work in Australia,[2] present-day Indigenous and non-Indigenous social and political relations – and the colonial structures in which they operate – are rarely discussed through the analytical lens of genocide. Yet, while direct physical killing and genocidal child removal practices may have ceased, some Indigenous people contend that genocide *is a continuing process* in an Australia that has failed to decolonize and continues to actively promote assimilation.[3] Such a contention is predicated on a victim's understanding of a culturally genocidal dimension of settler colonialism and, in particular, the central importance of land to Indigenous peoples' cultural survival *as peoples*. Such views are in keeping with Raphael Lemkin's original concept of genocide, that he developed in the 1940s, and appreciate that 'cultural' destruction can be a key *method* of genocide rather than a lesser form of genocide. Moreover, such an understanding appreciates that there is an inherent relationship between colonization and genocide – a point which was central to the work of the term's originator.

Lemkin (1944) titled his book on the Nazi Empire *Axis Rule in Occupied Europe* in order to place it, as Dirk Moses points out, in the 'tradition of criticizing brutal conquests. Indeed, genocide for Lemkin was a special form of foreign conquest and occupation. It was necessarily imperial and colonial in nature. In particular, genocide aimed to permanently tip the demographic balance in favor of the occupier' (Moses 2008: 9–10). A key strand of recent genocide scholarship focuses on the nexus between colonization processes[4] and genocidal practices.[5] Lemkin viewed genocide as an 'intrinsically colonial' product (Moses 2008: 9), and he clearly appreciated the importance of culture to group life and that destruction of such life would have dire *physical* consequences – which is especially true of colonized Indigenous peoples. I have argued elsewhere (Short 2010) that a Lemkin-inspired understanding of genocide is an important analytical tool for understanding the situation of Indigenous peoples both historically and also today – not simply because the concept itself has a rich intellectual history, but because it emphasizes what is at stake for many Indigenous peoples in settler colonial contexts, that is, their very survival as distinct peoples.

The 'logic of elimination' (Wolfe 2006: 387) that informed frontier massacres in places like Australia and North America, and the assimilationist agendas that emerged when the natives survived the onslaught, can in more recent times be found underpinning settler colonial expansionist land grabs driven by the logic of global capitalism. In the years after 1945, traditional forms of colonial terror transformed into a '"genocide machine" as the nature of capitalist domination became less overtly racist and more attuned to ... corporate imperatives' (Davis and Zannis quoted in Moses 2008: 24). Even today, governments frequently dispossess Indigenous groups through industrial mining and farming, but also through military operations and national park schemes – all of which routinely take no account of core Indigenous rights.[6]

In Australia today, the issue of genocide is not just an academic matter, nor is it simply relevant to settler state attempts to atone for *past* practices; rather, it is also relevant to understanding the political functions and human consequences of *contemporary* policies and practices that routinely undermine Indigenous peoples' basic human rights as peoples, whilst talking of 'reconciliation', atonement and 'improving the lot' of the Aborigines. In the following sections, I will explore the links between the official reconciliation process, the apology to the Stolen Generations, genocide and the need to decolonize.

Historical context of Indigenous–settler relations

The First Fleet of European colonizers arrived on Gamaraigal land on 26 January 1788. The early reports of William Dampier, the English pirate/explorer, and Captain James Cook (and others) generally portrayed the 'natives' of New Holland, as the continent was then called, as small in number, wandering nomadically with no fixed territory and with no recognizable system of laws and customs (Dampier 1927 [1697]: 312), and so the colonizers applied the legal doctrine of *terra nullius*, meaning 'land of no one', to the Australian continent. The philosophical eurocentric underpinnings of this assertion were based on John Locke's seventeenth-century notion of property ownership. In his *Two Treatises of Government*, Locke proposed that property in land originated from tilling the soil, 'mixing labour with land' (1970 [1689]), and the apparent absence of such activities led to the colonizer's conviction that the natives had no investment in the soil and hence no legitimate claim to it. This outlook served to legitimize the widespread use of the *terra nullius* concept in eighteenth-century international law, facilitating colonial expansion and the dispossession of native peoples.

The application of the *terra nullius* doctrine in uninhabited lands was clear; a European power that discovered a new *uninhabited* territory was entitled to claim the land for its empire. However, where lands were inhabited by 'uncivilized natives', the British adopted Lockean ownership principles to discount the moral claims of the Indigenous inhabitants. In other parts of the British Empire, where the inhabitants were not regarded as quite so 'uncivilized' (e.g. New Zealand), the Crown claimed sovereignty over, but not ownership of, the land.

In an attempt to 'legitimately' gain land, the Crown would ordinarily enter into treaties with the Indigenous inhabitants. Even so, in many cases these treaties merely reflected the unequal bargaining position facing the Indigenous peoples and were often violated in practice. Nevertheless, in the United States and Canada, for example, the British recognized and treated with the natives. In Australia, however, the *terra nullius* doctrine prevailed even though the reality of Indigenous organization was quite different to that implied by the doctrine. It is estimated that, when European colonizers first arrived, there were between 300,000 and 1,000,000 Aborigines in Australia and around 500 different regional groups.[7] The culture of traditional Aboriginal people was diverse in terms of language, totems, food and daily routine, but with a communality of territoriality, kinship, spirituality, 'Dreaming', art, family structures, education, initiation and ceremonies. Moreover, anthropological and historical studies of Australian Aborigines have demonstrated that they, over tens of thousands of years, developed complex forms of social organization, including laws relating to land use and management (Greer 1993).

Disregarding this reality, the *terra nullius* doctrine formed the basis for European settlement along the coast and gradually penetrated into the farthest reaches of the continent. The often unauthorized settler 'squatting' of herds and flocks on areas well beyond established settlement boundaries led to the inevitable, and frequently disastrous, conflict with the Indigenous peoples of the continent (see Reynolds 1981). As Charles Rowley states, the native inhabitants of Australia did not 'melt away magically before the tide of European settlement like fairy floss ... the hard reality is that we killed them' (Rowley 1970: 154). Between 1788 and 1884, the Indigenous death toll in the conflict is estimated to have been around 20,000. In addition to the physical killing, their dispossession from their lands and the destruction of the natural environment also destroyed the basis of Indigenous peoples' spiritual, cultural and legal systems. Aborigines had a spiritual attachment to the land and considered themselves as belonging to the land, as many still do. It is an integral part of their mythology as well as being their home, hunting ground, recreation place, cathedral or temple, court of law, cemetery and the place to which their spirits return after death (Greer 1993).

In 1872, the colonial authorities introduced a system of 'pastoral leases', a form of tenure tailored for the peculiar conditions of Australia, in a bid to regulate uncontrolled occupation of vast tracts of land by squatters and minimize conflict with the Aborigines. The squatters were allowed to use the land only for grazing, while the Aborigines had access to the land for their traditional practices and certain other permitted activities. The new legal arrangement, however, did not stop the conflict. Massacres, poisoning of flour and waterholes and the banishment of Aboriginal people from traditional sources of food and water were used by pastoralists and others as 'dispersal' measures (Rowley 1970: 154).

Aborigines were tolerated when they could act as a pool of cheap labour for the emerging pastoralists (see May 1996; Reynolds 1981). Given their intimate knowledge of the land and ability to survive under harsh conditions, the Aborigines made excellent stockmen and became the backbone of the livestock industry. Yet their wages were usually around half those of White workers, and such employment did little to halt the general trend of dispossession, which was accelerated by government resettlement programmes and assimilation policies (see Haebich 2001). The general settler view by the end of the century was that there was a direct relationship between colonial progress and the destruction of Aboriginal society (Johnston 1992: 10.4).

The loss of their lands and autonomy along with the resultant cultural erosion and welfare dependency led to a startling decline in the health and well-being of many Indigenous groups. Faced with such a position and coupled with the failure of violent resistance, Indigenous groups began to mobilize politically. The modern movement for Indigenous rights began in the 1920s with the formation of several Aboriginal political organizations.[8] They focused their attention on government 'protection' policies (controlling where people could live and work, what they could do and who they could meet or marry) that were effectively destroying their communities and cultures. They campaigned for justice, citizenship rights, land rights and freedom from the restrictions imposed on them by various pieces of discriminatory state legislation.

In the mid-1960s, inspired by the 'Freedom Riders' of the civil rights movement in the United States, Charles Perkins and a group of Aboriginal and White students conducted the fact-finding and protest-oriented 'freedom rides' of 1964 and 1965 throughout the north-west of New South Wales. The rides brought an end to many discriminatory practices and a new awareness of the power of active protest (see Curthoys 2002). The success of the freedom rides, coupled with frustration at failed attempts by the Gurindji and Yirrkala people in the Northern Territory to protect their traditional lands from mining exploration, led to a new, more forthright direction in Aboriginal activism.

In 1966, poor working conditions and low wages of Indigenous pastoral workers prompted the Wave Hill strike in the Northern Territory, which eventually led to the Commonwealth Conciliation and Arbitration Commission ruling for equal wages. Unfortunately, the decision led pastoralists to mechanize stock management, employ European stockmen, and sack Indigenous workers on a large scale. Since Aboriginal people were no longer a cheap 'on-site' labour pool, there was increasing pressure to move Aboriginal communities off the land.

A significant, and arguably positive, development came on 27 May 1967, when a referendum that was called by the government of Prime Minister Harold Holt approved two amendments to the Australian Constitution that related to Indigenous peoples. The Federal Parliament was given a constitutional power, under which it could make special laws 'for' Aboriginal people (for their benefit, but importantly it did not preclude laws that worked to their detriment) in addition to other 'races'. On Australia Day 1972, in a more symbolic but nonetheless enduring development, with the aid of the Communist Party of Australia, four Aboriginal activists travelled to Canberra to establish the 'Aboriginal Tent Embassy' in protest at their continuing dispossession and severely disadvantaged status. Such forthright protests gradually began to draw attention to the plight of Indigenous peoples, whose focus was firmly on regaining their political autonomy and a land base from which to regenerate their culture.

Unlike the other settler colonial contexts discussed above, no treaties with Indigenous peoples were signed by the British colonies in Australia in the late eighteenth or nineteenth centuries or subsequently on the foundation of the Australian Commonwealth in 1901. Since the absence of a treaty challenged the legitimacy of the settler state itself, it was perhaps unsurprising that Indigenous political mobilization eventually sought to campaign for a treaty or treaties. The notion of a treaty had significant potential. Whilst many Indigenous groups had been totally dispossessed of their traditional lands and relocated to government-designated 'reserves', there still existed the possibility of returning land and political autonomy to those that *had* managed to maintain traditional connections to their land. Significant tracts of vacant 'crown' land and Indigenous-occupied reserve land could also be returned to Indigenous ownership and control.

In 1979, the National Aboriginal Conference, a government-established forum for the expression of Aboriginal views, instigated a concerted campaign for a treaty that would recognize and restore Aboriginal rights to land and political autonomy, and that would compensate Aboriginal peoples for the loss of and damage to their traditional lands and way of life – all while protecting Aboriginal identity, languages, law and culture. The notion of negotiating a 'treaty' brought strong opposition from prominent politicians concerned that it would imply an agreement between two 'sovereign nations', which was of course problematic as, from the time of conquest up to the present, Aboriginal people have never officially been regarded as possessing nationhood or sovereignty. As Roediger and Wertsch (2008: 13) confirm, 'national narratives of one sort or another help organise historical memories of a people', and since the nineteenth century, the dominant nationalist settler 'narrative template' has been the 'one nation and one state, in one territory' formula of nationhood (Moran 1998: 107). Legally and culturally, the settler state constituted itself as the only sovereign nation within the territory, a situation that resulted in no significant dialogue on the notion of a treaty. In 1988, John Howard, the then opposition leader (later to become prime minister), suggested that 'it is an absurd proposition that a nation should make a treaty with some of its own citizens'.

This type of attitude gradually led government ministers to use the equivocal, more open-ended terms 'compact' or 'agreement,' a dilution signalling the political demise of the treaty campaign. From these debates emerged a new policy direction fuelled by the influential 1983 Senate Standing Committee report, which dismissed the treaty idea and concluded that societal 'attitudes' lay at the heart of the 'Aboriginal problem'. In 1988, the government reneged on a prior commitment to a treaty, suggesting that non-Indigenous Australians needed to be 'educated' about the Aboriginal problem before they would be ready for a treaty.

Australian reconciliation

In early ministerial discussions on the nature of the reconciliation process, the Federal Minister for Aboriginal and Torres Strait Islander Affairs, Robert Tickner, suggested that 'there can be no reconciliation without justice' (2001: 29). Even so, the need for cross-party consensus made sure that 'education' for the non-Indigenous rather than 'justice' for the Indigenous emerged as the dominant focus of the process. And yet the preamble to the enabling legislation, the Council for Aboriginal Reconciliation Act (CARA) 1991, outlined the rationale for the process, clearly identifying the injustice that necessitated a formal reconciliation process – the original act of colonial dispossession and its legacy of Aboriginal social and political disadvantage, although as would be expected of a settler-state-led process, any acknowledgement of a 'colonial genocide' was absent, as was any commitment to specific measures to address the issues it did mention. All that remained of the treaty idea was the vague aspiration to produce a 'document of reconciliation' by the end of the ten-year process.

While an entirely Indigenous reconciliation council was initially envisaged (Short 2008: 36), the eventual format was a twenty-five-person council consisting of businessmen, government employees, academics and high-profile Aboriginal people, most of the latter having a background in the churches. The Council primarily had a dual role that involved devising community-wide education initiatives and advising the minister on possible policies that might further the reconciliation process.

A formal equality approach was adopted by the Council, which sought to balance Indigenous and non-Indigenous interests. This contrasted starkly with the 'victim group'-oriented treaty campaign of the late-1980s, from which the reconciliation process emerged. From the outset, Council rhetoric had a broad focus that sought to include the 'wider society' wherever possible (Short 2008: 110). Contrary to the more obvious approach of other reconciliation processes, such as the Truth and Reconciliation Commission of South Africa, official Australian reconciliation focused less on the needs of the victims and more on the educational needs of non-Indigenous Australians. Furthermore, and somewhat perversely for a top-down initiative instigated without serious consultation with Indigenous peoples (see Short 2008), the Council envisioned its process as 'bottom up', a process in which significant change would percolate through existing structures once non-Indigenous society had been sufficiently educated in Indigenous issues. Once again, this was far from the concrete practical measures demanded by the Treaty movement, which included land rights, self-determination, restitution, compensation and acknowledgement of the harms of colonization and their legacy.

In 1992, the High Court handed down the landmark Mabo judgement (*Mabo and Others* v. *Queensland* (No. 2) 1992), which exposed the colonial myth of *terra nullius* and held that in certain situations Indigenous groups *might* have rights to land, or 'native title', that had survived colonization. However, the burden of proof for native title fell on Indigenous groups. In order to acquire this group-specific right, they had to demonstrate their 'distinctiveness' by proving their 'traditional, and continuing, physical and spiritual connection' to their land. The laws and customs of the Indigenous peoples provided the content of native title. In the ruling, Justice Brennan stated:

> Native title has its origin in and is given its content by the traditional laws acknowledged by and the traditional customs observed by the indigenous inhabitants of a territory. The nature and incidents of native title must be ascertained as a matter of reference to those laws and customs.
>
> (Quoted in Mabo 1992: 42)

While the Court implicitly recognized the continuance of traditional laws and customs, it did not recognize any concomitant political autonomy or sovereignty, or value which such laws and customs had in their own right. Native title is merely a right of occupation. Dispossessed Indigenous groups stand no chance of regaining lost land. Even if they can prove 'traditional connection', they are still required to be in occupation. Following the Mabo decision, Prime Minister Paul Keating stated his desire to enact legislation to give legislative effect to the landmark decision (see Keating 2000).

On 10 December 1992, Keating delivered a speech in Sydney's Redfern Park to mark the Australian launch of the United Nations International Year of the World's Indigenous People. The speech has subsequently become known as the Redfern Park Statement (reproduced in Keating 2000). It was the first significant national governmental act of official remembrance during the reconciliation era. Many Indigenous people felt that the speech, combined with the Mabo case, represented valuable acknowledgement of colonial injustice and provided hope that the government would legislate measures to facilitate return of Indigenous lands to Indigenous control. To his credit, Keating pointed to the incongruous nature of contemporary Australia and highlighted what many would call the genocidal (although he did not use the word) aspects of Australian history:

> The starting point might be to recognise that the problem starts with us non-Aboriginal Australians. It begins, I think, with that act of recognition, that it was we who did the dispossessing, we took the traditional lands and smashed the traditional way of life. We brought the diseases. The alcohol. We committed the murders. We took the children from their mothers. We practised discrimination and exclusion.
>
> (Keating 2000)

The speech, as an official act of remembrance, provided public acknowledgement of certain key aspects of the historical facts of Australia's genocidal past, the like of which had never before been spoken by an Australian prime minister. The symbolic acknowledgement of harm was followed later in the speech by the hint of possible substantive structural change in the colonial relationship when Keating argued that the Mabo case could be 'the basis of a new relationship between Indigenous and non-Aboriginal Australians' (Keating 2000). Thus, the speech raised Indigenous expectations for a favourable national legislative response to Mabo that would facilitate dispossessed Indigenous peoples to regain lands and allow them to control their natural resources and veto any unwanted development.

Even so, the 1993 Native Title Act that followed was shaped in no small part by the interests of a powerful farming and extractive industry lobby that sought guarantees that future land negotiations would be conducted within the parameters set by existing power inequalities (Short 2007). Indeed, Prime Minister Paul Keating had earlier asserted that 'Aboriginal people understood that a generalised veto was never on and that there was some doubt that they even deserved a right of consultation and negotiation.'[9] Without a right to veto future development, land rights are largely meaningless, and such a denial of a meaningful land base is, I have argued, part of a continuing colonial genocidal process (Short 2010). Thus, despite Keating's Redfern talk of Mabo providing the 'building blocks of change' and a 'new relationship', when it came to the follow-up legislation, the decolonizing rhetoric which accompanied the apologetic official act of remembrance did not match the reality. As has been the case throughout Australian history, Indigenous interests were trumped by the settler need for territory. As Patrick Wolfe (2006) observes, 'territoriality' is settler colonialism's single irreducible element.

Significant inconsistencies between political rhetoric and political action are a pervasive feature of Australian state-driven initiatives which purport to further the cause of 'reconciliation'. The much-lauded, and belated, formal state apology to the Stolen Generations offers another illustration of this point, and it is to this that I will now turn.

Apology to the Stolen Generations

National remembrance initiatives, and 'apologies' more specifically, are politically important for several reasons: the way the past is presented and represented conveys information about present relations, while apologies define victims and perpetrators, and demarcate lines of acceptable conduct – which in turn send signals about future behaviour. With official acts of remembrance, such as apologies, national governments can influence the way societies remember the past, which in turn has implications for present and future public policy.

If we want to better understand the various interrelated dimensions of speech acts like apologies, it is useful to consider the influential work of J.L. Austin. His landmark 1962 study *How to Do Things with Words* outlined a theory of speech acts[10] which distinguished between those utterances which were 'constative' – used for stating things or conveying information – and those which, like an apology, were 'performative' – used for doing things or performing actions. Even so, merely saying a performative word does not accomplish the act, and while a performative utterance is neither true nor false, speech act theory highlights a set of conditions which allow us to consider such performative utterances 'felicitous' or 'infelicitous'. 'Felicity conditions' are vital to the success of many speech acts. Felicity conditions can be subdivided into three categories: preparatory conditions, conditions for execution and sincerity conditions. 'Preparatory conditions' can include the authority or status of the speaker to perform the speech act, the situation of other actors and the like, while 'conditions for execution' often refer to an accompanying act (often a ritual or ceremony) without which the speech act itself is seen as lacking. 'Sincerity conditions' are those which demonstrate that the speaker must really mean what they say and are thus of vital importance when considering certain performative speech acts such as official acts of remembrance and apology.

The theory and practice of reconciliation, as articulated in academic (e.g. Minow 1998) and practitioner (e.g. Lederach 1999) writing, attaches much importance to the reconciliatory potential of official acts of remembrance which acknowledge responsibility and express remorse via official apologies and reparations. Suitable reparations, within such a formula, will be for many (but of course not necessarily all) a vital *felicity condition* for a formal state apology – they may be a sincerity condition and, given the interrelated nature of apologies and reparations, a *condition for execution*. An apology without reparations runs the risk of seeming less sincere since *reparations themselves express implicitly or explicitly an apology* for wrongdoing or for failing to do more to resist atrocities. The symbolic dimension of reparations acknowledges the harms and accepts a degree of responsibility while guaranteeing non-repetition. Tavuchis (1991: 17) argues that 'to apologise is to declare voluntarily that one has no excuse, defence, justification, or explanation for an action (or inaction)'; and so the full acceptance of responsibility by the wrongdoer is the hallmark of a genuine apology, a crucial *sincerity* condition; and full acceptance of responsibility is often demonstrated by accompanying words with material compensation in a concrete demonstration of sincerity.

Apologies, as official acts of remembrance, can function to correct the public record, afford public acknowledgement of a violation, assign responsibility and reassert the moral baseline by defining the actions in question as violations of basic norms. Even so, they are less good at warranting any promise about the future, given the shifts in office holders (Muldoon 2009). Chancellor (1998: 8) argues that 'apologising is now the rage the world over, especially in the US, where it has long been a standard means of winning favour without paying any real price for one's mistakes'. However, whoever offers an apology cannot compel forgiveness, since it is still the surviving victim's right to withhold forgiveness. It is safe to say that unless vital felicity conditions are met – like direct and immediate material actions (payments of compensation and the like) that manifest responsibility for the violation, an official apology may seem superficial, insincere or meaningless (Minow 1998: 117).

During the second half of the official reconciliation process in Australia, there was much pressure on the government to issue a formal apology for one specific dimension of Indigenous–settler 'relations of genocide' (Barta 2000) – the issue of the 'Stolen Generations'. The Stolen Generations is the now-common term for the victims of a systematic, state-sanctioned, forcible removal policy in which thousands of Aboriginal babies and children of mixed descent were taken from their mothers, families and communities,[11] and yet despite the systematic and widespread nature of the 'removal' policies, they were shrouded in a great silence.

In 1969, W.E.H. Stanner observed that Australian history was a narrative silent about the relations between Aborigines and settlers, and he called upon historians to break what he termed the 'cult of forgetfulness' or 'the great Australian silence' (Stanner 1969: 25). By the late 1980s, the silence was being broken in the cultural realm with musicians like Archie Roach writing about the child removal policies in his song, 'They Took the Children Away'. In the academic realm, historian Peter Read coined the term 'Stolen Generations' in one of the first studies of child removal policies (1981) and with Coral Edwards produced a landmark book *The Lost Children* (Edwards and Read 1989). In 1996, Doris Pilkington wrote the now-famous book *Follow the Rabbit-Proof Fence* (an acclaimed film – *Rabbit-Proof Fence* – based on the book followed in 2002) about the living conditions in children's institutions in Western Australia, describing them as 'more like a concentration camp than a residential school for Aboriginal children' (Pilkington 1996: 72). And, as mentioned previously, it was not until 1997 that the silence was truly broken with the publication of Bringing Them Home (BTH), the Human Rights and Equal Opportunity Commission's national inquiry report into the Stolen Generations.

BTH contained harrowing evidence, finding that forcible removal of Indigenous children was a gross violation of human rights that continued well after Australia had undertaken international human rights commitments. In particular, the report concluded that the removal constituted *an act of genocide* contrary to the 1948 Convention (which forbids 'forcibly transferring children of [a] group to another group' with the intention of destroying the group).[12] Child removal was racially discriminatory because it only applied to Aboriginal children on that scale. The report linked the finding of genocide to the question of an apology, and both were discussed in the context of 'reparations'; the inquiry recommended further steps rather more concrete than saying sorry or pledging 'never again': it argued for monetary compensation (Barta 2008a: 208).

The power of Stanner's 'great Australian silence', with regard to the Stolen Generations in particular, was in evidence back in 1991 with the reconciliation process enabling legislation (CARA 1991) which omitted any reference to this particular genocidal episode. Given the magnitude of this particular colonial injustice, it was an astonishing omission for a national 'reconciliation' process. By some estimates, up to 100,000 children were removed under the policies from the early years of settlement up until the late 1970s. Even so, following publication of BTH the issue of the Stolen Generations became inextricably linked to the notion of 'reconciliation'. Indeed, a few years after the report Colin Tatz (1999) argued that Aborigines in general considered the Stolen Generations one of the most serious issues in their lives and, as such, that it must be addressed in a genuine attempt at reconciliation.

When the John Howard government (1996–2007) was faced with the publication of BTH (1997) and the widespread calls for an official apology, Howard chose to attack the report's findings with a form of what Cohen (2001: 109) has termed 'implicatory denial'. The closest Howard came to an official apology was to express regret for the 'blemish' of the past, since for him there was little to regret about an Australian history that broadly constituted an 'heroic and unique achievement against great odds' (Howard

2000: 90). For Howard, any voicing of concerns over postcolonial legitimacy simply displayed a lack of national self-confidence (Short 2008).

As the national election approached in November 2007, however, the then opposition leader Kevin Rudd promised to issue a formal state apology if the Labor Party returned to power. Even so, there was some surprise that Rudd made it the first order of business for the new parliament when the Howard government was ultimately defeated (Barta 2008a: 204). As Tony Barta (2008a: 204) writes:

> In the long years of waiting, and in the last weeks of consultation about the exact wording, Aborigines of the stolen generations made clear that 'sorry' was the only word that would do. Rudd did not fail them.

The fanfare surrounding the apology was truly extraordinary. As a television event, it was widely promoted; in major cities across Australia, giant screens were erected in the manner of a major sporting event so that crowds could gather. Schools allowed children out and Indigenous people from far and wide converged on Canberra to witness this historic event which finally took place on Wednesday 13 February 2008. The following is an extract from Rudd's speech:

> Today we honour the Indigenous peoples of this land, the oldest continuing cultures in human history. We reflect on their past mistreatment. We reflect in particular on the mistreatment of those who were Stolen Generations – this blemished chapter in our nation's history. The time has now come for the nation to turn a new page in Australia's history by righting the wrongs of the past and so moving forward with confidence to the future. We apologise for the laws and policies of successive Parliaments and governments that have inflicted profound grief, suffering and loss on these our fellow Australians.
>
> We apologise especially for the removal of Aboriginal and Torres Strait Islander children from their families, their communities and their country. For the pain, suffering and hurt of these Stolen Generations, their descendants and for their families left behind, we say sorry. To the mothers and the fathers, the brothers and the sisters, for the breaking up of families and communities, we say sorry. And for the indignity and degradation thus inflicted on a proud people and a proud culture, we say sorry. We the Parliament of Australia respectfully request that this apology be received in the spirit in which it is offered as part of the healing of the nation. For the future we take heart; resolving that this new page in the history of our great continent can now be written.
>
> We today take this first step by acknowledging the past and laying claim to a future that embraces all Australians. A future where this Parliament resolves that the injustices of the past must never, never happen again. A future where we harness the determination of all

> Australians, Indigenous and non-Indigenous, to close the gap that lies between us in life expectancy, educational achievement and economic opportunity. A future where we embrace the possibility of new solutions to enduring problems where old approaches have failed. A future based on mutual respect, mutual resolve and mutual responsibility. A future where all Australians, whatever their origins, are truly equal partners, with equal opportunities and with an equal stake in shaping the next chapter in the history of this great country, Australia.

When Rudd finished his further remarks, the house and the crowds outside erupted in applause. Ultimately, however, the most important issue was the apology's reception by the people to whom it was directed. While it was a significant and emotional event, not least because it brought to an end the Howard years of denial, the impact of the apology on an emotional level was perhaps more acute for many Indigenous people due to the tremendous difficulty in getting the Australian government to make such a simple gesture. In general terms, Indigenous responses to the apology fell into one of three categories:[13] some received it unreservedly,[14] while others felt it was a welcome but seriously belated 'first step' – one that should see compensation follow quickly – and still others who felt it a hollow gesture without accompanying compensation. For example, Christine Fejo-King said that the apology 'for many of us … (brought) the relief and peace we had been searching for, for so long … Saying "Sorry" was the right thing to do. Past government policies and practices of removing Indigenous children have damaged so many peoples' lives. Saying "Sorry" acknowledged the past, the trauma it caused at the time, and the hurt and suffering it continues to cause today' (quoted in Moses 2011: 153).

Chairperson of the Journey of Healing Association of South Australia, John Browne, was of the 'first step' persuasion: 'People are saying (that) an apology is hollow without reparations or compensation. Well, I say it may be hollow but it's a start. I mean, just to get the federal government to apologise is a big thing' (quoted in de Tarczynski 2008). Kathy Mills, however, argued that 'the apology was empty because in the same breath Rudd took all the goodness out of the intention by saying there will be no compensation … Removing children from their family is a crime against humanity that has not been addressed' (quoted in Hall and Perpitch 2010). Similarly, Lyn Austin, chairperson of Stolen Generations Victoria, argued that:

> The forced removals, the atrocities that our people have suffered in the institutions and the church homes and wherever (as) victims of sexual and physical abuse and the trauma and the pain, are reasons for compensation … I could walk out on the street tomorrow and trip over the footpath and sue the local council. I'd get compensated for that, so why not compensation for stolen generation members?
>
> (Quoted in de Tarczynski 2008)

The empirical reality was that some Indigenous peoples accepted the 'compensationless' apology unreservedly, while many others did not. The lack of accompanying financial restitution was, and still is, a major issue for many Indigenous peoples.[15] The lack of accompanying compensation to the victims of the forced removal policies has meant that they are left to try their luck in the courts – if they can afford it. For some Indigenous people, this situation significantly diminishes the quality and sincerity of the apology: the lack of accompanying reparations means that a necessary felicity condition has not been met.

Throughout the official reconciliation process, Howard sought to minimize Australia's genocidal history whenever possible, and rather than offering a formal state apology he simply regretted this 'blemished' aspect of Australian history. Unfortunately, Rudd used the same word in his apology, which diminished its acknowledgement of the enduring *deep wound* created by a genocidal policy that spanned a century. Indeed, there is also another sense in which the apology failed to describe the harm inflicted accurately and in the terms favoured by many of the victims and the BTH report – 'genocide'. In this sense, Barta (2008b) argued that the apology 'buried a history of genocide', for the apology itself constructs a narrative of the past, as it is both 'a form and function of remembering the past' (Roediger and Wertsch 2008: 9). When the Rudd government firmly rejected a compensation fund and omitted the 'G word' in the formal apology, it effectively severed the important moral connections made by the BTH report when it had argued that its finding that genocide had been committed necessitated a formal and explicit apology coupled with appropriate reparations.

Rudd failed to mention 'genocide' in his apology, as he feared 'electoral suicide', which arguably highlights the failure of the reconciliation process on its own terms. The stated objective of the reconciliation process was to educate the non-Aboriginal population to better understand Indigenous issues (see Short 2006) and eventually to back a treaty, and yet it seems that non-Indigenous support was a political precondition for making an official apology. For instance, prior to Rudd's apology polls suggested that the public was roughly split 50/50 on the issue of an apology for the Stolen Generations; however, after he made the apology, the majority supported it.[16] So, it is highly likely that if Rudd had included the word 'genocide', the majority of Australians would have rejected the apology and punished him at the next election, since BTH's genocide conclusion was the most controversial aspect of the report's findings. Previously, the Howard government and its supporters had launched swathes of attacks on that aspect of the report alone (Manne 2001). And yet, as Barta (2008b: 208) argues:

> The government changed, and the apology was pushed into the limelight without the legal argument that had helped place it on the national agenda. The nation, it is safe to say, did not want to know. The Rudd government, striving for maximum consensus, was not about to rub open a bitter controversy.

Yet again, the settler colonial context in which such acts of remembrance are made is in evidence here, for as long as Aboriginal people remain a persistently marginalized minority in Australia, the possibility of a genuinely decolonizing reconciliation process (that includes treaties between the settler state and Indigenous nations – as had been requested by the treaty campaign of the late-1980s which led to the reconciliation process) remains dependent on the mobilization of support of a wider non-Indigenous public.

Going beyond the issue of genocide, a campaign group, the Stolen Generations Alliance, has called for an audit of the progress in implementing BTH's fifty-four recommendations and has pointed to another function of the apology – it gave the impression that everything had been done for the Stolen Generations survivors, when most of the recommendations had not been implemented.[17] In addition to these issues, another governmental policy provided a backdrop to the apology, which many Indigenous people felt rendered the apology deeply hypocritical, since the policy in question was racially discriminatory. Indeed, the day before the apology was delivered thousands of Indigenous people marched in protest in Canberra against the continuation of a now-infamous Howard government initiative. Without consulting the targeted Indigenous communities and under the auspices of protecting children from abuse, in 2007 the Howard government introduced the Northern Territory National Emergency Response Act (often referred to as the 'Intervention') – a discriminatory package of changes to Indigenous welfare provision, law enforcement, land tenure and basic freedoms, which the United Nations has since denounced as racially discriminatory.[18] I have argued that the Intervention is genocidal (Short 2010) – if one adopts a Lemkin-inspired understanding of the concept and takes seriously the culturally destructive impacts of certain measures such as the compulsory land acquisition policies contained in the Act. For Lemkin, the cultural method of genocide was at the heart of his understanding (see Moses 2008; 2010; Short 2010), as it is a group's culture that animates the 'genos' in genocide. The Intervention and its associated measures has had such a culturally destructive impact on many Indigenous communities, that some spokespersons have talked in terms of genocide. Indeed, as John Ah Kit, the first Indigenous minister in the Northern Territory's history, put it: the Intervention 'is about the beginning of the end of Aboriginal culture; it is in some ways genocide' (see Short 2010).

Colonial remembrance and the Indigenous sovereignty challenge

From the outset, the Australian reconciliation process since the 1990s exhibited an overt nation-building agenda, an approach which ignored the fact that at the time of invasion Indigenous peoples were self-governing political entities or 'sovereign nations' (Reynolds 1996),[19] and in spite of over two hundred years of colonialism many Indigenous groups can still claim, and prove, such status.[20] As Reynolds pointed out, Australia 'has never been *one* nation, popular rhetoric notwithstanding. We share a country, a continent and a state, but not a nation' (1996: 178). Rudd's apologetic act of remembrance continued this colonial construction with frequent references to a singular 'nation'. In a similar vein, Indigenous nationhood was written out of official reconciliation so as to avoid the accusation of 'separatism' and discourage Indigenous peoples' 'claims' based on difference (Moran 1998; Short 2008) – Rudd's apology continued this approach. The failure to accord Indigenous nationhood equal recognition and respect during the official reconciliation process, and the apology's construction of a singular 'national' memory highlights an important issue that remains unaddressed, but which underpinned the treaty campaign in the late-1980s – what Howard in 1988 described as the 'absurd proposition of Aboriginal sovereignty'. Aboriginal sovereignty in this context is 'absurd' because the settler state constituted itself as *the only* sovereign on the continent and because no treaties were signed with Indigenous peoples.

Thus, the crux of the Indigenous sovereignty challenge is that settler state sovereignty was not legitimately established and that Aboriginal sovereignty was, *and continues to be*, illegitimately ignored: the latter is a key dimension of Australia's continuing relations of genocide (see Short 2010). Such a denial has profound implications for a reconciliation process originally instigated *because of the injustice of Australian settlement and colonial dispossession* as an alternative to a treaty (see Short 2008). Indeed, a reconciliation process that does not address the Indigenous sovereignty challenge cannot be considered decolonizing and will do little to alter a key element of the continuing genocidal relationship between many Indigenous peoples in Australia and the settler state (see Short 2010). That is not to suggest all aspects of Australian reconciliation are therefore devoid of value: there may be many important symbolic (like the apology) and practical acts that go some way to addressing the injustices of the past *for some people*, but if they do not confront the constitutional issue, a fundamental aspect of Indigenous–settler relations will remain unaddressed (see Gunstone 2007; Muldoon 2009) and inherently colonial and genocidal for many groups. As Muldoon and Schaap (2012: 185) write:

> While the apology provided a measure of recognition (both of the suffering endured by Indigenous people and of the value of their culture), it was marred by an ongoing failure on the part of the Australian state to properly acknowledge what the history of its relations with Indigenous people disclosed about *its* identity.

Such criticism of the apology has come from some within Australia; however, due to the high-profile nature of the apology, it also attracted similar attention from overseas. As Moses (2011: 149) writes, 'Some Indigenous intellectuals outside Australia were unimpressed with the apology, not only because compensation was not in the offing, but because it did not seriously question the terms of the Australian nation-state'. Because the Australian apology did not set out on this course, it 'did not succeed in transforming existing colonial relationships with Indigenous people' (Moses 2011: 149). It was a 'distraction' (Corntassel and Holder quoted in Moses 2011: 149). Moses, however, disagrees with this critique and suggests that such a position is 'non-falsifiable in the sense … that it *presumes* the persistence of colonial domination, irrespective of legal and policy changes … (asserting) that colonialism by definition cannot tolerate Indigenous alterity' (Moses 2011: 146).

This is an important challenge for a reading of the formal reconciliation process, and its official acts of remembrance for genocidal practices, as a process formed and underpinned by fundamental colonial impositions, assumptions, constructions and 'relations of genocide'. And yet, the *enduring* problem is that Indigenous sovereignty is not recognized or respected in Australia. Its existence is only implicitly recognized in the notion of 'native title', which gains its content from observable Indigenous 'traditional' laws and customs that have continued to survive colonization. Constitutional recognition of Indigenous sovereignty (e.g. via a set of treaties) with a concomitant political right to self-determination is unfortunately still an 'absurd proposition'. Moreover, legal and policy changes such as the Native Title legislation and the Intervention are inherently colonial and culturally destructive in their denial of meaningful land rights and cultural and political autonomy (and hence, I have argued, genocidal) in ways that are observable and not simply presumed (see Short 2010). The Native Title legislation, following the Mabo case, presumed legitimate settler state sovereignty, placed the burden of proof on Indigenous people to demonstrate they have a right to their land and, even if they are successful, denied them a veto over development – all achieved without consulting those most likely to be affected by such policies. It is difficult to see these measures as 'postcolonial' and a break from prior relations of genocide, as indeed is construing the recent Northern Territory Intervention as such. The latter is a racially discriminatory top-down imposition which includes arbitrary land acquisition and does not enjoy the support of those affected by it even though a small minority of Indigenous people welcomed its measures (Short 2010). Moreover, this racially discriminatory Intervention was endorsed by the Rudd government at the same time as its apology sought to consign such paternalistic colonial discrimination to the past.

Conclusion

Two well-received acts of official remembrance conducted in the spirit of 'reconciliation', Keating's Redfern Park speech and Rudd's formal apology, were heralded as signalling a new era in Indigenous–settler relations. While they both included postcolonial sentiment and sought to imagine a new direction for Australia in this regard, they both occurred in a colonial political context which contradicted their narratives. Rudd's official apology, in effect, not only 'buried a history of genocide' (Barta 2008a), but it imagined Australia as postcolonial when no meaningful structural or functional change to the colonial order had occurred. The relationship continues to be, as Wolfe (2006) argues, a 'structure not an event', and a structure so deeply embedded that it will take a lot more than words to change it. When the time came to follow up on the apologetic sentiment with deeds, the settler state was found wanting. After the Redfern Park speech, the Keating government enacted legislation to limit the impact of common law land rights in favour of powerful commercial interests to such an extent as to render these rights largely meaningless. The official apology, for many, failed to meet important felicity conditions, as it was not accompanied by reparations and, to make matters worse, it occurred at the same time as the government presided over the continued suspension of Australia's (only) Racial Discrimination Act – so as to maintain the discriminatory package of measures known as the Intervention. As such, the incongruous nature of these acts at best renders the symbolic gestures somewhat empty and at worst renders them cynically self-serving.

This chapter has argued that acts of official acknowledgement and remembrance for past human rights abuses and genocide by a settler state – allegedly seeking to decolonize its relationship with Indigenous peoples – are considerably diminished by the positively *colonial, and arguably genocidal*, contemporary political context in which they were made. Until the Australian settler state goes further than mere apologetic words, the symbolic reconciliatory power of such acts of remembrance will always be diminished; and until Aboriginal sovereignty is formally acknowledged and respected, claims that Australia has decolonized its genocidal relationship with Aboriginal people are premature.

Notes

1 After Barta's paper, the next serious consideration of the issue, although somewhat under-theorized, was that of Tatz (1999). But it was Dirk Moses's work on the topic and Tony Barta's second essay that really brought a new level of understanding and insight to the issue (see Moses 2000).

2 Barta (1985: 249) ends his paper suggesting that 'relations of genocide are alive', while Tatz (1999: 1) suggests more broadly that much of Australia's 'inter-racial history I call "genocide"'while Patrick Wolfe (quoted in Tatz 1999: 1) argues, correctly in my view, that settler colonialism is structure not an event; in John Pilger's television documentary 'Welcome to Australia' (Carlton Television, UK), Tatz categorically states that 'Australia has been at this (genocide) for over 200 years'.

3 Such as Kevin Buzzacott and Darren Bloomfield from the Tent Embassy, and Michael Anderson and John Ah Kit, to name a few.

4 For an interpretation of the difference between 'colonization' and 'colonialism', see Fieldhouse (1981: 4–5).

5 See, for example, Kuper (1981); Barta (1985); Docker (2008); Curthoys (2008) and Moses (2008).

6 In particular, the right to 'free prior and informed consent' of those Indigenous peoples affected by them – now an established international core principle most recently enshrined in Article 19 of the United Nations Declaration on the Rights of Indigenous Peoples – available at: http://www.un.org/esa/socdev/unpfii/en/drip.html.
7 The upper estimate of 1,000,000 was made by Noel Butlin (cited in Manne 2001: 103) and has not been endorsed by anyone else. Nevertheless, it is frequently cited as the estimated upper limit: see, for example, Manne (2001: 103).
8 For example, the Australian Aborigines Protection Association, the Association for the Protection of the Native Races of Australia and Polynesia, and the Aboriginal Union were all formed around this time.
9 SBS Dateline 28/07/93.
10 For more on speech act theory, see Austin (1962), Levinson (1980, 1983) and Searle (1969).
11 The policies and practices of removal were in effect throughout the twentieth century until the early 1970s. There are many Indigenous people, now in their late twenties and early thirties, who were removed from their families under these policies. Although the official policies and practices of removal have been abandoned, the Bringing Them Home report reveals that the past resonates today in Indigenous individuals, families and communities (HREOC 1997).
12 Convention on the Prevention and Punishment of the Crime of Genocide, 1948, Article 2 (e). Available at: http://www.oas.org/dil/1948_Convention_on_the_Prevention_and_Punishment_of_the_Crime_of_Genocide.pdf.
13 I have formed this broad classification of responses from my own post-apology interviews with Indigenous peoples, from mainstream media quotations, from Indigenous media reports, from online discussion forums and from activist networks – hence I cannot claim them to be irrefutable. Moreover, in the absence of systematic quantitative and qualitative social research into Indigenous responses to the apology, I don't think it is possible to say which of the strands I tentatively identify is numerically dominant.
14 See Moses (2011) for examples of such responses.
15 See Pearson (2008) on this as well as Hall and Perpitch (2010), who cite over 500 members of the Stolen Generations Alliance still seeking compensation. See www.sgalliance.org.au/website/index.php?option=com_content&view=article&id=47&Itemid=53. Accessed: 26 March 2012.
16 See www.creativespirits.info/aboriginalculture/politics/stolen-generations-sorry-apology.html.
17 See Stolen Generations Alliance. (2010) 'Stolen Generations Alliance says BTH Audit is the Next Step', Media Release. 25 May. Available at: www.sgalliance.org.au/website/index.php?option=com_content&view=article&id=49&Itemid=55. Accessed: 26 March 2012.
18 See UN Special Rapporteur James Anaya's comments available at http://www2.ohchr.org/english/issues/Indigenous/rapporteur/docs/ReportVisitAustralia.doc.
19 For a discussion on Aboriginal 'nationhood' and the misconception that Aboriginal groups were not 'distinct political entities' at the time of conquest, see Reynolds (1996).
20 As of 17 June 2013, there have been 178 determinations that native title exists in the entire determination area or in parts of the determination area. Thus, 178 Indigenous groups in Australia that have proven that they have a continuing attachment to their land and that live by observable 'traditional laws and customs' can be traced back to pre-colonial times (see http://www.nntt.gov.au/Applications-And-Determinations/Search-Determinations/Pages/Search.aspx). Their sovereignty provides the content of native title, but is not officially recognized for what it is or respected in its own right.

Bibliography

Austin, J.L. (1962) *How to Do Things with Words*, Cambridge: Harvard University Press.

Barta, T. (1985) 'After the Holocaust: Consciousness of Genocide in Australia', *The Australian Journal of Politics and History*, 31.1: 154–161.

——. (2000) 'Relations of Genocide: Land and Lives in the Colonization of Australia', in I. Wallimann and M. Dobkowski (eds) *Genocide and the Modern Age: Etiology and Case Studies of Mass Death*, New York: Syracuse University Press: 237–252.

——. (2008a) '"They Appear Actually to Vanish from the Face of the Earth": Aborigines and the European Project in Australia Felix', *Journal of Genocide Research*, 10.4: 519–539.

——. (2008b) 'Sorry, and not Sorry, in Australia: How the Apology to the Stolen Generations Buried a History of Genocide', *Journal of Genocide Research*, 10.2: 201–214.

Behrendt, L. (2001) 'Genocide: The Distance between Law and Life', *Aboriginal History*, 25: 132–147.

——. (2009) 'Home: The Importance of Place to the Dispossessed', *South Atlantic Quarterly*, 108.1: 71–85.

CARA (Council for Aboriginal Reconciliation Act) 1991, No. 127. Available at: http://www.comlaw.gov.au/Details/C2004A04202. Accessed: 26 March 2012.

Celermajer, D. (2008) 'Apology and the Possibility of Ethical Politics', *Journal of Cultural and Religious Theory*, 9.1: 14–34.

Chancellor, A. (1998) 'Pride and Prejudice: Easier Said than Done', *The Guardian*. 17 January: 8.

Cohen, S. (2001) *States of Denial: Knowing about Atrocities and Suffering*, Cambridge: Polity.

Curthoys, A. (2002) *Freedom Ride: A Freedom Rider Remembers*, Sydney: Allen & Unwin.

——. (2008) 'Genocide in Tasmania: The History of an Idea', in D. Moses (ed.) *Empire, Colony, Genocide: Conquest, Occupation and Subaltern Resistance in World History*, Oxford: Berghahn Books: 229–252.

Dampier, W. (1927 [1697]) *A New Voyage Round the World*, London: Argonaut Press.

De Tarczynski, S. (2008) 'Apology, No Compensation For Lost Generations', *Inter Press Service*. 27 January. Available at: http://ipsnews.net/news.asp?idnews=40955. Accessed: 26 March 2012

Docker, J. (2008) 'Are Settler-Colonies Inherently Genocidal?', in D. Moses (ed.) *Empire, Colony, Genocide: Conquest, Occupation and Subaltern Resistance in World History*, Oxford: Berghahn Books: 81–101.

Edwards, C. and P. Read. (1989) *The Lost Children: Thirteen Australians Taken from their Aboriginal Families Tell of the Struggle to Find their Natural Parents*, Sydney: Doubleday.

Fagenblat, M. (2008) 'The Apology, the Secular and the Theologico-Political', *Dialogue: The Journal of the Social Sciences in Australia*, 27.2: 16–32.

Fieldhouse, D.K. (1981) *Colonialism, 1870–1945: An Introduction*, New York: St Martin's Press.

Gooder, H. and J.M. Jacobs. (2000) '"On the Border of the Unsayable": The Apology in Postcolonizing Australia', *Interventions: International Journal of Postcolonial Studies*, 2.2: 229–247.

Greer, S. (1993) 'Australian Aboriginal Societies and Heritage', in N. Loos and T. Osanai (eds) *Indigenous Minorities and Education: Australian and Japanese Perspectives of their Indigenous Peoples, The Ainu, Aborigines and Torres Straight Islanders*, Tokyo: Sanyusha Publishing: 187–204.

Gunstone, A. (2007) *Unfinished Business: The Australian Formal Reconciliation Process*, North Melbourne: Australian Scholarly Publishing.

Haebich, A. (2001) *Broken Circles: Fragmenting Indigenous Families 1800–2000*, Fremantle: Arts Centre Press.

Hall, L. and N. Perpitch. (2010) 'Stolen Generations Compensation Still a Sore Point', *The Australian*. 27 May. Also available at: http://www.theaustralian.com.au/news/nation/stolen-generations-compensation-still-a-sore-point/story-e6frg6nf-1225871772507. Accessed: 26 March 2012.

Harris, S. (1979) 'It's Coming yet ... ', Aboriginal Treaty within Australia between Australians, Canberra: Aboriginal Treaty Committee. Also available at: http://www.aiatsis.gov.au/collections/exhibitions/treaty/m0020366_a.html. Accessed: 26 March 2012.

Howard, J. (1988) 'Treaty is a Recipe for Separatism', in K. Baker (ed.) *A Treaty with the Aborigines?* Melbourne: Institute of Public Affairs Limited.

——. (2000) 'Practical Reconciliation', in: M. Grattan (ed.) *Essays on Australian Reconciliation*, Melbourne: Black Books: 88–96.

Human Rights and Equal Opportunity Commission (HREOC). (1997) *Bringing Them Home: Report of the National Inquiry into the Separation of Aboriginal and Torres Strait Islander Children from Their Families*, Canberra: Commonwealth of Australia. Available at: http://www.humanrights.gov.au/publications/bringing-them-home-report-1997. Accessed: 26 March 2012.

Johnston, E. (1992) Commissioner QC, 'Frontier Period: Disease and Violence', *National Report of the Royal Commission into Aboriginal Deaths in Custody*, Vol. 2–10.4, Canberra: AGPS.

Keating, P. (2000) 'Redfern Park Speech', in M. Grattan (ed.) *Reconciliation: Essays on Australian Reconciliation*, Melbourne: Black Inc.: 60–64.

Kuper, L. (1981) *Genocide: Its Political Use in the Twentieth Century*, New Haven and London: Yale University Press.

Lederach, J.P. (1999) *Sustainable Reconciliation in Divided Societies*, Washington DC: United States Institute of Peace Press.

Lemkin, R. (1944) *Axis Rule in Occupied Europe: Laws of Occupation, Analysis of Government, Proposals for Redress*, Washington DC: Carnegie Endowment for International Peace.

Levinson, S. (1980) 'Speech Act Theory: The State of the Art', *Language Teaching and Linguistics: Abstracts*, 13.1-2: 5–24.

——. (1983) *Pragmatics*, Cambridge: Cambridge University Press.

Locke, J. (1970 [1689]) *Two Treatises of Government*, Second Edition Reprint, Cambridge: Cambridge University Press.

Manne, R. (2001) 'In Denial: The Stolen Generations and the Right', *Quarterly Essay*, 1: 1–113.

May, D. (1996) *Aboriginal Labour and the Cattle Industry: Queensland from White Settlement to the Present*, Cambridge: Cambridge University Press.

Minow, M. (1998) *Between Vengeance and Forgiveness*, Boston: Beacon Press.

Moran, A. (1998) 'Aboriginal Reconciliation: Transformations in Settler Nationalism', *Melbourne Journal of Politics* 25: 101–132.

Moses, D. (2000) 'An Antipodean Genocide? The Origins of the Genocidal Moment in the Colonization of Australia', *Journal of Genocide Research*, 2.1: 89–107.

——. (2004) 'Genocide and Settler Society in Australian History', in D. Moses (ed.) *Genocide and Settler Society: Frontier Violence and Stolen Indigenous Children in Australian History*, Oxford: Berghahn Books: 3–48.

——. (2008) 'Empire, Colony, Genocide: Keywords and the Philosophy of History', in D. Moses (ed.) *Empire, Colony, Genocide: Conquest, Occupation and Subaltern Resistance in World History*, Oxford: Berghahn Books: 3–54.

——. (2010) 'Raphael Lemkin, Culture, and the Concept of Genocide', in D. Bloxham and A.D. Moses (eds) *The Oxford Handbook of Genocide Studies*, Oxford: Oxford University Press: 19–41.

——. (2011) 'Official Apologies, Reconciliation, and Settler Colonialism: Australian Indigenous Alterity and Political Agency', *Citizenship Studies*, 15.2: 145–159.

Moses, D. and D. Celermajer. (2010) 'Australian Memory and the Apology to the Stolen Generations of Indigenous People', in A. Assman and S. Conrad (eds) *Memory in a Global Age: Discourses, Practices, and Trajectories*. Abingdon: Routledge: 32–58.

Muldoon, P. (2009) 'Past Injustices and Future Protections: On the Politics of Promising', *Australian Indigenous Law Review*, 13.2: 2–17.

Muldoon, P. and A. Schaap. (2012) 'Confounded by Recognition: The Apology, the High Court and the Aboriginal Embassy in Australia', in A. Hirsch (ed.) *Theorizing Post-Conflict Reconciliation: Agonism, Restitution and Repair*, London and New York: Routledge: 184–201.

Pearson, N. (2008) 'When Words Aren't Enough', *The Australian*. 12 February. Also available at: http://www.cyp.org.au/downloads/noel-pearson-papers/when-words-arent-enough-130208.pdf. Accessed: 26 March 2012.

Pettigrove, G. (2003) 'Apology, Reparations and the Question of Inherited Guilt', *Public Affairs Quarterly*, 17.4: 319–348.

Pilkington, D. (1996) *Follow the Rabbit-Proof Fence*, Brisbane: University of Queensland Press.

Read, P. (1981) 'The Stolen Generations: The Removal of Aboriginal People in New South Wales 1883 to 1969', (New South Wales) *Ministry of Aboriginal Affairs*: Occasional Paper No. 1, Sydney: Ministry of Aboriginal Affairs.

Reynolds, H. (1981) *The Other Side of the Frontier*, Townsville: James Cook University of North Queensland.

——. (1996) *Aboriginal Sovereignty: Three Nations, One Australia*, New South Wales: Allen & Unwin.

Roediger, H.L. and J.V. Wertsch. (2008) 'Creating a New Discipline of Memory Studies', *Memory Studies* 1.1: 9–22.

Rowley, C.D. (1970) *The Destruction of Aboriginal Society*, Canberra: Australia National University Press.

Rudd, K. (2008) 'Apology to Australia's Indigenous Peoples', Parliament of Australia, House of Representatives, *Parliamentary Debates*. 13 February: 167–177.

Schaap, A. (2009) 'The Absurd Proposition of Aboriginal Sovereignty', in A. Schaap (ed.) *Law and Agonistic Politics*, Farnham: Ashgate Publishing: 209–224.

Searle, J. (1969) *Speech Acts: An Essay in the Philosophy of Language*, Cambridge: Cambridge University Press.

Short, D. (2003) 'Australian "Aboriginal" Reconciliation: The Latest Phase in the Colonial Project', *Citizenship Studies*, 7.3: 291–312.

——. (2005) 'Reconciliation and the Problem of Internal Colonialism', *Journal of Intercultural Studies*, 26.3: 267–282.

——. (2006) 'Reconciliation as Education: The Council and the "People's Movement"', *Journal of Australian Indigenous Issues*, 8.1: 33–52.

——. (2007) 'The Social Construction of Indigenous Native Title Land Rights in Australia', *Current Sociology*, 55.6: 857–876.

——. (2008) *Reconciliation and Colonial Power: Indigenous Rights in Australia*, Farnham: Ashgate Publishing.

——. (2010) 'Australia: A Continuing Genocide?', *Journal of Genocide Research*, 12.1-2: 45–68.

Stanner, W.E.H. (1969) *After the Dreaming: Black and White Australians – An Anthropologist's View*, Boyer Lecture Series, Sydney: Australian Broadcasting Commission.

Stolen Generations Alliance. (2010) 'Stolen Generations Alliance says BTH Audit is the Next Step', Media Release. 25 May. Available at: www.sgalliance.org.au/website/index.php?option=com_content&view=article&id=49&Itemid=55. Accessed: 26 March 2012.

Tatz, C. (1999) 'Genocide in Australia', *AIATSIS Research Discussion Papers No. 8*. Available at: http://www.kooriweb.org/gst/genocide/tatz.html. Accessed: 26 March 2012.

Tavuchis, N. (1991) *Mea Culpa: A Sociology of Apology and Reconciliation*, Stanford: Stanford University Press.

Tickner, R. (2001) *Taking a Stand: Land Rights to Reconciliation*, London: Allen & Unwin.

Vivian, A. and B. Schokman. (2009) 'The Northern Territory Intervention and the Fabrication of "Special Measures"', *Australian Indigenous Law Review*, 13.1: 78–106.

Wolfe, P. (2006) 'Settler Colonialism and the Elimination of the Native', *Journal of Genocide Research*, 8.4: 387–409.

10 Bodies of evidence

Remembering the Rwandan genocide at Murambi

Nigel Eltringham

Introduction

On a warm Sunday afternoon in December 2007, my driver navigated the rough road down to the site of the half-completed Murambi Technical School in southern Rwanda, where an estimated 50,000 Tutsi men, women and children were murdered between 20 and 21 April 1994 by the interahamwe militia and gendarmes (ICTR 2005: para 88). Although I had first travelled along the road from Butare to Cyangugu ten years earlier while conducting doctoral fieldwork, only now did I take the opportunity to visit the site, one of six national memorial sites in Rwanda and the largest after the Kigali Memorial Centre (see Sodaro 2011).[1]

Although I had not been there before, I was nonetheless familiar with Murambi through non-fiction and fiction. In 2006, Murambi had become an internationally recognizable name with the publication in English of the Senegalese author Boubacar Boris Diop's novel *Murambi, The Book of Bones* (the French original, *Murambi, le livre des ossements*, was first published in 2000; see Hitchcott in this volume). In addition, in 2007 the non-governmental organization (NGO) African Rights had published a 213-page report entitled *Murambi: 'Go. If You Die, Perhaps I Will Live'* to coincide with the national commemoration of the genocide, which was held at Murambi in April of that year.

At Murambi I entered the twenty-four classrooms which housed around 800 corpses of the victims of the massacre preserved in lime. Having been exhumed from mass graves in 1996, the bodies are misshapen, the signs of violent death apparent. Standing close to those remains, I was struck again by a tension within the crime of genocide. On the one hand, a distinct feature of the crime is that it is 'a denial of the right of existence of entire human groups' (United Nations 1946). And yet, both scholars and judges have come to recognize that groups marked for elimination are often fantasies in the minds of perpetrators (Chalk and Jonassohn 1990: 23; ICTR 1999: para 98). In encountering anonymous remains at Murambi, my overwhelming sense was that the ultimate victory of the perpetrator is the erasure of the individual. The individual was, after all, real, whereas the image of the targeted group propagated by the perpetrator was an abstract fantasy.

At that time, there were no information boards at Murambi. This made the three, apparently recently installed, maroon-painted shields conspicuous. In English, French and Kinyarwanda they read: 'FRENCH SOLDIERS WERE PLAYING VOLLEY HERE'; 'MASS GRAVE OF VICTIMS' and 'PLACE OF FRENCH FLAG DURING OPERATION TURQUOISE'. I was aware that the Rwandan president, Paul Kagame, had denounced the French government's alleged complicity in the genocide in his speech at the annual commemoration held at Murambi in April 2007. I also knew why he had chosen to do this. In November 2006, I had witnessed – while conducting fieldwork at the International Criminal Tribunal for Rwanda (ICTR)[2] in Arusha, Tanzania – the political fallout over the issue of arrest warrants by a French anti-terrorist judge for nine of Kagame's close associates, accusing them of conspiring to shoot down the plane carrying President Juvénal Habyarimana on 6 April 1994, an event that triggered the genocide (ICTR 2004). I realized that these newly installed signs spoke not to me, the physically present visitor, but were engaged in a long-distance confrontation with the Tribunal de Grande Instance de Paris.

Returning to Kigali that evening, I had dinner with a prosecution lawyer of the ICTR. Interested in my visit to Murambi earlier in the day, the lawyer proceeded to recount, in extensive detail, a narrative of the events at Murambi on 20–21 April 1994. The geography of the site still fresh in my mind, I asked a question about the attack related to the layout of the buildings. 'I don't know', replied the lawyer, 'I've never been there'. Together with Diop's novel and the African Rights report, witness testimony at the ICTR had begun to create a distinction between Murambi as a place and Murambi as a body of text(s).

Taking my visit as a starting point, this chapter will consider three elements of genocide remembrance. First, when promoted as acts of remembrance, to what extent are fictional accounts, human rights advocacy and law distinct genres? Second, is the display of the remains of the victims of genocide necessary for the preservation of memory, or is it a recuperation of the anonymizing gaze of the perpetrator? And, finally, given that sites are appropriated for ever-changing political objectives, can remembrance ever be insulated from wider political interests or is it always contaminated by the vagaries of political instrumentalization?

Remembrance through textualization

It would be conventional to provide a narrative of what happened at Murambi Technical School. And yet, the temptation to provide such a 'history' in order to distinguish it from a reflection on 'remembrance' would be to ignore a key lesson from the contributions to this volume, namely, that an account of 'what happened' cannot be sequestrated from 'remembrance'. Murambi is part of the 'global political economy of traumatic storytelling' (Colvin 2006: 172) through three textual forms: a human rights report, a novel and transcripts/

judgement from a criminal trial. As vehicles of remembrance, what is distinctive about these three genres and what, if anything, do they have in common?

African Rights' 2007 report, *Murambi: 'Go. If You Die, Perhaps I Will Live'*, is harrowing and unrelenting, drawing on the testimony of 91 Rwandese (survivors and perpetrators) collected between 2004 and 2006. For the authors, the report is explicitly a document of remembrance. They state that in 'recording these memories, we hope to ensure that the victims of Murambi are remembered within Rwanda and internationally' (African Rights 2007: 7).

The effect of the chronological narrative is one of unremitting immediacy, the statements of those testifying displaying the qualities of unmediated recall – a '"pure" utterance and "authentic" transmission of experience' (Douglass and Vogler 2003: 56). Scholars, however, have critiqued, on a number of grounds, the genre of the human rights report that is produced by a variety of human rights NGOs. First, to claim that the report contains 'forensic' and unmediated truth does not take account of the way in which memory works. Second, such a claim ignores the processes through which information is acquired, selected and arranged by the human rights advocate. Finally, as a literary genre, the human rights report may disempower those for whom it purports to speak; alienate those who testify from their

Figure 10.1 The half-completed Murambi Technical School in southern Rwanda, December 2007. © Nigel Eltringham.

own stories; and its production is a result of power inequalities (Schaffer and Smith 2004: 27, 36–37, 45; Wilson 1997).

As regards how memory works, remembrance is not 'pure' unmediated utterance. As Michael Jackson (2002: 15) observes, 'To reconstitute events in a story is no longer to live those events in passivity, but to actively rework them, both in dialogue with others and in one's own imagination' (see Douglass and Vogler 2003). Under such circumstances, a witness's factual understanding of what they actually heard or saw is always evolving, including the incorporation of secondary 'foreign material' (Levi 1986: 130), that is, stories from others, or what the survivor reads (see Eltringham 2013). As a consequence, memory is transformed 'as it is replayed, recited, reworked and reconstrued in the play of intersubjective life' (Jackson 2002: 22). Part of the reason for this is that the survivor speaks to 'multiple audiences – survivors in the local community, perpetrators in the local community, the dead, national government officials, and international human rights advocates', so that the narrative is transformed by differences in relative power and intimacy between the testifier and these different audiences (French 2009: 98).

The human rights report relies for its affect on the use of testimonial narrative that generates a sensation of immediacy (see Maclean in this volume). The story the report wishes to tell could be conveyed in third-person prose alone. Testimonial narrative is, however, used intermittently. For example, the African Rights report (2007: 90) quotes a survivor: 'I would leave the storied building but then find myself returning to see if anyone had survived. I kept tripping over bodies of people I knew'. While such extracts are presented as spontaneous personal monologue, such testimony is, in reality, elicited and produced dialogically as a co-production with an 'auditor' or interviewer (Eastmond 2007; Jackson 2002: 22; Langfield and Maclean 2009; Vansina 2006 [1961]: 29). This process, of course, is influenced by the intent and prior knowledge of the person doing the interviewing (Laub 1992: 61). Making memory legible, therefore, always relies on the framing grammar of the interviewer, so that stories are the 'result of a relationship, a common project in which both the informant and the researcher are involved together' (Portelli 1981: 103). The central role of the interviewer, however, is erased as the questions the interviewer asks are excised from the published testimony and what was a two-way conversation is presented as a monologue (Gelles 1998: 16). Furthermore, the utterance of the witness goes through a process of 'entextualization' in which, for example, an oral testimony is translated from one language to another and then transcribed; then extracts are taken from that transcript and inserted into a report which may, in turn, be selectively quoted in other reports (French 2009: 97). The human rights report, therefore, reflects a 'collage of intervening presences – witness, editor, transcriber, translator, reader', so that the text 'reflects the different voices, styles of expression, perceptions of "truth", and political agendas of each and every participant in its chain of production' (Douglass and Vogler 2003: 68).

This raises questions about the agency of the victim in the 'collage of intervening presences' that generates textual artefacts of genocide remembrance. Writing in the context of the Khulumani ('Speak Out') Support Group that represents victims and survivors of gross human rights violations committed during Apartheid, Tshepo Madlingozi (2010) sees a relationship between human rights reporting and the 'rescuing' mission of colonialization (see Abu-Lughod 2002; Spivak 1988: 297). Madlingozi (2010: 210) suggests that the 'practice of speaking for and about victims further perpetuates their disempowerment and marginality', given that those who 'mine' the stories of victims do so 'by dint of our geopolitical and institutional privilege'. Madlingozi (2010: 210) suggests that the human rights advocate ('entrepreneur') gets to speak on behalf of victims:

> not because the latter invited and gave her a mandate but because the entrepreneur sought the victim out, categorized her, defined her, theorized her, packaged her, and disseminated her on the world stage. Having 'mined' the story in order to use it in the First World … the entrepreneur reinforces her status as the authoritative knower who is ordained to teach, civilize and rescue the benighted, hapless victim.

As a consequence, the victim *constructed* in the process of writing the human rights report is a 'hapless, passive victim dependent on NGOs and others to speak for her' (see discussion in the chapter by Frieze in this volume of 'Aurora's' manipulation). This, Madlingozi (2010: 213) argues, reproduces colonial relations of 'disempowerment and trusteeship'. According to French (2009: 96), part of this disempowerment relates to an 'ideologically loaded conception of human language' which is concerned only with the content of what is said, and not with *how* it is said. As a consequence, self-appointed experts ('analysts, activists, and human rights workers') (French 2009: 96) decode testimony for 'objective' facts and discard anything 'cultural' that distorts the isolation of objective facts. At the ICTR, for example, experts in the form of judges refer to the expert testimony of a Rwandan social scientist:

> According to the testimony of Dr Ruzindana it is a particular feature of the Rwandan culture that people are not always direct in answering questions, especially if the question is delicate. In such cases, the answers given will very often have to be 'decoded' in order to be understood correctly. This interpretation will rely on the context, the particular speech community, the identity of, and the relation between, the orator and listener, and the subject matter of the question.
>
> (*ICTR Prosecutor* v. *Jean Paul Akayesu* 2 September 1998. Para 156)

There is, therefore, a process of 'tacit erasure' in which 'culturally specific ways of knowing and telling' are delegitimated, ignored and implicitly censored (French 2009: 105).

Madlingozi's (2010) analysis suggests that the figure of the 'victim' around which the human rights report is organized is a subject position created by the international human rights movement. Likewise, David Kennedy (2001: 112) notes that application of the label 'victim' erases both differences *among* victims and 'the experience of their particularity and the hope for their creative and surprising self-expression', replacing it with a 'sanctified vocabulary for their self-understanding, self-representation and representation as "victims"'. As with the display of anonymous bodies bereft of names and biography (see below), so the application of 'victim' can deprive individuals of what makes them exemplars of humanity, against which a crime can be committed. The arguments of Madlingozi, Kennedy and French indicate that those who have experienced extreme violence are offered a subjectivity that promises recognition, but subjects them to a relationship of dependency.

This also has implications for that other set of texts, witness testimony preserved in the transcripts at the ICTR. This affinity is not surprising, given that because human rights reports aspire to set in motion a legal reckoning (even if they rarely achieve this purpose), they mimic the accusatory structure of a criminal indictment (Dudai 2006; Wilson 1997). It is no surprise, then, that the victim-witness in international criminal trials is a similarly ambivalent position of (dis)empowerment.

In contrast to domestic criminal trials, trials for mass atrocity (genocide, crimes against humanity and war crimes) have been promoted as acts of remembrance in themselves because they produce a 'historical record' (Eltringham 2009). At the ICTR, that record is the (heavily mediated) testimony of the approximately 2,000 witnesses who have given testimony. This includes, for example, the witnesses in the trial of Colonel Aloys Simba, a retired army officer who was appointed the head of civil defence in Gikongoro and Butare in 1994, and who was found guilty on 13 December 2005 of genocide and extermination as a crime against humanity at Murambi Technical School and sentenced to twenty-five years' imprisonment (ICTR 2005).

A curious feature of the Statute of the ICTR (United Nations 1994) is the use of the term 'victims and witnesses'. Given that just 'witnesses' would have sufficed, a distinct category of *victim*-witness was intentionally marked. This is not curious, however, if one recognizes that 'victim' brings with it the 'rescuing' quality noted by Madlingozi and implies the presence of 'rescuers'. Kamari Clarke (2009: 13) suggests that without a 'victim' the 'moral – and thus institutional – power' of tribunals like the ICTR and their memorializing 'historical record' would be weakened. In other words, international tribunals require a 'tragic spectacle of suffering – the spectre of a victim representing the condition of oppression in need of salvation' (2009: 15).

Such an analysis suggests that the organizing principle of 'victim' in both human rights reporting and international criminal justice does not refer primarily to the men, women and children who were targeted, but to a *depersonalized* and *disembodied* figure that calls forth a rescuing discourse. As Clarke (2009: 61) notes, 'humanitarianism requires an object to be saved'. To take this position to its natural conclusion, those engaged in human rights advocacy/international criminal justice do not 'only represent and speak for victims but "produce" the victim' (Madlingozi 2010: 225.) because they *need* the 'victim' (a category of their own construction) in order for their (civilizing) projects to make sense. In this process, therefore, the agency of the 'victim' is 're-assigned to the institutionally powerful in their name' (Clarke 2009: 4).

None of these observations should be misread as devaluing the testimony collected in the African Rights report or the trial proceedings of the ICTR. These critiques do, however, alert us to a clear tension between the necessity of recording and disseminating testimony without further disempowering those who testify. These critiques are equally relevant to me, given that, as a researcher, I have acted as an 'entrepreneur' in the way Madlingozi describes. There is a need, therefore, to acknowledge the two hidden aspects of how these texts are produced. To recognize that the figure of the victim, seemingly an *a priori* starting point, is in reality a product of the process of reporting warns against inadvertently disempowering the testifying subject. Likewise, attention to the 'collage of intervening presences' between raw experience and preserved testimony draws attention to the *affected* qualities of such documents and the reasons why they resonate with those who consume in the 'global political economy of traumatic storytelling' (Colvin 2006: 172).

While the human rights report and the trial transcript/judgement share certain features, one would assume that, as a fictional account, Diop's novel is distinct in that it does not claim to convey objective, forensic truth. Attention to Diop's reflection on why he wrote *Murambi, The Book of Bones* and why he organized it in a particular manner, however, suggests important affinities between all three of these texts of remembrance. As a journalist and novelist, Diop could have written either a fictional or factual account. He chose fiction because:

> When you are a journalist [the] facts command the story. When you are a novelist, [your] imagination commands the facts … When I wrote this novel, I was commanded by the facts. But if I had decided to write a journalistic account, I would have to check everything – numbers, dates, who said what. I wouldn't be free to tell the story. For me, the most important thing was to underline the human side of the story. After genocide, it is important to give a face, to give a name, to give blood and flesh to the people who were killed. I felt I could do this better as a novelist, but I also wanted to be trusted by my readers. I didn't want them to see my novel as something fake. I wanted readers to confront reality. The story wasn't just from my imagination. I wanted people to read the book and know that everything I had to work with in the novel was true.
>
> (Quoted in Morris 2011)

I suggest that this statement could apply to all three texts considered here. All three 'work with' what is true for those who are asked to testify, but all three texts mediate that truth with different degrees of transparency. Testimony at the trial of Aloys Simba at the ICTR was created through the public, transparent mediation of a lawyer's question and a witness's answer, which were then selected and paraphrased for the judgement (Eltringham 2009). While the presence of the interviewer is retained in the trial transcript, the presence of the interviewer is erased from *Murambi: 'Go. If You Die, Perhaps I Will Live'*. In the report, specific questions asked of individual witnesses are erased as the continuous testimony of an individual witness is disassembled into fragments of speech that are reassembled into a composite, continuous narrative, in which the fragments of recalled individual memory no longer attest to a unique individual perspective, but are made to act as touchstones of 'authenticity' linked by the editors' bridging glosses.[3]

While the ICTR judgement and the human rights report rely on 'direct' testimony to disguise mediation, Diop's mediation is there for all to see: 'everything I had to work with in the novel was true'. While the ICTR judgement and the human rights report take disparate testimony and create a composite, realist, omniscient narrative, Diop 'resists a reductive interpretation of the events' (Hitchcott in this volume) and maintains the disparate experience of the single witness. Of thirteen chapters in Diop's book, eleven are narrated in the first person by separate characters (the remaining two are narrated in the conventional third person). Diop resists the creation of a composite – something that we find in the ICTR judgement and the human rights report. Such indirect portrayal, it has been argued, avoids the 'deceptive immediacy' of the realist narrative and increases the 'potential for genuine ethical witness' (Gregory 2006: 203) because in reality no eyewitness experiences an event in its entirety (Jay 1992: 104). For the human rights advocate to reconstruct a meaningful narrative of an event or series of events, they must take a wider view than that accessible to any single eyewitness or participant (Passmore 1974: 148). In contrast, Nora Strejilevich (2006: 704), a survivor of the 'Dirty War' (1976–1983) in Argentina, suggests that 'a truthful way of giving testimony should allow for disruptive memories, discontinuities, blanks, silences and ambiguities'. All three of these texts mediate, but because Diop resists a fabricated composite, his 'fiction' is closest to the 'true' experience of the eyewitness who witnesses, from an idiosyncratic location, the chaotic unfolding of events that only later, with the benefit of hindsight, are recognized as genocide.

Bodies on display

Immediately after the massacre, the Gikongoro *Préfectural* office provided two bulldozers, which were used to bury the dead in order to prevent disease; burial took four days (African Rights 2007: 116). According to Shannon Scully (2012: 15), during exhumations in 1995 one mass grave was found in which the bodies had barely begun to decompose. The survivors of the massacre, along with the Government of Rwanda and the National Museum of Rwanda stopped the decomposition by covering the bodies in limestone and putting them on display. From this perspective, it was survivors who chose to display the bodies because 'they are the only way desperate survivors can convey the tragedy' (Smith 2006; see Ibreck 2010: 338). This decision to display human remains from 1996 onwards 'transgressed in an unheard of way traditional relationships with the dead' (Vidal 2004: 578; see Eltringham 2012). Like the victims of political violence in Zimbabwe, the refusal to bury disturbs the 'material, social and symbolic processes and techniques through which things and substances become human remains, bodies become bones, and living people become safely dead' (Fontein 2010: 439).

Rachel Ibreck (2010: 337), however, also notes that the display of remains is controversial and 'in contradiction with the survivors' determination to honour and rebury the dead' (see also Rozen's discussion of the display of bodies in this volume). The same tension can be seen in the way that, on the one hand, Célestin Kanimba Misago, director of the National Museum, initially worked with survivors to preserve the remains (Ibreck 2010: 338), but, on the other hand, he has also written that a 'reburial ceremony is, for those who suffer from the trauma of not having buried their own, the opportunity to publicly honour their memory, and is thus a kind of therapy' (Misago 2007: 10). These contradictory positions may be explained by the fact that survivors are not homogeneous and do not agree on whether or not to display remains (Meierhenrich 2011: 284; see Longman and Rutagengwa 2006: 252).

On the one hand, there is historical precedent for the display of bodies. In his study of funeral rites in Rwanda, Gerard van't Spijker (1990) notes that the preference is to bury the body in the family compound, but that the term used for this rite, *gushaka ishyamba*, translates as 'look for a forest', which recalls the 'old custom of exposing the corpse in a non-cultivated place, forest or marsh' (Spijker 1990: 61). According to Aléxis Kagame (1954: 307), the Tutsi exposed their dead because they had a horror of decomposition and preferred to be 'eaten by hyenas' rather than by worms. On the other hand, the relevance of this precedent to Murambi is not, however, self-evident given that, as Spijker notes, *gushaka ishyamba* now refers to *burial* rites, not to exposure of the corpse.

The anthropologist Claudine Vidal (2004: 580–582) argues that the decision to put the remains at Murambi on display in 1995 and 1996 must be understood within a confrontation between the post-genocide government and the Roman Catholic Church which has been accused of being an institution of complicity with the government which oversaw the genocide (see Eltringham 2000). In 1995, elements of the Roman Catholic Church had denounced the opening and re-internment of mass graves, often involving the forced labour of the local population, as unnecessarily traumatic, disrespectful to the dead and lacking a sacred element. Vidal (2004: 585), therefore, sees the display of bodies, including those at Murambi, as part of a campaign by the post-genocide government against the Roman Catholic Church.

Another explanation is that such display was due to the emergence of denial in 1995 and 1996. This has remained a key explanation. Freddy

Mutanguha, country director for the Aegis Trust (a UK genocide prevention charity) in Rwanda, has stated: 'There are those who feel that only reburial can offer dignity for the dead, but [they] fear that unless the ultimate evidence of genocide is there to see, it could be denied and perhaps one day happen again' (Aegis Trust 2011). Conversely, the decision to display also corresponded with emerging criticism of the post-genocide government. On 29 August 1995, several prominent Hutu politicians resigned from the coalition 'Government of National Unity' in protest at extra-judicial killings and human rights violations by the Rwandan Patriotic Army (RPA).[4] Jens Meierhenrich (2011: 288) suggests that the decision by the government to display 'macabre' remains was, and continues to be, a means to 'disable comprehension', that 'by appealing to emotions rather than reason', such displays disable reflection on the post-genocide regime. Displaying remains is intended to 'facilitate a forgetting of the present' (Meierhenrich 2011: 289; see Guyer 2009: 170) in a context in which the post-genocide government has been severely criticized for its internal human rights record and its military involvement in neighbouring Congo since 1996 (Meierhenrich 2011: 289; see Straus and Waldorf 2011). As Sara Guyer (2009: 162) suggests, the 'traumatic silence that [the bodies] generate can be difficult to distinguish from the enforced silence that the regime demands and indeed operates as a supplement to it'.

Whatever the reason for the display of the bodies, their presence raises difficult questions. Uli Linke (2009) has reflected upon the relationship between genocide and the 'Body Works' exhibition (launched in 1995 in Tokyo) designed by Gunther von Hagens in which, real dissected bodies are made into anonymous anatomical models through a process of 'plastination'. Linke (2009: 150) reflects on how this exhibition replicates elements of Nazi genocide, that 'the exhibit uncannily plays out a multiplicity of themes associated with the atrocities of the Nazi regime: the negation of humanity, the dehumanization of bodies [and] depersonalization as a formative category of identity'. Given that each body on display in the 'Body Works' exhibition is 'frozen in time, without personal identity and life history, robbed of its humanity' (Linke 2009), the exhibition replicates practices of the Nazi (and other) genocides that dehumanized the victims. The preservation of the bodies at Murambi is analogous to the plastination of bodies in 'Body Works' in that the 'commemoration of the dead subject's life history' is suppressed (Linke 2009: 175).

Saru Guyer (2009: 163) sees this as an 'essential predicament' of memorials in Rwanda, including Murambi, in that they:

> cannot and do not memorialize individual deaths and proper names. Yet, by refusing to return names, identities, or individualities to the dead, they … recur to genocide's logic (which also is colonialism's logic) – that is, the logic of impersonality whereby persons are recognized only as members of a population.

This anonymization is reflected in other genocide memorial sites. In Cambodia, for example, the two main sites of Tuol Sleng and Choeung Ek 'are alienating because of their lack of any personal accounts or stories of lost lives' (Williams 2004: 250; see Lesley-Rozen this volume). This is in contrast with the Srebrenica-Potočari Memorial Room in Bosnia and Herzegovina, where anonymization is resisted by displaying an object (e.g. lighter, watch, glasses) alongside a photo and personal story of twenty of the 8,000 men and boys killed by Serbian forces in July 1995 (Simic 2009: 278; see Bardgett 2007).

As noted earlier, there is a clear tension between remembering genocide as an act against a population aggregated and anonymized by the perpetrator and remembering the humanity of each victim. Sara Guyer (2009: 174), speaking in the context of Murambi, notes that to view the bodies on display is to privilege the anonymizing element because it places the observer into the position of the perpetrator, 'leading us to see the dead as the perpetrators of the genocide saw the living', as an anonymized mass. Such displays, it can be argued, achieve the opposite of Diop's wish that 'after genocide, it is important to give a face, to give a name, to give blood and flesh to the people who were killed' (quoted in Morris 2011).

But a tension remains. Scully (2012) defends the display of the remains as the 'right of an affected group'. According to Scully, the majority of the ten survivors of the massacre support the bodies remaining on display even though the remains of their children and spouses may be among them. For one survivor, Emmanuel Nshimyimana, 'originally we didn't like having our people on display. But we know it is for the future and therefore it is important that they are preserved for future generations' (Scully 2012: 17). As with the tension between recording testimony and avoiding disempowering survivors, the display of bodies also involves a, possibly irresolvable, tension.

Political instrument

When I visited Murambi, the three signs mentioned in the introduction were the only information available on site. The lack of information/interpretation is noted by Vidal (2004: 585):

> The design of these memorials to the genocide gave immediate physical and emotional evidence. But this evidence is no substitute for another dimension, also essential: to know how, by what political paths, this state crime had been perpetrated, and with what active and passive complicities.

At the time of my 2007 visit, there was an exhibition at Murambi produced in the UK, drawing on the text of the African Rights report and described on the Rwandan government museum website as:

> A simple narrative outlining the development of the genocidal ideology from pre-colonial and colonial times through to the post-colonial policies

> of division between ethnic groups. It describes the role of propaganda and the systematic organization of the killing during the genocide.[5]

In other words, the exhibition contained a standardized history of Rwanda propagated by the Rwandan Patriotic Front (RPF) which maintained that ethnicity had been created, or substantially distorted, by colonial authorities, thereby disrupting a pre-colonial unity and that the Genocide had begun in 1959 with the overthrow of the Tutsi monarchy (see Buckley-Zistel 2009: 34–41; Eltringham 2004: 163–177; Sodaro 2011: 80–81; Zorbas 2009).

The only problem was that the exhibition had been closed. In February 2003, the Aegis Trust had been invited by the Rwandan government to 'take over responsibility for the creation of the Kigali Genocide Memorial, the Murambi Memorial Centre and preservation work at an additional five major sites around the country'.[6] The Murambi memorial was intended to be completed by 2004, the tenth anniversary of the genocide. The exhibition, however, was criticized by an 'ad hoc commission' for having 'grammatical errors' and 'photographs that do not make any sense'; further, it did 'not reflect the truth about history, politics or Rwandese culture' (Laville 2006). However, Aimé Kayinamura, who coordinated the project, stated:

> The contested photos had to do with the story of a young Tutsi boy who lost his parents, survived his machete wounds, and was taken in by a Hutu family. After the genocide, the family fled to the former Zaire, taking the boy with them. The depiction of the family's journey included scenes of large-scale suffering of Hutu refugees in the former Zaire.
>
> (International Justice Tribune 2008: 2)

According to Kayinamura, the 'ad hoc commission' had 'felt that these photos could suggest a double genocide and we had to remove them'.

As Dacia Viejo-Rose (2011: 469) notes, in a post-conflict context 'an edited version of history is constructed and attempts are made to mould memories in order to give legitimacy to the post-war administration', that selective 'choices are made about what to explicitly "remember" or deliberately silence' (see Logan in this volume). Given the negative response of the Rwandan government to the (re)publication of United Nations reports alleging RPA involvement in the massacre of Rwandan refugees in Congo in 1996–1998 (Eltringham 2004: 118–142; Office of the UN High Commissioner for Human Rights 2010), the photos of those same refugees appearing in the exhibition was not acceptable. As Elizabeth King (2010: 293) notes, 'in order to legitimate its rule, the Rwandan government selectively highlights some civilian memories of violence, and represses others' (see Conway 2011). In the case of the exhibition, those associated with the Rwandan government appear to have imposed an absence at Murambi.

But, with the three notice boards something was made present or, more correctly, re-presenced. The significance of those three boards goes back to the moment the 1994 genocide began. On 6 April 1994, Rwandan President Juvénal Habyarimana, President Ntaryamira of Burundi and various members of their staff were returning to Kigali from a summit in Dar es Salaam, where Habyarimana had apparently consented to establish a power-sharing government. His aircraft was shot down around 8:23 p.m. having been hit by surface-to-air missiles launched from a location near Kigali Airport. There were no survivors. The killing of Hutu politicians committed to a peace process commenced immediately and was soon after followed by the widespread killing of Tutsi.

On 23 June 1994, 2,200 French paratroopers entered Rwanda through Bukavu and Goma in Congo under the name 'Operation Turquoise', which had been approved by the UN Security Council under Resolution 929 (1994) (African Rights 2007: 142–150). Given the extensive assistance that the French government had given to the pre-genocide Rwandan government (see Kroslak 2007) and that by the end of June 1994 the RPF was clearly going to militarily defeat the genocidal government, the French government's decision to intervene was highly controversial. Murambi Technical School was one of the French bases.

Twelve years later, on 17 November 2006, the French anti-terrorist Judge Jean-Louis Bruguière, who had been conducting an investigation since 1998 on behalf of the families of the three French crew[7] killed in the attack on Habyarimana's plane, issued international arrest warrants against nine close associates of President Paul Kagame for the plane attack, adding that he thought Kagame should also stand trial, but that, as serving head of state, he was immune.[8] Although experts commissioned by a French judge concluded in 2012 that the missile was fired from a position held by the Presidential Guard and not the RPF (Oosterlinck et al. 2013), Murambi was to play an important role in the Rwandan government's response to Judge Bruguière's accusations.

It was the combination of the French soldiers at Murambi and Bruguière's arrest warrants that gave Paul Kagame the opportunity to denounce the French government at the April 2007 national commemoration of the genocide held at Murambi:

> The international community has not only responsibility for what was genocide, but a part of the international community has participated in the Rwandan genocide … What proof is there? There is much evidence. There is what we have been told by those who were present here at Murambi. To play on the graves of those who were killed during the genocide, play ball on their graves, play volleyball on their graves … It shows first of all that they came here with another objective. It was not to only save people, as they proclaimed they had come to save people, on the contrary it was to kill them … They want to attempt a trial by saying that Rwandans have killed when it was they who have killed them … Because these, these foreigners, these are those which have that

> part of the responsibility, those that want to be the investigating judge, and also the prosecutor and even to be the judges in the same trial. They kill and after they judge the 'victims', those that they have just killed!
>
> (Government of Rwanda 2007)

It appears that to ensure that the link was beyond doubt, the three signs were erected: 'FRENCH SOLDIERS WERE PLAYING VOLLEY HERE'; 'MASS GRAVE OF VICTIMS' and 'PLACE OF FRENCH FLAG DURING OPERATION TURQUOISE'.

As the obverse of the erasure of the Hutu refugees in Congo in the exhibition, the re-presencing of the French paratroopers through these signs is further testament to Dacia Viejo-Rose's (2011: 469) observations about the malleability of such sites. These signs are remarkable, given that in 2007 this was the only information provided and it is of limited value due to the fact that key information is missing: when were French soldiers playing volleyball?; what was Operation Turquoise? One assumes that their intended consumers are not casual visitors, but the foreign dignitaries and press who attended the commemoration ceremony in 2007.

Conversely, the cynical use of Murambi in this way – to deflect a political attack on an elite rather than honour the memory of the victims – can be

Figure 10.2 Sign in English, French and Kinyarwanda at Murambi, December 2007. © Nigel Eltringham.

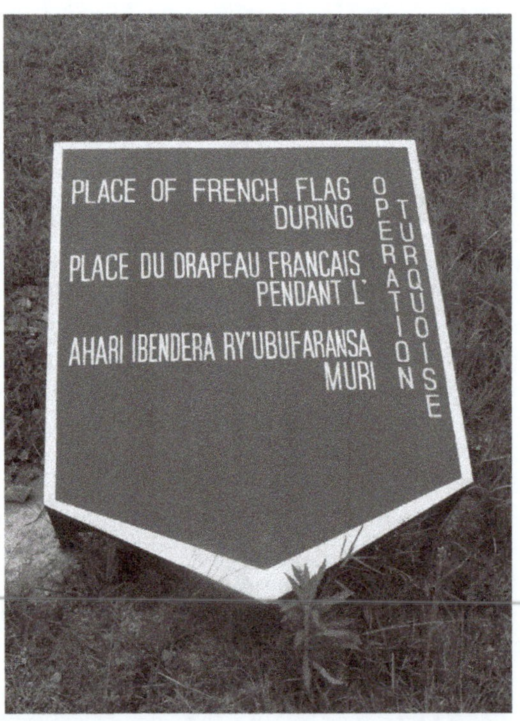

Figure 10.3 Sign in English, French and Kinyarwanda at Murambi, December 2007. © Nigel Eltringham.

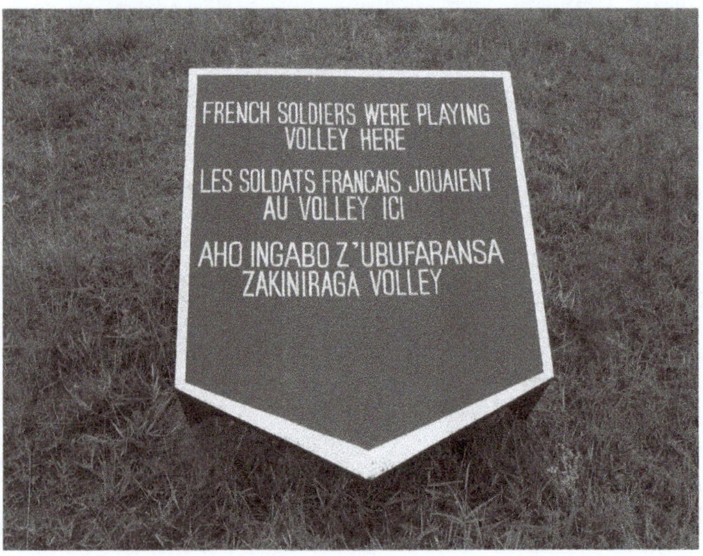

Figure 10.4 Sign in English, French and Kinyarwanda at Murambi, December 2007. © Nigel Eltringham.

interpreted as abhorrent. And yet, it fits into a well-known pattern. As Paul Williams (2004: 248) notes, the Tuol Sleng memorial site in Cambodia was designed by the Vietnamese to justify the invasion by portraying the Khmer Rouge as 'fascist'. By presenting the genocide as 'resembling the Holocaust, rather than the murder of political enemies that blotted the histories of the Soviet Union, China and Vietnam' (2004: 248), communism could be absolved. Sites are inherently susceptible to such manipulation, and this marks another irresolvable tension.

Conclusion

The uses to which Murambi will be put in the future are unpredictable. Writing in the context of Holocaust memorialization, James Young (1993: 154) notes 'no memorial is ever-lasting: each is shaped and understood in the context of its time and place, its meaning contingent on evolving political realities'. The way in which Murambi has changed demonstrates the need to see 'memorials as processes rather than objects' (Viejo-Rose 2011: 469), that they are transient. Dacia Viejo-Rose (2011: 467) observes that 'through use, new meanings get added to them yet these do not entirely replace the previous ones which are still part of their symbolic capital, to intermittently wax and wane in different contexts with each use and reuse'. The meaning sites communicate may appear to be relatively fixed, but 'these sites prove to be far more malleable, the meanings associated with them changing with use and over time' (2011: 471). As Elena Lesley-Rozen (in this volume) demonstrates, Tuol Sleng and Choeung Ek in Cambodia were 'repurposed' from initially being sites that justified the Vietnamese occupation of the country to serve as explanatory devices for the work of the Extraordinary Chambers in the Courts of Cambodia.

As with other genocide sites, three constituencies vie with one another in how events at Murambi are remembered: 'Global memory entrepreneurs' – African Rights, ICTR and the Aegis Trust; 'Local memory entrepreneurs' – the Government of Rwanda – and the survivors (Mannergren Selimovic forthcoming). The relative power and ascendancy of these groups shifts over time. As a consequence, Murambi as place and as text will continue to change. As James Young (1993: 3) states:

> On the one hand, official agencies are in a position to shape memory explicitly as they see fit, memory that best serves a national interest. On the other hand, once created, memorials take on lives of their own, often stubbornly resistant to the state's original intentions … New generations visit memorials under new circumstances and invest them with new meanings.

Notes

1 For a guide to the national sites, see http://cnlg.gov.rw/-Genocide-.html. For a guide to different kinds of memorials, see http://genocidememorials.cga.harvard.edu/home.html.

2 The International Criminal Tribunal for Rwanda was created by the United Nations Security Council in November 1994. Its mandate was to put on trial *any person* accused of committing the following in Rwanda in 1994: genocide (as defined by the 1948 UN Convention for the Prevention and Punishment of the Crime of Genocide); crimes against humanity (a widespread or systematic attack on a civilian population) and 'war crimes' (Article 3 common to the 1949 Geneva Conventions).
3 This is in contrast to unedited videotestimony (see Maclean in this volume).
4 These were: Prime Minister Faustin Twagiramungu (non-Hutu Power MDR), the Interior Minister Seth Sendashonga (RPF) and the Minister of Justice Alphonse-Marie Nkubito. Nkubito had been the public prosecutor in 1990, but was considered too liberal and replaced by Révérien Mukama. Targeted in the Genocide, Nkubito had escaped to the French Embassy and was evacuated to Bujumbura.
5 http://www.museum.gov.rw/2_museums/murambi/genocide_memorial/pages_html/page_murambi_exibit.htm. Accessed: 24 October 2007.
6 http://www.aegistrust.org/index.php/What-we-do/what-we-do.html.
7 Jacky Héraud (pilot), Jean-Pierre Minoberry (co-pilot) and Jean-Michel Perrine (engineering officer).
8 http://news.bbc.co.uk/1/hi/6168280.stm.

Bibliography

Abu-Lughod, L. (2002) 'Do Muslim Women Really Need Saving? Anthropological Reflections on Cultural Relativism and its Others', *American Anthropologist*, 104.3: 783–790.

Aegis Trust. (2011) *Genocide Memorial Opens at Murambi, Rwanda*, Nottingham: The Aegis Trust.

African Rights. (2007) *'Go. If You Die, Perhaps I Will Live': A Collective Account of Genocide and Survival in Murambi, Gikongoro, April–July 1994*, Kigali: African Rights.

Bardgett, S. (2007) 'Remembering Srebrenica', *History Today*, 57.11.

Buckley-Zistel, S. (2009) 'Nation, Narration, Unification? The Politics of History Teaching after the Rwandan Genocide', *Journal of Genocide Research*, 11.1: 31–53.

Chalk, F. and K. Jonassohn. (1990) *The History and Sociology of Genocide: Analyses and Case Studies*, New Haven: Yale University Press.

Clarke, K.M. (2009) *Fictions of Justice: The International Criminal Court and the Challenge of Legal Pluralism in Sub-Saharan Africa*, Cambridge: Cambridge University Press.

Colvin, C.J. (2006) 'Trafficking Trauma: Intellectual Property Rights and the Political Economy of Traumatic Storytelling', *Critical Arts: A Journal of South-North Cultural and Media Studies*, 20.1: 171–182.

Conway, P. (2011) 'Righteous Hutus: Can Stories of Courageous Rescuers Help in Rwanda's Reconciliation Process?', *International Journal of Sociology and Anthropology*, 3.7: 217–223.

Douglass, A. and T.A. Vogler. (2003) *Witness and Memory: The Discourse of Trauma*, London: Routledge.

Dudai, R. (2006) 'Advocacy with Footnotes: The Human Rights Report as a Literary Genre', *Human Rights Quarterly*, 28.3: 783–795.

Eastmond, M. (2007) 'Stories as Lived Experience: Narratives in Forced Migration Research', *Journal of Refugee Studies*, 20.2: 248–264.

Eltringham, N. (2000) 'The Institutional Aspect of the Rwandan Church', in D. Goyvaerts (ed.) *Conflict and Ethnicity in Central Africa*, Tokyo: Tokyo University of Foreign Studies: 225–250.

——. (2004) *Accounting for Horror: Post-Genocide Debates in Rwanda*, London: Pluto Press.

——. (2009) '"We are not a Truth Commission": Fragmented Narratives and the Historical Record at the International Criminal Tribunal for Rwanda', *Journal of Genocide Research*, 11.1: 55–79.

——. (2012) 'Exhibition, dissimulation et « culture ». Le traitement des corps dans le génocide rwandais', in É. Anstett and J.-M. Dreyfus (eds) *Cadavres impensables, cadavres impensés. Approches méthodologiques du traitement des corps dans les violences de masse et les génocides*, Paris: Éditions Pétra.

——. (2013) '"Illuminating the Broader Context": Anthropological and Historical Knowledge at the International Criminal Tribunal for Rwanda', *Journal of the Royal Anthropological Institute*, 19.2: 338–355.

Fontein, J. (2010) 'Between Tortured Bodies and Resurfacing Bones: The Politics of the Dead in Zimbabwe', *Journal of Material Culture*, 15.4: 423–448.

French, B. (2009) 'Technologies of Telling: Discourse, Transparency, and Erasure in Guatemalan Truth Commission Testimony', *Journal of Human Rights*, 8.1: 92–109.

Gelles, P.H. (1998) 'Testimonio, Ethnography and Processes of Authorship', *Anthropology Newsletter*, 39.3: 16–17.

Government of Rwanda. (2007) 'Discours de son Excellence le président de la République Paul Kagame prononcé à Murambi le 7 avril', Kigali: Office of the President.

Gregory, S.A.M. (2006) 'Transnational Storytelling: Human Rights, WITNESS, and Video Advocacy', *American Anthropologist*, 108.1: 195–204.

Guyer, S. (2009) 'Rwanda's Bones', *Boundary 2: An International Journal of Literature and Culture*, 36.2: 155–175.

Ibreck, R. (2010) 'The Politics of Mourning: Survivor Contributions to Memorials in Post-Genocide Rwanda', *Memory Studies*, 3: 330–343.

ICTR. (1999) *The Prosecutor v. Clément Kayishema and Obed Ruzindana*. Arusha: ICTR.

——. (2004) *The Prosecutor v. Theoneste Bagosora, Gratien Kabiligi, Aloys Ntabakuze, Anatole Nsengiyumva Case No. ICTR-98-41-T. Defence Exhibit DK125. Delivrance De Mandats D'arret Internationaux – Ordonnance De Soit Communique.*

——. (2005) *The Prosecutor v. Aloys Simba Case No. ICTR-01-76-T. Judgement and Sentence.*

International Justice Tribune. (2008) 'Shaming the World at Murambi', *Radio Netherlands Worldwide*. 1 December. Available at: http://www.rnw.nl/international-justice/article/shaming-world-murambi. Accessed: 26 July 2013.

Jackson, M. (2002) *The Politics of Storytelling: Violence, Transgression, and Intersubjectivity*, Copenhagen: Museum Tusculanum Press.

Jay, M. (1992) 'Of Plots, Witnesses, and Judgements', in S. Friedlander (ed.) *Probing the Limits of Representation: Nazism and the 'Final Solution'*, Cambridge: Harvard University Press: 97–107.

Kagame, A. (1954) *Les Organisations socio-familiales de l'Ancien Rwanda*, Bruxelles: Académie Royale des Sciences Coloniales (ARSC).

Kennedy, D.W. (2001) 'The International Human Rights Movement: Part of the Problem?', *Harvard Human Rights Journal*, 15: 101–126.

King, E. (2010) 'Memory Controversies in Post-Genocide Rwanda: Implications for Peacebuilding', *Genocide Studies and Prevention*, 5.3: 293–309.

Kroslak, D. (2007) *The Role of France in the Rwandan Genocide*, London: Hurst & Co.

Langfield, M. and P. Maclean. (2009) 'Multiple Framings: Survivor and Non-Survivor Interviewers in Holocaust Videotestimony', in N. Adler, S. Leydesdorff, M. Chamberlain and L. Neyzi (eds) *Memories of Mass Repression: Narrating Life Stories in the Aftermath of Atrocity*, New Brunswick and London: Transaction Publishers: 199–218.

Laub, D. (1992) 'Bearing Witness or the Vicissitudes of Listening', in S. Felman and D. Laub (eds) *Testimony: Crises of Witnessing in Literature, Psychoanalysis, and History*, London: Routledge: 57–74.

Laville, S. (2006) 'Two Years Late and Mired in Controversy: The British Memorial to Rwanda's Past', *The Guardian*. 13 November. Available at: http://www.guardian.co.uk/world/2006/nov/13/rwanda.sandralaville. Accessed: 26 July 2013.

Levi, P. (1986) 'The Memory of Offense', in G. Hartman (ed.) *Bitburg in Moral and Political Perspective*, Bloomington: Indiana University Press: 130–137.

Linke, U. (2009) 'The Limits of Empathy: Emotional Anesthesia and the Museum of Corpses in Post-Holocaust Germany', in A.L. Hinton and K.L. O'Neill (eds) *Genocide: Truth, Memory, and Representation*, Durham: Duke University Press: 147–191.

Longman, T. and T. Rutagengwa. (2006) 'Memory and Violence in Post-Genocide Rwanda', in E.G. Bay and D.L. Donham (eds) *States of Violence: Politics, Youth, and Memory in Contemporary Africa*, Charlottesville: University of Virginia Press: 236–260.

Madlingozi, T. (2010) 'On Transitional Justice Entrepreneurs and the Production of Victims', *Journal of Human Rights Practice*, 2.2: 208–228.

Mannergren Selimovic, J. (2013) 'Making Peace, Making Memory: Peacebuilding and Politics of Remembrance at Memorials of Mass Atrocities', *Peacebuilding*, 1.3: 334–348.

Meierhenrich, J. (2011) 'Topographies of Remembering and Forgetting: The Transformation of *Lieux de Mémoire* in Rwanda', in S. Straus and L. Waldorf (eds) *Remaking Rwanda: State Building and Human Rights after Mass Violence*, Madison: University of Wisconsin Press: 283–296.

Misago, C.K. (2007) 'Les instruments de la mémoire Génocide et traumatisme au Rwanda', *Gradhiva: Revue d'anthropologie et d'histoire des arts*, 5.

Morris, A. (2011) 'Boubacar Boris Diop: Interview', *TriQuarterly*. 18 July. Available at: http://www.triquarterly.org/interviews/interview-boubacar-boris-diop. Accessed: 29 July 2013.

Office of the UN High Commissioner for Human Rights. (2010) *Report of the Mapping Exercise documenting the most serious violations of human rights and international humanitarian law committed within the territory of the Democratic Republic of the Congo between March 1993 and June 2003*, Geneva: Office of the United Nations High Commissioner for Human Rights.

Oosterlinck, C., D. van Schendel, J. Huon, J. Sompayrac and O. Chavanis. (2013) *Rapport D'Expertise: Destruction En Vol Du Falcon 50 Kigali (Rwanda)*. Paris: Cour d'appel de Paris, Tribunal de Grande Instance de Paris. Also available at: http://ddata.over-blog.com/xxxyyy/2/93/44/38/rapport-ballist-attentat-contre-habyarimana-6-4-19-copie-1.pdf. Accessed: 25 March 2014.

Passmore, J. (1974) 'The Objectivity of History', in P. Gardiner (ed.) *The Philosophy of History*, Oxford: Oxford University Press: 145–160.

Portelli, A. (1981) 'The Peculiarities of Oral History', *History Workshop Journal*, 12.1: 96–107.

Schaffer, K. and S. Smith. (2004) *Human Rights and Narrated Lives: The Ethics of Recognition*, Basingstoke: Palgrave Macmillan.

Scully, S. (2012) 'The Politics of the Display of Human Remains: Murambi Genocide Memorial, Rwanda', paper presented at the International Network of Genocide Scholars' Biennial Conference, San Francisco, 28 June–1 July.

Simic, O. (2009) 'Remembering, Visiting and Placing the Dead: Law, Authority and Genocide in Srebrenica', *Law Text Culture*, 13.1: 273–310.

Smith, J. (2006) 'Our Memorial to 50,000 Dead is no Empty Historic Exercise', *The Guardian*. 21 November. Available at: http://www.guardian.co.uk/commentisfree/2006/nov/21/comment.rwanda. Accessed: 29 July 2013.

Sodaro, A. (2011) 'Politics of the Past: Remembering the Rwandan Genocide at the Kigali Memorial Centre', in E.T. Lehrer, C.E. Milton and M.E. Patterson (eds) *Curating Difficult Knowledge: Violent Pasts in Public Places*, Basingstoke: Palgrave Macmillan: 72–90.

Spijker, G. van't. (1990) *Les usages funéraires et la mission de l'Église: Une étude anthropologique et theologique des rites funéraires au Rwanda*, Kampen: J.H. Kok.

Spivak, G.C. (1988) 'Can the Subaltern Speak?', in C. Nelson and L. Grossberg (eds) *Marxism and the Interpretation of Culture*, Urbana: University of Illinois Press: 271–313.

Straus, S. and L. Waldorf (eds). (2011) *Remaking Rwanda: State Building and Human Rights after Mass Violence*, Madison: University of Wisconsin Press.

Strejilevich, N. (2006) 'Testimony: Beyond the Language of Truth', *Human Rights Quarterly*, 28.3: 701–713.

United Nations (1946) *Resolution 96(1) The Crime of Genocide*, New York: United Nations General Assembly.

——. (1994) *Resolution 955 (1994) Adopted by the Security Council at its 3453rd Meeting*, New York: United Nations Security Council.

Vansina, J. (2006 [1961]) *Oral Tradition: A Study in Historical Methodology*, New Brunswick: Transaction Publishers.

Vidal, C. (2004) 'Les commémorations du génocide au Rwanda', *Cahiers d'Études Africaines*, 44.175: 575–592.

Viejo-Rose, D. (2011) 'Memorial Functions: Intent, Impact and the Right to Remember', *Memory Studies*, 4.4: 465–480.

Williams, P. (2004) 'Witnessing Genocide: Vigilance and Remembrance at Tuol Sleng and Choeung Ek', *Holocaust and Genocide Studies*, 18.2: 234–254.

Wilson, R. (1997) 'Representing Human Rights Violations: Social Contexts and Subjectivities', in R. Wilson (ed.) *Human Rights, Culture and Context: Anthropological Perspectives*, London: Pluto Press: 134–160.

Young, J.E. (1993) *The Texture of Memory: Holocaust Memorials and Meaning*, New Haven: Yale University Press.

Zorbas, E. (2009) 'What Does Reconciliation after Genocide Mean? Public Transcripts and Hidden Transcripts in Post-Genocide Rwanda', *Journal of Genocide Research*, 11.1: 127–147.

Index

NOTE: Page numbers in italics are for illustrations